United States National Security Policy in the Decade Ahead

INTRODUCTION BY
Frank Barnett

EDITED BY
James E. Dornan, Jr.

Crane, Russak
New York

United States National Security Policy
in the Decade Ahead
Published in the United States by
Crane, Russak & Company, Inc.
347 Madison Avenue
New York, New York 10017
ISBN 0-8448-1302-8
LC 77-90924

Printed in the United States of America

TABLE OF CONTENTS

Preface

For more than a decade the United States has been caught up in a "great debate" over profound issues of national security policy. The range of the debate has varied: The Vietnam War brought to the fore questions concerning the appropriate role for the United States in Third World conflicts, while more recently the state of Soviet-American relations, SALT, and the significance for the United States of growing Soviet military power have been the focus of attention. Such debates have of course occurred before in the twentieth century—at the time of the Spanish-American War, before the United States's entry into World War I and World War II, and over the United States commitment of ground forces to NATO.

The present debate, however, is unusual and perhaps even unique in several respects. It has been sustained for a longer period than any previous debate. A wider segment of the public appears to be engaged than was the case with most earlier controversies over foreign policy. Discontent with recent American statecraft spans the political spectrum from Left to Right (although, to be sure, the reasons for the unhappiness of critics on the Left vary considerably from those of persons on the Right). Finally, the scope of the public discussion has transcended particular problems and embraced the most fundamental of questions concerning America's role in world politics.

In the fall of 1976 the Department of Politics at the Catholic University of America arranged under my direction a series of lectures on Capitol Hill for senior staff members of the United States Senate and House of Representatives who have professional responsibilities in the area of United States national security policy. The lectures examined various dimensions of the current American world role, with emphasis on identifying alternatives to recent and current policies. They were revised for publication during the spring and summer of 1977, and constitute, in my view, an important contribution to the continuing debate over the future of United States foreign policy.

I would like to thank Dr. John Tierney of the National Security Research Group for providing essential "logistical" support for the lectures.

JAMES E. DORNAN, JR.

The Catholic University of America
August 1977

*United
States
National
Security
Policy
in the
Decade
Ahead*

Chapter One

Alternatives to the Past: An Overview of the United States National Security Policy

Frank R. Barnett

INTRODUCTION

In the age of detente, it might seem almost as if Washington has unwittingly produced a one-scene parody of the monumental five-act epic of the decline of Pax Britannica. In the self-confident years of the Eisenhower era, let alone the exhilarating months of the Kennedy interval, the public was frequently reminded by its pundits that "the American President is the most powerful man on earth." Since the supremacy of the dollar, the putative strength of a global—if largely untested—alliance system, and the unquestioned superiority of United States strategic and naval forces combined to give the White House global reach, there was material substance to the boast. Today, few would reassert the claim, now that oil seems mightier than the dollar, our alliances are in disarray, and the president is armed with a dubious "sufficiency" of arms in the face of a Soviet military buildup that knows no peacetime parallel since the feverish activity of Nazi Germany in the late 1930s.

Some will dismiss this thesis as reflecting the stark language and obsolete concerns of the cold war. Ironically, such critics are correct; one should be using harsher terms to portray the sterner reality of today. The cold war, after all, was waged with élan, by a united and confident America, from a position of relative superiority, against an opponent inferior in every element of strength save its capacity for political and propaganda warfare. The cold war was of lesser danger and

1

smaller scope than the present conflict. Today, we are simultaneously engaged in a research and development war, a resource war, a struggle between economic systems on a global stage, plus two separate levels of an arms race (strategic and conventional). Although we have not yet entered the event, we are also being challenged to an intense intellectual competition in the field of military doctrine. Would that we had the comfortable options and strategic cushions of the bygone era of the cold war, when the USSR spent merely 9 percent of its GNP on military might, and when only the president of the United States had an intercontinental airlift and world navy at his command.

It is only fitting that an "overview," to save the reader's time, should have the decency to offer its own summary. This paper will argue that, since containment is dead and detente is failing, the United States must now embrace a national security policy based on (*a*) defense *innovation* and military reform, (*b*) selective *engagement*, and (*c*) a new alliance of the committed and the competent. To muster and focus scarce resources for such a policy we must "think lean" and rid our strategy of the impedimenta of sentimentality and utopianism characteristic of much of United States national security policy since 1945 and which even America can no longer afford.

For a start, we might redefine the USSR not as a respectable adversary, but as the manifest enemy she proclaims herself to be in both word and deed. The input of American food, credits, and technology to the Soviet "military-commissar complex" has in no wise impeded the increased output of Soviet missiles, main battle tanks, and submarines, nor was the Politburo effectively "enmeshed" in Secretary Kissinger's web of detente politics in Portugal, Angola, or Vietnam. It is thus imperative to drop the pretense that euphemisms can paper over protracted conflict as usual.

Congress has already partially nullified the impulse to pay any price and oppose every foe on the world stage; but there is still a need to define objectives more clearly and set priorities. For example, with the aim of applying scarce resources to truly vital interests, we should consider that benign neglect may be more appropriate to many areas of foreign policy than to domestic affairs and that the root causes of hunger, poverty, and tribal or ethnic antagonisms in large parts of the world may be beyond our powers to prescribe or allay.

Moreover, since societal continuity is a precondition for helping others, we should be wary of those sermons warning us to choose between becoming the breadbasket for the world and deploying cruise missiles. Prudent defense and international largesse are not necessarily incompatible. Let us continue, or even expand, food for peace programs; but we should not imagine that humanitarian acts are a counterpoise to the USSR's design of at least seven new missile systems since SALT I.

"Closing the gap" between the Third World and the West via gratuities is simply not a feasible priority for the United States, although the success stories in Taiwan and South Korea should encourage us to support self-help societies. But if the advertised void between some of the less developed countries (LDCs) and the West is ever to be bridged it will take many generations; and, if Maoist cults and the dead weight of Marxist dogma continue to suffocate Third World efficiency, it may never happen. Adjusting the North/South imbalance may be the task of a century, whereas the East/West rivalry could be settled in Russia's favor within a decade if present military trends are not reversed.

There is a bleak line about religious faith from nineteenth-century poetry that suggests the untenable state of current United States defense strategy—". . . Wandering between two Worlds; One dead, the other powerless to be born." The policy of military containment, which enjoyed bipartisan support for the first two decades following World War II, was mortally wounded in Vietnam and received the *coup de grace* in Angola. Its remains may yet be indecently interred in southern Africa, Korea, and Taiwan. Can anyone doubt that the policy of Truman, Eisenhower, and Kennedy, Acheson, Dulles, and Rusk is now dead?

What policy then is "powerless to be born?" The Nixon Doctrine at first glance seemed to offer an authentic alternate policy: America would no longer police the world unilaterally[1] but would act as the reliable senior partner of a "Self-Help Interpol" and tolerate no blackmail of small neighbors by an ideological Mafia. But how reliable and vigorous is the senior partner? Weighing the end games in Vietnam, Cambodia, Laos, Mozambique, and Angola, noting the active insurgencies in Burma, Thailand, Malaysia, and the Philippines, and assessing the new potency of Castroism throughout the Caribbean and Sub-Sahara Africa, many of our small neighbors must feel that the Nixon Doctrine was shredded before its tenets could be memorized by State Department public affairs officers. Nor is there anything to take its place. Detente is less a policy than an increasingly threadbare rationale for ad hoc retreats from the grave sites of containment.

SEATO officially buried itself in June of 1977; CENTO is moribund; our bilateral defense treaty commitments to Korea and Taiwan command declining support among our own foreign policy elites; and, despite growing Soviet maritime strength in the Persian Gulf theater, Congress is reluctant to undergird American "naval sufficiency" in the Indian Ocean. Although we are a Pacific power, the future of that vast theater is shadowed by uncertainty as to our operational commitment to defense treaties with Australia, New Zealand, the Philippines, and Japan, even as the USSR speeds development of Siberian resources targeted for Soviet naval facilities on the Sea of Japan.

Inside our blue-chip alliance, NATO, Greece and Turkey are dubious and sullen partners; Canada is sometimes an economic rival and political adversary; Iceland, Portugal, Italy, and the Netherlands are partially neutralized by the frictions of internal leftist politics; Denmark and Norway appear to be more geographical expressions than substantive allies; and gallant Britain is so enervated by the troubles in Ireland and her own productivity crisis that she is barely able to fulfill her commitment to NATO's defense. The impressive strength and high competence of West Germany's forces on the central front do not materially lessen the danger to NATO's flanks, especially at a time when a succession crisis in Yugoslavia may soon present Moscow with options to reach the Adriatic directly or through a more pliant ally. The Baltic and Mediterranean, if not yet Soviet lakes, at least now offer Moscow outflanking opportunities almost as much as they afford strategic access to United States fleets.

Surely, as we begin America's third century, we owe anxious friends, nervous allies, and ourselves a nobler prospect than passively to await the Gulag Ice Age, on the shorelines of Tartar oceans. Moscow's contemptuous disregard for the human rights provisions of Helsinki—the more outrageous in that the new czars pluck intensified repression from "basket three"—should animate decent people to rebuild the barricades against ancient barbarism modernized only with psychiatric yoke and electronic knout. What sort of people are we that we are willing to confer prestige and legitimacy on such a monstrous mutation of the ideal of progress?

Of course we have problems other than those of foreign policy and defense; and articulate spokesmen who press the claims of domestic reform as deserving high priority should be heard and, as appropriate, heeded. But defense of the realm can scarcely be deferred until "our own house is in order," or regarded as a simple trade-off for more desirable welfare programs. In the 1930s the American people endured a plague of problems. In voices of fear and sometimes hatred, Americans talked of unemployment, lockouts, and sit-ins—of that man in the White House, unfair taxes, and packing the Supreme Court—of share-croppers and the Dust Bowl—of the Ku Klux Klan, lynchings, and the Capone mob. As a committee of the whole, Americans worried about the clear and present blips on their personal radar screens.

Perhaps fewer than .1 percent of the American people were concerned about the marshaling, in Nazi Germany, of the Stuka dive bombers and Tiger tanks whose combined capacity for blitzkrieg was soon to revolutionize military strategy and place all of Europe under the boot of Berlin. Nor were Americans in the 1930s troubled by the mass production of the German U-boats that very shortly would send thousands of British and American seamen to early graves and nearly snap the spine of the Atlantic Alliance.

If German submarines had been nuclear powered, if V-2 buzz bombs with atomic tips could have overarched the Atlantic as well as the English Channel, our failure in the 1930s to take seriously the menace of the Third Reich might have enabled Hitler to include the American people in his Final Solution. The moral of the story is that an open society of individualists and pressure groups will tend to magnify its internal problems, so long as it continues to be a living civilization. But, while there is no plausible "worst case" scenario in which the United States would be extinguished by domestic race war, crime, pollution, or recession, by the mid-1980s there may be imaginable conditions under which the Republic could be terminated by a Soviet first-strike capability. Even more likely are a number of scenarios in which our allies could be neutralized or "decoupled" from the United States in time of crisis if there is further deterioration in the strength and credibility of United States deterrent forces.

Many commentators, of course, argue that our security is guaranteed by the "balance of terror"; but the old balance of terror is coming unhinged. Given the energetic Soviet civil defense program, the USSR's superiority in air defense systems, the massive Soviet ICBM megatonnage advantage, Moscow's proliferation of advanced missiles, and a Soviet military doctrine that features "secrecy, shock, and surprise," the so-called balance of terror might prove out at 80 million Americans dead against, say, 20 million Russians. True, 20 million deaths would be a fearful price for political leaders to pay for overcoming their nation's chief enemy; yet we should be wary of accepting uncritically the proposition that a Judeo-Christian-rooted definition of "unacceptable" losses would necessarily govern the calculations of people tutored by Stalin and themselves veterans of a war against Germany in which the USSR suffered at least 20 million casualties while remaining a viable society.

Three recent secretaries of defense (Messrs. Laird, Schlesinger, and Rumsfeld) have warned us that—while we still cling to an increasingly precarious parity—the military *trend* lines strongly favor the USSR. This means there can come a time—not much later than 1980—when Moscow will have pushed open a "window" of strategic opportunity. (One thinks by analogy of the "space-window" of the astronauts—those finite moments when all the forces of gravity and rocket thrust are in proper correlation to maximize the success of a moon shot—those finite moments that must be either exploited quite decisively or foregone.) Our danger would be compounded if the opening of the Soviet "opportunity window" should coincide with some further deterioration in relations between Moscow and Peking; for, in that instance, the Kremlin might feel compelled to preempt one or both of her enemies before the full nuclear potential of the People's Republic of China (PRC) could be developed on the Russian flank. Our own destiny, ironically, might thus become dependent, not on detente diplomacy between Moscow and Washington, but on the unpredictable clash of Leninist and Maoist-fed nationalist passions on the Sino-Soviet border, over which we have little control. (If, on the contrary, rapprochement between Moscow and Peking should coincide with an era of even "presumed" Soviet arms superiority, the USSR's imperial pressure on the Middle East and elsewhere could prove irresistible.)

The "opportunity window" of Moscow, once unambiguously open, will be difficult for us—and impossible for anyone else—to close. Indeed, if it opens too far, we might be precluded from even the prototype stage of adequate countermeasures. One can easily imagine Soviet strategists warning a future Politburo that such and such an American weapons design, if allowed to get beyond the blueprint step, would close Moscow's "strategic window" four years hence.

At such an hour, Moscow would not necessarily need to mount, or even threaten, a preemptive strike. If the Kremlin chose to be subtle, a handful of hapless and overawed policymakers in Washington could be urged *privately* to allow the new American weapons design to be gracefully nullified at, say, a SALT IV. Casuistry and public relations would prevail. Given the manifest need for secrecy during delicate negotiations, no face would be lost by American leaders; no shock waves of alarm or indignation would animate an uninformed populace—and the bountiful flow of grain, technology, and credits from an *undestroyed* America to a needy USSR could be institutionalized as a permanent feature of world politics. (The postulated Soviet "window of opportunity," of course, leads to a score of alternate scenarios, none of them particularly comforting.)

Gloomy as these prognostications sound, however, it is worth stressing that there is nothing inevitable about the decline of the West. Communist Russia, like all totalitarian states, has hidden flaws, unreliable "allies," and internal weaknesses that could become future vulnerabilities. There is nothing in our stars that ordains NATO to detrain at the Finland station. It is USSR, not the West, that confronts a "two-front" contingency; and it is the Communist economy that is $40 billion in debt to its capitalist adversaries.

What, then, might be some positive United States objectives in the coming decade, as we recognize that we can no longer afford to pay every price and are unwilling to mount every barricade? My list contains eight proposals.

First, regain strategic *superiority,* if possible by research finesse and defense innovation, if necessary by allowing SALT to lapse (a perfectly legal option) and devoting 10 percent instead of 6 percent of our GNP to a contest in which the Russians are already spending between 15 and 20 percent of their own. Instead of deploring the arms race, we can and should win it if the Soviets remain intransigent about symmetrical arms control. The inexact verbal formula of "rough equivalence" will not do. Since we cannot, in an open society, match the secrecy, central control, and indifference to casualties of the Leninist state, high technology is one of the few assets we possess. (We gave up a clear advantage in ABM technology at SALT I, and presumably the Soviets are eager to eliminate our decisive edge in cruise missile technology at SALT II.) Together with our skilled labor, economic strength, and creative management, we could translate that "high technology edge" into strategic superiority, a condition under which the world lived in relative peace for a quarter of a century.

Second, safeguard the stability of the Persian Gulf theater and access to those fuel tanks of the West and Japan whose outlets run across the Indian Ocean.[2] The Middle East is no longer another geographical square on the chessboard, comparable to Southeast Asia or Latin America. Owing to the geo-economics of energy, that region instead is now the wood and ivory of the chessboard itself. The Persian Gulf is inseparable from the future of NATO and the destiny of Japan. For at least another fifteen years, Middle East policy is United States energy policy; and energy policy is intimately linked to United States domestic employment, and to our economic and defense policy broadly considered. Not even NATO is more important to our security than the Persian Gulf, for if the Gulf's energy reserves were denied to the West, NATO would cease to be viable.

Saudi Arabia, for example, with at least a quarter of the world reserves, can produce oil at the cost of about 20 cents a barrel. In the United States it costs $6.50. If, through proxy war or coup or insurrection, the USSR could gain control of Saudi oil, Moscow would have incalculable economic leverage on the world market. Despite Communist mismanagement and the efficiency of United States firms, nothing could make up for the disparity in the cost of production factor.

Third, upgrade the military defenses of NATO in terms of doctrine and hardware, recognizing that we need precision-guided *ideas* as well as weapons. Defense intellectuals should note that Senator Sam Nunn, in forcing the Pentagon to rethink its "long-war premise" for NATO, may have done more to alter strategy than the last $10 million worth of DOD's contract research. We are entering an era in which those who perceive the enormity of the Soviet threat are precisely those who must be willing to criticize the Pentagon on systems and doctrine and suggest constructive options. We need task forces on "military reform," composed of members of Congress, labor leaders, business people, and academic experts who are sympathetic to the need for improved defense but are also able to compel bureaucracies to seek innovation.

Unhappily, in a society whose politicians and intellectuals tend to polarize on defense/welfare issues, the United States public too often must choose between uncritical support of its military establishment and polemics directed against war in general and an American (never a Russian) weapons system in particular. "Stronger defense through innovation and military reform" is a better rallying point for the future.

Fourth, prevent NATO's internal collapse or self-paralysis at the hands of popular front coalitions of Communists and the Marxian or Maoist wings of European Socialist parties. This is a formidable and delicate task; some say it is an "impossible" one for an alliance of democracies. Yet, in the case of Portugal, it was demonstrated (chiefly by European social democrats) that international communism is not the only force that can coordinate "transnational politics." Nor has the AFL-CIO been impotent in bolstering and cooperating with anti-Communist labor organizers in Europe and other parts of the world. It remains to be seen if the parties of the Center and moderate Right, which espouse private capitalism and middle-class values, can also learn to transfer "practical politics" and public affairs "technology" across frontiers. Some beginnings have been made in France, Spain, and the United Kingdom, with the initiative coming from industrialists and publishers. It is imperative that responsible private groups in the United States engage themselves in this political struggle to avert the erosion of NATO's defenses by nonmilitary means. History has scarcely ordained that democratic parties must never "transgress" a frontier to safeguard human rights, while Communist political machines are free to orchestrate international lobbies to support each other in local power grabs.

Fifth, maintain, even enhance, the credibility of our military presence in the northwest Pacific. From the viewpoint of what the British used to call grand strategy, additional United States military power in this theater can be justified on four grounds: (1) there is neither trip-wire nor buffer zone between the superpowers on the air and sea lanes of the Pacific "front"; (2) United States trade with partners across the Pacific is rising at an astonishing rate, and a goodly share of our future economic well-being will depend on a healthy investment climate in an Asia uncoerced by Moscow; (3) owing to the Sino-Soviet ideological conflict, the sixty-plus divisions massed in the border zone on both sides, and the manifest peril to all of Asia that would ensue if an enlarged Soviet fleet were to be unopposed in the seas adjacent to Japan, China, and the Philippines, no other quarter of the globe will be so quickly and dangerously destabilized by a cutback in American military power; and (4) no prudent Soviet planner could eye the apparent weakness of NATO without reflecting that a Red Army thrust into Europe could well bring a riposte from NATO's senior partner from the direction of the Pacific as well as on the western front.

It is imperative, above all, to prevent Japan from despairing over United States intentions and as a consequence seeking alternate sources of security for herself in some new arrangement with one or both of the Communist giants in her neighborhood. Given the magnitude and quality of her GNP, a neutralist Japan—to whose high technology either the Chinese or Russian military had easy access—could shift the balance of power permanently against us in the Pacific Basin. Inasmuch as South Korea (ROK) and the Republic of China on Taiwan (ROC) are shields for Japan, and Japan is the *sine qua non* of our own defense perimeter in Asia, this necessitates our continued and ungrudging adherence to our defense treaties with the ROK and ROC. Otherwise, we must prepare ourselves for the bleak options to which Japan might be driven if she concludes we are an uncertain ally— options that might range from accommodation with Moscow to the acquisition of a Japanese nuclear deterrent. Support for independent and non-Communist governments in South Korea and Taiwan, despite our dislike for some of their authoritarian politics, offers a much more attractive future than creating such a climate of alarm and despondency in Asia that Japan, the third-ranked economic force in the world, chooses to decouple from America.[3]

Sixth, begin now to revise doctrine, refine technology, and prepare military equipment for the possible battlefields of the 1980s, a period in which—despite all arms control measures—as many as 15 nations may possess nuclear weapons. There is growing evidence that, notwithstanding the rhetoric employed at the UN, a number of nations have concluded that the Nonproliferation Treaty is dying if not already dead. One can imagine tragic but plausible scenarios in which tactical nuclear weapons might some day be used in southern Africa or in the Middle East by new members of the "nuclear club." Of course, our diplomacy should struggle against and attempt to delay that prospect as long as possible. It would be folly, however, to handcuff American military doctrine and troop training to the premise that—apart from an all-out strategic conflict between the superpowers—all future war zones will be nonnuclear. A good case can be made, for example, for the proposition that to upgrade the defense of NATO against the Soviets' preferred offensive tactics and "short-war" doctrine we need more contingency planning incorporating the potential of a new generation of dial-a-yield "mininukes" that minimize fallout effects and thus substantially reduce expected civilian casualties. We should also speed the provision of antitoxic devices for American battle tanks and armored personnel carriers in order to give United States soldiers survival parity on the European battlefield: the Soviets are already considerably ahead of us in designing doctrine, war-game exercises, and "equipment in the field" based on their own premise that *both* chemical and radiation weapons will be used in early conjunction with conventional firepower in any major contest. The technology to catch up is already in hand and is relatively inexpensive; but first we must overcome a curious American taboo that somehow permits saturation bombing with napalm but inhibits the use against a military target of a laser-guided mininuke with no fallout and little collateral damage to civilian facilities.

Seventh, prevent the realignment of Moscow and Peking against the United States by maintaining enough power in the Pacific to discourage Soviet expansion and offering economic and possibly military aid of modest dimensions to the PRC. In her hostility toward the democratic societies of the "capitalist" West, and in her encouragement of militant subversion, Chinese communism is no more savory than the Soviet brand, although much of Peking's political warfare is now directed against Moscow. But the People's Republic of China does not, at this time, directly menace the United States militarily. Communist China has no ICBMs, no far-flung navy, no intercontinental airlift; its army is essentially defensive and clearly ill-equipped for distant adventures. As long as we are firm in insisting on restrained PRC behavior toward Taiwan and other Asian allies, a United States "tilt toward China," while ideologically distasteful, would be the classic move of checking a powerful enemy with a lesser rival.

Is it worth the risk? Perhaps one can answer only with another question: What happens to the balance of power if the Moscow-Peking axis is reestablished and the Soviets are freed from their two-front anxieties? To avert that catastrophe, even a substantial gamble is justified. Of course we should not delude ourselves that the Communist Chinese and the United States will work together because Peking likes us. It is rather that Peking's leaders appear genuinely afraid of a Soviet preemptive strike against China. Therefore, Peking's leadership—for perhaps a decade—needs at least a demi-alliance with the United States to create uncertainty in Moscow concerning possible United States reactions to a war between China and the USSR. (And the United States can cultivate this ambiguity, in our own interests, by being firmer in our relations with allies and adversaries alike.)

A tilt toward Peking raises the question of Taiwan and our commitment to old friends there. If we can believe some private sources, and a good deal of public evidence, Peking is in no hurry to ingest Taiwan militarily. (Indeed, many Asian scholars feel that, paradoxically, the immediate result of a Washington betrayal of Taiwan would be to generate grave doubts in Peking about United States reliability and the value of the United States–PRC relationship. For now, security needs have clear priority in Peking's policy calculations, and American support is far more valuable to Peking as a counter to Soviet aggression than would be the PRC's early possession of Taiwan. Despite the Shanghai Communique (which, of course, is not a treaty), diplomats and scholars have found a formula by which our relations toward the Chinese Communists need not compromise our continued protection of the Republic of China. Indeed, the time may be ripe for a low-key diplomatic initiative by Washington that would transcend the status quo and promote a more lasting settlement of the "two Chinas" problem. For this, we can resort not only to the precedent developed by Willy

Brandt for resolving the issue of the two Germanys, but to some of the
principles shared by both Chinas as well. Since both Peking and Taipei
agree there is but one China, why not encourage discussion of the
Willy Brandt solution for the problem of divided Germany? That solution was "one nation, two states, and someday peaceful reunion." Although relations between the two Germanys are still marred by Communist espionage against the Federal Republic of Germany (FRG)
and the refusal of the East to adhere to Helsinki's human rights clauses,
Willy Brandt's diplomatic invention has led to a less tension-charged
modus vivendi. There is now at least some economic and human
traffic between the divided halves, whereas ten years ago East Germany
and West Germany refused absolutely to recognize each other, stood
bayonet to bayonet, and traded the same sort of polemics that Taiwan
and the PRC now exchange. Today, the two Germanys have agreed
on mutual recognition and limited additional relations on the basis of
the formula "one nation, two states." Could a similar design be applied
to Peking and Taipei? Admittedly, this would be an awkward and am-
biguous "nonsettlement" of the China issue for the present, but perhaps that is our best option.[4]

Eighth, to avert a Soviet strategy of "divide and Finlandize," bring
into being a new alliance linking North America and Europe to Japan
and the Persian Gulf. This would not be a substitute for NATO but
rather an imperative adjunct to it. Such a Grand Alliance would serve
as an enlarged means both of defending NATO's energy flank in the
Middle East and safeguarding certain other nations whose security is
indivisible from NATO's own owing to their oil reserves or geostrategic
position.

This initiative would remedy a weakness in our common defense
that was already obvious in 1958 to Gen. Charles de Gaulle. At that time
the French president proposed to Eisenhower and Macmillan that the
United States, Britain, and France should coordinate allied action during crises on a scale far wider than the geographical limits established
in the NATO treaty. Although de Gaulle's concept was rejected, its
logic is even greater today when Marxist regimes in Angola and Mozambique, friendly to the USSR, dominate African shores on both sides
of the oil route around the Cape of Good Hope.

The new alliance, of course, cannot be a form of NATO paternalism. Instead, it must generate a truly global partnership, based not on the bipolar and regional politics of the 1950s, but on a multinational *realpolitik* that links the economic, energy, and security concerns of NATO to those of such other "strong points" in the non-Communist world as Japan, Australia, Indonesia, Iran, and Saudi Arabia.[5] The alliance would recognize the major status of the Persian Gulf states as the "sixth power" in the world, as well as the need to substitute cooperation for hostility in the West's relationships with the key forces of OPEC. (Iran, Saudi Arabia, the Persian Gulf sheikdoms, and Indonesia are at least as concerned about expanding Soviet power as we are. Thus, while disputes over oil pricing and the high cost of industrial goods divide us, the paramount security concern should unite us. The task of statesmanship, therefore, is to innovate a diplomatic framework inside which mutual security trade-offs can compensate for economic forbearance by all partners.)

It is difficult to think of a simple phrase to describe a vast naval alliance of the southern oceans, designed for the era of energy scarcity and based on vital interests that stretch from North America and Britain to Australia and Japan. APIODA would be the acronym for the geographical scope of the treaty required—the Atlantic/Pacific/Indian Ocean Defense Agreement—although doubtless a less unwieldy term can be found. But if the title is awkward, the political rationale for APIODA is clearcut: to confront Soviet power, expanding from its interior heartland against isolated "targets" on the rim, with a cohesive global alliance rather than disparate regional groupings that have no military obligations to each other.

It is self-evident that NATO—dependent on Third World oil, minerals, and raw materials—is vulnerable to the disruption of production and trade outside NATO boundaries. Japan's overwhelming reliance on foreign sources of raw materials beyond her control is even more apparent. Finally, it is clear that some states in the Persian Gulf—despite large imports of armaments—lack either the manpower or the military sophistication to protect themselves in certain contingencies. In the absence of APIODA, the USSR can always concentrate against the weakest state on her periphery, using her four-ocean navy to complement her sheer central mass as a continental power spanning Eurasia and fronting on the Persian Gulf. In the wake of her success in Angola,

Russia may also assume she can with impunity again use Cuban and other proxies to wage a full-scale "resource war" throughout the southern hemisphere.[6] Against these multiple threats, a Grand Alliance of the scope indicated would more than match Soviet naval deployments and would confer overwhelming advantages on the non-Communist side in GNP, manpower, resources, and technology. APIODA would be our means to redress the purely military balance with an alliance that linked the competent and committed of the non-Communist world, east and west, north and south.

In summary, despite the relentless buildup of Soviet armament, the Communist wave of the future is no more likely to succeed than the Nazi version that collapsed more than a generation ago, provided we convert our extraordinary assets into working options. The West and its allies in all parts of the world have incalculable advantages in high technology, economic efficiency, and human resources, not to mention food that the Communist system produces so inefficiently for its toiling masses.

Moreover, for all its missiles and warships, the Soviet empire is still weakened by rival nationalisms. Scores of millions of the peoples of the USSR resent what is known as Great Russian chauvinism. The Ukraine is potentially Russia's "Ireland"; and there are Baltic, Armenian, Georgian, Mongol, Muslim, and Christian minorities, as well as Jewish, inside the belly of Mother Russia. In addition to the growing dissent of many intellectuals, there are the political heresies of Titoism and Maoism, and now a "Protestant revolt" among West European Communists. If we can muster the national will to exercise the constructive options that lie between nuclear war and one-sided detente, the weaknesses in the Soviet system will compound themselves. Marxist idealism inside the USSR is long since dead, and a totalitarian state smothers the impulse for self-renewal generated in pluralistic societies. Only our own lack of nerve and high purpose will enable the Russian Politburo to gain further success for its sick and shabby enterprise.

NOTES

1. A self-evident historical fiction, since a number of allies in Europe and Asia had always made substantial contributions (in terms of relative GNP and manpower) to the common cause.

2. A specific proposal on how to do this, via a new Grand Alliance, is outlined below.

3. The somewhat less immediate, but still vitally important, problem of devising ways to support friends in Australia, New Zealand, Indonesia, Singapore—and elsewhere in the ANZUS and ASEAN region—is treated in the eighth proposal, an outline for a new Atlantic, Pacific, and Indian Ocean Defense Arrangement.

4. This concept—presented here in simplistic outline—has been developed more fully by such noted scholars as Ray Cline of Georgetown's Center for Strategic and International Studies, Frank Trager of New York University, Richard Walker of the University of South Carolina, and Franz Michael of George Washington University. What is more, such policy proposals have at least been heard by leaders from Peking and Taipei, and it is encouraging to note that the proponents have not been blacklisted by those who listened.

5. While these states suggest the geographical reach of the Grand Alliance, this list is not intended to be definitive. For example, the states in the ASEAN and ASPAC groupings should be invited to join.

6. Although the USSR and PRC are semirivals, both are still hostile to non-Communist systems. Each in its own way may be tooling up to conduct a "resource war" against the United States, Japan, and the Common Market: (1) the USSR by using diplomacy, naval power, and a Cuban foreign legion to seal off key mineral areas of the Third World and/or sit astride the fuel lifelines with Russian warships; (2) the PRC by tutoring and supporting the anticapitalist bloc in the UN in its attacks on private investment, multinational corporations (MCNs), and capitalist banking.

Chapter Two

Diplomacy and United States Foreign Policy

Robert L. Schuettinger

A realistic and effective diplomatic strategy is at least as important to a nation as its military and economic power. In fact, without an effective diplomacy, the gains won in the marketplace or on the battlefield can be lost at the negotiating table. In analyzing the role that American diplomacy must therefore play in furthering our national security in the coming years, we must first define the nature of the diplomatic craft, and then face the central problem confronting all democracies: how democratic can, or should, our diplomacy be? Next, we will examine the dangers to which diplomacy in a democracy is particularly susceptible, and how this country has fared in its pursuit of its primary diplomatic objectives since 1945. The essay will conclude with a consideration of certain proposals for the adaptation of our diplomacy to the changing requirements of the coming decade.

THE ART OF DIPLOMACY
It has often been remarked that while diplomacy has always played an important role in the life of a nation, the nature of diplomacy itself has changed drastically since the Congress of Vienna in 1815. A commercial attaché busily promoting British wool to Japanese business people, we are told, is an altogether different kind of diplomat from the German princes who lounged around the palaces of Vienna. The rise of mass democracy (or, at a minimum, the need for dictators to placate their people), the rapid development of technology and the shift from a European-centered to a truly global political world have all combined, it is argued, to give rise to a "new" diplomacy that grad-

17

ually replaced the "old" by the end of World War I. Secrecy is thus presumed to be outdated, or at least inappropriate and censurable where practiced, while ambassadors and lesser diplomats are now simply messengers for foreign ministers and heads of government who are able to decide important matters among themselves on short notice. Professionalism is therefore reduced to the implementation of details while policy is made at political (and hopefully democratic) centers of power. Many even maintain that the concerns of diplomacy have been so transformed in the twentieth century that modern-day practitioners devote the bulk of their time to such mundane matters as press relations, educational and cultural affairs, trade issues, and the promotion of tourism.[1]

A distinguished French diplomatist, on the other hand, took a more cautious view. "To talk," M. Jules Cambon wrote, "about new and old diplomacy is to make a distinction without a difference. It is the outward appearance, or, if you like, the make-up of diplomacy which is gradually changing. The substance will remain—firstly because human nature never changes; secondly because there is only one way of settling international differences and lastly because the most persuasive method at the disposal of a government is the word of an honest man."[2]

There is an underlying tradition in diplomacy that has always insisted that the prime qualities of a good diplomat are truthfulness and honesty,[3] reinforced, in the words of Sir Harold Nicolson, by "calm, patience, good temper, modesty and loyalty."[4] Yet this diplomatic style is also not without its problems. As Sir Harold himself observed,

> The dangers of vanity in a negotiator can scarcely be exaggerated. It tempts him to disregard the advice or opinions of those who may have longer experience of a country, or of a problem, than he possesses himself. It renders him vulnerable to the flattery or the attacks of those with whom he is negotiating. It encourages him to take too personal a view of the nature and purposes of his functions and in extreme cases to prefer a brilliant but undesirable triumph to some ostentatious but more prudent compromise. . . . It lures its addicts into displaying their own verbal brilliance, and into such fatal diplomatic indulgences as irony, epigrams, insinuations and the barbed reply. . . . Of all diplomatic faults (and they are many) personal vanity is assuredly the most common and the most dangerous.[5]

Despite such problems, I am persuaded that there are real advantages to be gained by a reexamination of the classical tradition in diplomacy.[6] The primary task of our diplomats today is to follow the precepts of the wisest of their predecessors and cultivate the virtues of honesty, patience, and moderation. If they do this, a number of problems endemic in the contemporary world might at least be ameliorated. Members of democratic electorates, for example, are often castigated for impatience with regard to the art of diplomacy. But we sometimes forget that this is often caused by the arrogance and deceitfulness of some of the foreign policy elite—who, presumably, ought to know better.

The problem faced by a democracy of combining the efficient formulation and implementation of a foreign policy with the retention of popular support for that policy was noted by Tocqueville over a century ago. "A democracy can only with great difficulty," he wrote, "regulate the details of an important undertaking, persevere in a fixed design, and work out its execution in spite of serious obstacles. It cannot combine its measures with secrecy or await their consequences with patience. These are qualities which more especially belong to an individual or an aristocracy and they are precisely the qualities by which a nation, like an individual, attains a dominant position."[7] Moreover, as a contemporary analyst of the American character has concluded, "The rule to which there are few exceptions . . . is that at the critical junctures, when stakes are high, the prevailing mass opinion in a democracy will impose what amounts to a veto upon changing the course on which the government is at the time proceeding. Prepare for war in time of peace? No. It is bad to raise taxes, to unbalance the budget, to take men away from their schools or their jobs, to provoke the enemy."[8]

It has always been common in democracies for those outside the inner circle guiding our foreign policy to charge those within of excessive secrecy and ignorance of, if not hostility to, the values of the people. Those within the magic circle, however, have often jealously guarded their secrets in presumed self-defense against those whom they perceive as uninformed and impassioned meddlers in the affairs of professionals. Some members of the foreign policy elite go so far as to lay a claim to a near-monopoly on imagination, daring, and brilliance for themselves and their select cohorts.

Former Secretary of State Henry Kissinger outlined in clear terms this view in his first major work, *A World Restored.*

> For the spirit of policy is its contingency; its success depends upon the correctness of an estimate which is in part conjectural. The essence of bureaucracy is its quest for safety; its success is calculability. Profound policy thrives on perpetual creation, on a constant redefinition of goals. Good administration thrives on routine, the definition of relationships which can survive mediocrity. Policy involves an adjustment of risks; administration an avoidance of deviation. . . . The attempt to conduct policy bureaucratically leads to a quest for calculability which tends to become a prisoner of events. The effort to administer politically leads to total irresponsibility, because bureaucracies are designed to execute, not to conceive.[9]

The Wilsonian idealists, on the other hand, upheld the goal of "open covenants, openly arrived at" as the best medicine for the democratic weakness of impatience. If the people are fully informed and involved from the outset, they argue, then they will support the resulting policy, since they will have had a large hand in framing it.[10]

Upon reflection, it can be argued that both points of view have their merits. Perhaps the confusion would be lessened if all concerned could agree upon certain underlying premises. To return again to Tocqueville, the French political theorist once observed that democracies will normally pursue good ends in foreign policy but have imperfect means for carrying out these ends.[11]

The answer to this problem may well be to separate more clearly the formulation of foreign policy from the conduct of diplomatic negotiations. That is, diplomats should refrain from making (as opposed to recommending) policy, and politicians should refrain from implementing policies directly by taking part themselves in negotiations with other states. If this division of labor were observed, several fundamental problems could be resolved. Policymaking, which should never be secret in a democracy (except with reference to emergency responses to unexpected crises involving the survival of the nation), could be more democratic and open. Policy alternatives could be more freely debated. Politicians would derive the immense advantage of insuring popular support for policies that a solid majority were instrumental in forming. Political leaders who stated their goals clearly and defended them publicly against their critics might be better off in the long run than those leaders who dissimulated their goals in the false belief that a "moving target" is harder to shoot at. (Lyndon Johnson is the most obvious recent example.)

Once policy has been set by the elected leaders (president and Congress) in consultation with the people, however, professional diplomats would then be able to carry out that policy using their special skills. Negotiations to implement the democratically established policy could, and often would, be conducted in closed session. This would enable all participants to speak freely without "playing to the galleries"; negotiators would be allowed to "save face" in public even though they may be making some concessions in private. As is well known, in order to bring opposing groups together it is sometimes necessary for mediators to gain the confidence of opposing groups by showing sympathy for their position; this, of course, could not be done if all delicate negotiations were open to the public. The proper division of policymaking and policy-implementing responsibilities would be bound to benefit our foreign policy at all levels.

Having said this, at least six other considerations should be borne in mind by diplomats and political leaders alike. First, popular attitudes can be expected to lag behind the views of the foreign policy elite on most issues. This fact of life simply underlines the necessity for a continuous give-and-take between the leaders of a constitutional democracy and those who elected them to office. If the elected leaders cannot convince the electorate of the propriety of a proposed policy, then either that policy or the leaders, or both, should go.[12]

Second, an uncertain policy is always undesirable; since no one is sure of what it is, everyone is suspicious of it and not a few will take the opportunity to attack it. A secret policy, being unknown except to a few, is by definition uncertain and subject to all the problems of such policies.

Third, summit diplomacy can be dangerous and should be avoided if at all possible. Negotiations when conducted personally by political leaders naturally violate the division of labor discussed earlier, whatever appeal they might have in some circles. The risks in such ventures far outweigh the possible advantages. Whenever world-famous personalities gather, a "circus atmosphere" quickly develops; the media are attracted from near and far, and the temptation for politicians to behave in ways that will appeal to the media becomes almost overwhelming. Even more serious, there are strong pressures on the participants in such an "event" to come to some accord without full consideration of the viability of the agreement in the long run. So long as headlines are made, and immediate applause "earned," the world leaders will often be content. If a solution to a serious problem is too hastily put together, however, there is the very real danger that it may unravel all too quickly. There have been a number of recent major international agreements that come close to fitting the above description, most notably, perhaps, the Paris Accords on Vietnam in 1973. In addition, as a practical matter, decisions made at the summit allow for little or no change (except in a few cases where the home parliament must ratify a treaty), much less for more thoughtful reconsideration and analysis. All too often major political decisions are made in the most offhand manner, perhaps late at night (as was the case with the final version of SALT I in 1972) or with incomplete information. When heads of government are personally involved, the latitude for delay, maneuver, and reconsideration is limited.

Fourth, as Paul Eidelberg has pointed out in his recently published work, *Beyond Detente: Toward an American Foreign Policy*,[13] it is important to avoid agreements that cannot be enforced or that do not at least bring upon the violator an unwelcome consequence. Robert A. Lovett phrased this advice very well in testimony before a Senate committee. "I do not think," he noted,

> that there is any such thing as a "self-policing treaty," or "self-enforcing treaty" between two countries without similar ideas of law, order and political freedom. The right of inspection between two parties who distrust each other is essential. . . . Apparently the only valid protection against dishonesty between two great powers is to have a breach of a treaty carry its visible and tangible loss to the cheater. For example, an agreement to deliver oil against right of free passage through a canal. If the canal is blocked, oil delivery stops.[14]

Fifth, negotiators from democratic countries should beware the pitfall of assuming that the representatives from totalitarian regimes are not too dissimilar from themselves. In his book *American Foreign Policy*, Henry Kissinger warned that "anyone succeeding in Communist leadership struggles must be single-minded, unemotional, dedicated, and above all, motivated by an enormous desire for power. Nothing in the personal experience of Soviet leaders would lead them to accept protestations of good will at face value. Suspiciousness is inherent in their domestic position. It is unlikely that their attitude toward the outside world is more benign than toward their own colleagues."[15]

Sixth, practitioners of "public" or "political" diplomacy are, as we have seen recently, all too susceptible to *hubris*—to delusions of grandeur that cloud their judgment. In his biography of Lloyd George, Sir Charles Mallet suggested that "unvarying self-assurance tempered by an ever-varying opportunism is perhaps the most dangerous equipment that statesmanship can have."[16] While the line between necessary self-confidence and unwarranted *hubris* is often difficult to draw, the effort is well worth making—as recent American foreign policy clearly demonstrates.

RECENT AMERICAN DIPLOMACY

How well the United States has adhered to these principles can be determined in part by an assessment of the American postwar diplomatic record. Since the end of World War II, American diplomacy has had three goals: (1) creating an effective global collective security organization, supplemented by a system of American-led alliances, to control aggression, particularly of the Communist variety;[17] (2) halting the proliferation of nuclear weapons;[18] and (3) enhancing the economic development of the Third World nations to gain their friendship, or at least their neutrality, in our disputes with the Soviet Union.[19]

When we consider the present world situation, however, it is clear that our diplomacy has had at best mixed success. The dream of "collective security" has proved to be a chimera; and while most of our alliances (with the exception of SEATO) are still nominally intact, the reliability of many of our allies is questionable at best. At least five other nations (the USSR, the People's Republic of China, the United Kingdom, France, and recently India) have nuclear forces of varying capabilities, and the number of nuclear "threshold" states is growing. Finally, the number of American allies in the Third World is limited, regardless of the aid we have distributed to such nations. The fact that most Third World nations, which now comprise a majority of the UN, are petty police states whose leaders repress their own people and espouse (if often inexactly) assorted leftist ideologies only reduces the likelihood that they will associate themselves diplomatically with this country. Perhaps even a skillful American diplomacy could not have altered this situation appreciably. But the facts suggest that we could have done much better.

TOWARD A NEW AMERICAN DIPLOMACY

The question, of course, is how *can* we do better? To meet adequately the needs of American diplomacy in the years immediately ahead, there will have to be major institutional reforms in the State Department as well as in other governmental agencies directly connected with the conduct of foreign policy. As the recently appointed national security adviser, Zbigniew Brzezinski, has acutely pointed out, American international business firms are often more efficient and effective "diplomats" than equivalent agencies of the United States government. "What impresses me generally in foreign affairs," he recently told the Commission on the Organization of the Government for the Conduct of Foreign Policy," is that modern, large-scale, internationally active corporations have a far more effective way of operating internationally than the State Department. I would much rather deal abroad with the representatives of IBM than with many of our embassies, in terms of perspicacity of analysis, flexibility of operation, and rapidity of movements."[20]

The fundamental reason for this unfavorable comparison is not hard to find, and it applies to other departments of the government as well. That reason is the lack of flexibility in the civil service. Although there has been an increase in the number of late-entry persons coming into the civil service from other backgrounds, plus increases in the number of persons rotating from other departments, an ambassador still cannot draw on as large a talent pool as the manager of the branch office of a multinational corporation. If a private business needs the services of an exceptional person for a particular job, it will aggressively recruit that person, offer him or her working conditions and challenges (and, incidentally, the salary) that will interest the person, and put him or her to work. A foreign service executive, even the secretary of state himself, does not have such latitude. A career bureaucracy, protected by law from dismissal for all but the most flagrant incompetence, inevitably develops a mentality dominated by concern for personal security and by mediocrity—as Henry Kissinger often pointed out prior to 1969. The rewards for taking risks and for displaying exceptional ability are often not obvious to the career civil servant. Under those conditions, it is therefore entirely rational for a bureaucrat to "play it safe" and await automatic promotions based on seniority.

A more open foreign service, in which career officers spend several years at various times in universities or private businesses and in which military officers, business people, and scientists spend some time in the diplomatic service, will doubtless come about in the near future, not so much because it is a good idea but because it is an inevitable idea. Further, a stint on Capitol Hill early in the careers of diplomatic officers would provide insights into the nature of the democratic process that the foreign affairs specialists are not likely to have obtained at their universities or during their professional careers. Many congressional representatives and senators who serve on foreign-policy-related committees would probably welcome the assistance of such young officers both in the Congress itself and in their district offices. Our foreign service personnel would then learn firsthand that the interests of Washington are often different from those of the country at large and perhaps discover how to compensate for the differences.[21]

In addition, the tasks confronting our diplomacy have changed in recent decades. Before World War II, most of our diplomatic activity was concerned with traditional, usually bilateral, relationships between governments. Now, however, not only are negotiations conducted increasingly on a multilateral basis, but the range of these negotiations has widened correspondingly. There is now a more pressing need for expertise in scientific or economic problem areas, such as energy, population control, food supplies, resource conservation, and so forth. The great multinational corporations have responded to these challenges much more quickly and effectively than have governments. A larger representation in the State Department of experienced business executives and other experts would, therefore, give our foreign service the flexibility it needs to advance the interests of the United States under emergent conditions.

There is at least one more major lesson that the State Department could learn from leaders of business and industry. American business management is generally recognized as the best in the world mainly because our business community has combined entrepreneurial talent with systematic management techniques. (Until recently, there were few first-rate schools of business in Europe.) A major United States corporation would never think of going along from year to year without making advance surveys concerning consumer desires, the likely impact of long-term economic, social, cultural, and political trends on their industry, and the like. They would look upon themselves as "flying blind" if they did not obtain the best estimates available of the number and categories of skilled manpower that will be required five and ten years from now and of the kinds of plant and equipment that will be needed to meet projected demands. They also evaluate very carefully the likely activities of their competition, both foreign and domestic.

Within the government, only the Defense Department has maintained a file of "contingency plans" to deal with assorted eventualities, regardless of the likelihood that they might actually occur. Very little long-range planning, by way of contrast, is done by the State Department. As the president of the Council on Foreign Relations, Bayless Manning, has written, "in nonmilitary aspects of the nation's foreign policy, however, the . . . United States government does virtually no advance contingency planning in its foreign policy. And even less is done by way of national investment and commitment to long-term foreign relations programs that will produce results in the years ahead."[22]

All too often, as critics of American diplomacy have been pointing out for the past three decades, our foreign policy is dominated by reactions to current events and to the initiatives of other nations, with little thought of long-term consequences. The recent oil crisis is but one example out of many that could be cited. As long ago as the late 1940s, congressional committees received testimony that we could expect a crisis in energy supplies in about twenty-five years; yet in 1973, the United States government was caught almost totally unprepared for the predicted energy crisis. The old axiom that "operations drive out planning" is true for many institutions, but it is particularly pertinent to our foreign policy apparatus, divided as it is into dozens of semi-independent bureaucracies in several departments and agencies that all too often fail to cooperate effectively with each other. There is, of course, something to be said for competing and conflicting sources of ideas and recommendations for our policymakers. In the years ahead, however, there will be a greater need than ever before for close cooperation, especially in the area of long-range planning, among all the officials responsible for formulating the foreign policy of the United States, both in the executive and legislative branches.

In writing a small essay on a large subject, there are very obvious limitations. I have tried to set forth at least a few points that are not immediately self-evident, and to reiterate other points often made that cannot be made too often. As the title of one of Walter Lippmann's books in the 1940s proclaimed, our foreign policy is the "shield of the republic," our first line of defense. In addition to stressing the importance of diplomacy, I have tried to demonstrate that the underlying nature of the diplomatic arts has not and will not change. The centuries-old problem of how best to balance the need for leadership and some necessary secrecy with the equally impressive need in a democracy for an informed public opinion and freely given support must also be confronted by each generation. Finally, I believe that these concerns *can* be managed, and our diplomacy made more efficient, if we pay greater attention to the guidelines for diplomacy that I have outlined and reform the foreign policy apparatus to implement them effectively. If these steps are taken, I am confident that the record of American diplomacy will improve immeasurably in coming years.

NOTES

1. See, for instance, Harold Nicolson, "Diplomacy Then and Now," *Foreign Affairs* 40, no. 1 (October 1961): 39–49.
2. Jules Cambon, *Le Diplomate* (Paris: Hachette, 1926), pp. 119–20.
3. See especially the chapter "The Mission of Envoys," in Kautilya, *Arthasastra,* trans. Dr. R. Shamastry, 3rd ed. (Mysore: Wesleyan Mission Press, 1929). As one student of diplomacy has remarked. "There is no permanence in a relationship begun by promises which cannot be redeemed, and therefore, as I have said before, the use of deceit in diplomacy is of necessity restricted, for there is no curse which comes quicker to roost than a lie which has been found out." François de Callieres, *On the Manner of Negotiating With Princes* (South Bend, Indiana: University of Notre Dame Press, 1963), p. 130.

4. Harold Nicolson, *Diplomacy*, 3rd ed. (New York: Oxford University Press, 1963), p. 67.

5. Ibid., pp. 63–64.

6. The author is presently editing (with John J. Tierney) an anthology of such essays and memoirs, to be entitled *The Diplomatic Tradition*.

7. Alexis de Tocqueville, *Democracy in America*, 2 vols. (New York: Vintage Books, 1956), 1:243–44. It would be fair to assume that Tocqueville would lean toward the presidential side of the perennial executive-legislative tug-of-war. Members of the Foreign Service and such influential institutions as the Council on Foreign Relations and the Carnegie Endowment for International Peace would doubtless be pleased to read Tocqueville's observations on the importance of the foreign policy elite. "Almost all the nations that have exercised a powerful influence upon the destinies of the world," he wrote,

> by conceiving, following out, and executing vast designs, from the Romans to the English, have been governed by aristocratic institutions. Nor will this be a subject of wonder when we recollect that nothing in the world is so conservative in its views as an aristocracy. The mass of the people may be led astray by ignorance or passion; the mind of a king may be biased and made to vacillate in his designs, and besides, a king is not immortal. But an aristocratic body is too numerous to be led astray by intrigue, and yet not numerous enough to yield readily to the intoxication of unreflecting passion. An aristocracy is a firm and enlightened body that never dies. (Ibid., 1:245.)

8. Walter Lippmann, *The Public Philosophy* (Boston: Little, Brown and Co., 1955), pp. 19–20.

9. Henry Kissinger, *A World Restored* (New York: Grosset and Dunlap, 1964), pp. 326–27.

10. "It is this happy fact, now clear to the view of every public man," Wilson wrote, "whose thoughts do not still linger in an age which is dead and gone, which makes it possible for every nation whose purposes are consistent with justice and the peace of world to avow, now or any other time, the objects it has in view." Albert B. Hart, ed., *Selected Addresses and Public Papers of Woodrow Wilson* (New York: Boni & Liveright, 1918), pp. 247–48. For a critical analysis of Wilson's foreign policy approach, see Robert Osgood, *Ideals and Self-Interest in America's Foreign Relations* (Chicago: University of Chicago Press, 1953).

11. Tocqueville, *Democracy in America*, 1:246–48.

12. A valuable recent study of public opinion and foreign policy is *U.S.*

Foreign Policy: Principles for Defining the National Interest (A Public Agenda Foundation Report in association with the Carnegie Endowment for International Peace (New York: Carnegie, 1976).

13. Paul Eidelberg, *Beyond Detente: Toward an American Foreign Policy* (La Salle, Ill.: Sherwood Sugden & Co., 1977), chap. 8.

14. U.S., Congress, Senate, Subcommittee on National Security and International Operations of the Committee on Government Operations, *Negotiation and Statecraft: A Selection of Readings* (Washington, D.C.: Government Printing Office, 1970), p. 53. On a related point, Mr. Lovett observed at the time, "Do not give unilateral concessions, particularly to the Russians or the French. They will not feel gratitude. They will feel contempt for your gullibility."

15. Henry Kissinger, *American Foreign Policy* (New York: W.W. Norton, 1969), p. 37.

16. Sir Charles Mallet, *Lloyd George: A Study* (London: E. Benn, 1930), p. 156.

17. For a series of useful analyses of the founding of this worldwide system of alliances see Arnold Wolfers, ed., *Alliance Policy in the Cold War* (Baltimore: The Johns Hopkins University Press, 1959).

18. See, for instance, Lincoln R. Bloomfield, "Nuclear Spread and World Order," *Foreign Affairs* 53 (July 1975), 743–55.

19. For an interesting essay on America's relations with the Third World, see Daniel P. Moynihan, "The United States in Opposition," *Commentary* 59, no. 3 (March 1975): 31–44. For a perceptive comment on the recent demands for a "New Economic Order," see Irving Kristol, "The 'New Cold War,'" *The Wall Street Journal,* 17 July 1975. A fourth major goal of United States foreign policy has recently been added by the Carter administration—the protection and extension of human rights around the world. A former Brookings scholar, Ernest W. Lefevre, has written a penetrating analysis of this new policy in "The Trivialization of Human Rights," *Policy Review,* Winter 1978. See also Kenneth L. Ademan's overall critique of the Carter administration's foreign policy, "The Runner Stumbles: Carter's Foreign Policy in the Year One," *Policy Review,* Winter 1978.

20. Zbigniew Brzezinski, "The International Community in the Next Two Decades," *Appendices: Commission on the Organization of the Government for the Conduct of Foreign Policy,* vol. 1: *Appendix A: Foreign Policy for the Future* (Washington, D.C.: Government Printing Office, 1975), p. 17.

21. For a fascinating account of the interaction between the Foreign Service and the congressional staffs of Capitol Hill, see Frederick Poole, "Congress v. Kissinger: The New Equalizers," *The Washington Monthly* 7 (May 1975): 23. The author relates how a small but highly able

group of foreign service officers, frustrated at their inability to influence United States policy while at the State Department, secured key positions on Hill staffs, and later had considerable effect on such crucial legislation as the War Powers Act. Many of these same foreign policy specialists have recently returned to State as assistant secretaries, and so forth, in the Carter administration. See also a recent article on this subject by the present author, "The New Foreign Policy Elite," *Policy Review*, Summer 1977.

22. Bayless Manning, *The Conduct of United States Foreign Policy in the Nation's Third Century* (Claremont, Calif.: Claremont University Center for the Claremont Colleges, 1975), p. 68. A similar complaint (together with other interesting recommendations) is put forth in Senator Henry M. Jackson's *The Secretary of State and the Ambassador* (New York: Praeger, 1964). See also a perceptive critique of the State Department's bureaucracy by a newly retired foreign service officer, John Krizay, "Clientitus, Corpulence and Cloning—The Symptomotology of a Sick Department," *Policy Review*, Spring 1978.

Chapter Three

The Economic Factor in United States National Security Policy

Edwin J. Feulner, Jr.

INTRODUCTION

The systematic examination of the economic tools available to United States policymakers has fallen into disrepute since the early 1950s. At that time these subjects would have been discussed in unemotional terms, perhaps within the nomenclature of "economic warfare." Today, however, many policymakers, some in the executive branch and many in the legislature as well, denounce as cruel and heartless any suggestions involving the use of United States economic power to promote national security interests.

But conventional wisdom on this subject is far from consistent. Some commentators denounced the OPEC countries which used their economic power by stopping critical supplies of oil to the West in 1973, while displaying few scruples over the economic boycott of Rhodesia, the arms embargo against South Africa, and the limitation placed on credits to the Soviet Union because of its emigration policies.

Controversy over United States international economic policy, in fact, has increased considerably in recent years as world economic activity has increased. World trade now exceeds $800 billion per annum, and the international economic system is now truly universal, involving nearly all countries, large and small. Partly because it involves so many nations, each with its own noneconomic objectives, world trade has never approached the ideal of the free market espoused by laissez-faire economists. But that does not mean that interferences with free trade always go unnoticed. The Common Agricultural Policy of the European Community, for example, has led to the imposition of substantial restrictions upon the importation of United States agricultural products into Europe in order to protect less efficient European producers. This policy has evoked considerable resentment in the United States; and the oft-posed question, "if they won't even buy our crops at world prices, then why should our tax dollars be spent on their defense?" evokes sympathetic reaction among affected groups on the United States side of the Atlantic.

The complexity of worldwide economic interrelationships means inevitably that the use of economic means to achieve national security objectives will generate intense discussion. This has led some to conclude that economic issues should be separated as much as possible from national security questions.[1] To such commentators, the use of economic strategy for political objectives is impractical and probably unwise. A more careful examination of the possible advantages that can accrue from utilizing economic leverage to achieve foreign policy objectives, however, suggests a different view.[2] It is worth noting, for example, that, in comparison with military action, the use of economic policy as a national security tool affords a certain flexibility to the policymaker. It can often be stopped or even reversed almost instantly; and it does not normally do any immediate physical harm to the adversary. When used in combination with other tools, or when designed to achieve only limited objectives, it can yield considerable success.

However, as Professor Robert W. Tucker has noted, the prevailing attitude seems to be "a rising disinclination to use or to threaten force, whether from the belief that force is no longer expedient or from the conviction that force is no longer a legitimate instrument or, more likely, from a combination of the two."[3] Tucker points out that the growing disinclination on the part of the industrialized states of the West to use force to protect their interests extends not only to military force but also, to a lesser extent, to economic force. In a period when the military options available to United States policymakers are disappearing even more rapidly than our worldwide obligations, the possible advantages of alternative means of achieving our national objectives should be carefully examined.

ECONOMIC WARFARE TODAY

It is worth examining at the outset several recent efforts by nations to use economic power to achieve political goals. Almost all of these cases involve concerted efforts by at least several sovereign states, a further indication of the increasingly integrated nature of the structure of the world economy.

1. The Oil Embargo of 1973–74
The October 1973–July 1974 Arab oil boycott of the Western countries was a classic case of the use of economic pressure to achieve political objectives. The exercise of tight control over the allocation of a scarce and vital resource as a means of influencing international behavior had rarely before been attempted in history until the implementation of the embargo by the Arabs. The Arab embargo was directly tied to specific diplomatic objectives in a well-defined set of circumstances. The relationship between the changes in the behavior of the embargoed countries that were desired by the Arab states and the embargo was made explicit from the outset. It was clearly a success. Some of the nations most dependent on imported oil (particularly Japan and France) did cooperate with embargoing governments. This, in turn, increased the pressure on other embargoed countries. As Jerome Davis has stated:

> Oil was not so much an ultimate weapon as an instrument. The object was not so much to reduce the developed nations to poverty as to apply pressure to solve Arab problems and to deprive Israel of present and future support.[4]

At the time of the embargo the United States imported about 30 percent of its crude oil supply (not all of this from the Arab nations), and so the imposition of the embargo made Israel's primary ally directly vulnerable to coercion from the OAPEC (Organization of Arab Petroleum Exporting Countries) nations. It is easy, in hindsight, to argue that the embargo did not achieve total success, since the original Arab demands, including the removal of the Israeli military presence from the occupied territories and the establishment of a separate Palestinian state, were never met. But the discomfiture that the industrialized world suffered caused the consumer nations to break their common front on Middle East issues, and a strong case can be made that the more "even-handed" policy toward the region adopted by the United States recently is in part due to the embargo.

The domestic political and economic effects of the embargo, moreover, are still being felt. Some United States politicians, including members of the Carter administration, have called for gasoline rationing in order to reduce dependence on foreign oil. The announced posture of the United States government is to move toward energy independence which, at great cost, would attempt to make the United States independent of foreign energy sources. Naval petroleum reserves (such as Elk Hills, California) have been opened to commercial use, and massive sums of money have been allocated both in the private and public sectors for the purpose of developing alternative energy sources. Thus, the United States political apparatus has been forced to respond in several ways to economic pressure from the Arab countries.

2. United States Agricultural Exports
Following the 1973 oil embargo, a number of commentators suggested that the United States should begin to use its immense "food power" as a counterweight to oil power. Due to the unparalleled productivity of the agricultural sector in the United States, we can feed our own population and still export 60 percent of our wheat and rice crops, 50 percent of our soybeans, 25 percent of our grain sorghum, and 20 percent of our corn. Although we produce only 20 percent of the world's grain, our grain exports account for 50 percent of all trade in the world market. In 1974, the United States supplied 75 percent of the net global grain exports (with Canada accounting for an additional 15–20 percent). Some estimates suggest that the United States will be one of only two countries that will be self-sufficient in food in the 1980s.

With this kind of influence on the world food export market, it is clear that the utilization of such traditional means of economic warfare as preclusive buying—in accordance with which, for example, the United States might enter the world grain market and buy up the bulk of the Canadian exports—could give the United States even greater control over food supplies than the OPEC nations have over petroleum. Even President Carter has said: "Emergency food aid should not be used as a diplomatic tool. However, in trade discussions—with the Russians, for example—we should strive to obtain diplomatic concessions."[5] Domestic producers, however, are outspokenly opposed to the use of United States food power as a tool of foreign policy; responding to such pressures, the Ford administration also opposed it. The position of the producers stems from the belief that government manipulation of food markets will depress prices in a major sector of the market.

Recent proposals for a "world food bank," if adopted, would further reduce the leverage that might accrue from the use of United States food supplies as a political weapon since, presumably, the control of the food would be in the hands of "international civil servants," whose perspectives and/or interests would diverge substantially from those of the United States.

The ways in which United States agricultural power might be employed in the service of foreign policy objectives has been outlined by William Schneider in his monograph *Food, Foreign Policy and Raw Materials Cartels.*[6] In dealing with the objections of domestic producers, Schneider suggests creating an international reserve, disbursements from which would not be allowed to influence domestic prices. In addition, Schneider recommends that United States humanitarian relief be coordinated with that of other food-exporting nations, and that United States self-interest always be a factor even in the allocation of humanitarian aid.

The Schneider proposal and others like it allegedly found their way to the higher reaches of the State Department during the final year of the Ford administration. On 9 January 1976, Leslie Gelb, reporting in the *New York Times*, stated that Secretary Kissinger had initiated a policy linking United States foreign aid, including food aid, to voting records in the United Nations. He claimed that those countries that consistently voted against important interests of the United States would henceforth have difficulty negotiating new bilateral aid agreements. Gelb observed further that the majority of countries against which Kissinger's policy initiative was directed were those of the Fourth World (that is, those nations "most seriously affected" by the economic crisis that confronts many of the LDCs). There has been no indication, however, that Kissinger's approach will become the basis for United States policy during the Carter administration.

Moreover, both the Ninety-third and Ninety-fourth Congresses placed legal restrictions on the use of food as a tool of national security policy. Recent legislation provides that funds distributed in connection with the Food For Peace program cannot be used for security purposes by the recipient nations. The program was amended further in the 1976 Foreign Assistance Act, which requires that at least 75 percent of the commodities sold on long-term credit must go to the most needy nations (those with a per capita gross national product of $300 or less), regardless of their policy toward the United States. Further, the law specifically prohibits the United States from providing development assistance to any nation that engages in "a consistent pattern of gross violation of internationally recognized human rights." This provision, however, has been erratically enforced: stringently with regard to some countries such as Chile, but not at all against such states as Peru.

3. UN Sanctions and the Byrd Amendment

The importation of Rhodesian chrome has been a serious political issue in the United States since President Johnson formalized United States participation in the UN sanctions against Rhodesia in 1966. In 1971, Congress passed the Byrd Amendment, which permits the importation of chrome from Rhodesia. Supporters of the amendment made much of the fact that the only other important source of supply was the Soviet Union; reliance on the USSR was considered unacceptable because chrome is essential in the production of alloys for many military products, including jet engines, guns, and armor-piercing shells. Attempts in both the Ninety-third and Ninety-fourth congresses to undo the Byrd Amendment failed; it was finally repealed, after a strong lobbying effort by the administration.

The UN sanctions against Rhodesia in any case have had an adverse effect on the economy of that nation. From the time of the Unilateral Declaration of Independence (UDI) until 1976, the Rhodesian government was largely able to circumvent them, principally because of the continued support provided the Salisbury regime by South Africa. (South African support was particularly critical, since Rhodesia is a landlocked country and was totally dependent on South African air, rail, and road connections for purposes of foreign trade.) Living standards for both blacks and whites in the capital city of Salisbury remained among the highest on the African continent, and Rhodesian shops filled their shelves with goods not only from South Africa but also from many other industrialized countries; these goods were either transported through South Africa or supplied directly by that nation. Rhodesia was even able to obtain a modern fleet of commercial aircraft, in ostentatious disregard of the sanctions. But the sanctions extracted a considerable price in terms of reallocation of economic activity within Rhodesia; and more recently, South Africa has been less willing to cooperate with the Rhodesian government as fully as in the past. Thus Rhodesian trade has been considerably restricted, although Rhodesian farm products, particularly maize, are still exported in substantial quantities to her black African neighbors. History may yet judge the UN sanctions against Rhodesia to have been a successful application of economic power, in this case by a consortium of nations operating through an international organization, to achieve political objectives.

EAST-WEST TRADE

One of the principal examples of the use of economic power for political purposes since the end of World War II has been the effort by the NATO countries and Japan to regulate patterns of trade with Eastern Europe and the Soviet Union. Shortly after the war, working through the Coordinating Committee (COCOM), the Western nations, led by the United States, imposed extensive restrictions on trade with the Communist nations in many categories of industrial goods and raw materials. This was supplemented by stringent unilateral controls instituted by the United States under several laws, including the Export Control Act (now the Export Administration Act), the Trading with the Enemy Act, and the Battle Act.

While trade between the United States and the USSR increased under the Kennedy administration, the first systematic effort to expand trade relations with the Soviet Union and Eastern Europe began in 1968, under the theme of "building bridges with the Communists."[7] Although East-West trade did not initially approach the levels which some overly optimistic business people had been led to expect, more recently, under the policy of "detente," that trade has expanded greatly. It is concentrated in foodstuffs and sophisticated technology.

1. Agriculture

On three occasions in recent years the Soviets have been forced to purchase huge quantities of grain in foreign markets. In 1963–64, the USSR imported about 10 million tons of grain, including 1.8 million tons from the United States. Another disappointing harvest in 1965, plus the need to rebuild depleted reserves, led to additional massive grain purchases of 21.4 million tons by the Soviets in 1964–66. However, 1972 will be remembered as the year of the big grain sale. An unusually harsh winter and a short summer resulted in massive Soviet crop failures and the subsequent purchase of large quantities of grain, much of it from the United States. The United States sold 25 percent of its 1972 wheat crop to the Soviet Union, amounting to 13.7 million tons (almost half of total Soviet imports of 29 million tons). Not only the volume of the United States sales but also the credit that was extended to the USSR by the Commodity Credit Corporation (CCC) led to widespread criticism of the transaction. Credit was granted at interest rates as low as 6.125 percent, and a subsidy of some forty cents per bushel was given to the exporter. It is estimated that the total cost of the 1972 transactions to the United States taxpayers was $800 million, leading some critics in Congress and elsewhere to characterize the transaction as "the great grain robbery."[8]

The Jackson-Vanik Amendment to the Trade Act of 1974 prohibited CCC credits for future Soviet grain deals so long as the USSR pursues restrictive emigration policies. In addition, the Export Administration Act of 1974 clarified the president's right to institute export controls to safeguard against a temporary increase in foreign demand brought about by events such as a Soviet crop failure.

Soviet purchases since 1972 have ranged from 2.3 to 14 million tons per year. These large and erratic purchases by the Soviets have depleted American and world grain stocks and have interfered with the United States plan to establish a world grain reserve as called for by the 1974 World Food Conference held in Rome. United States officials have repeatedly asked that the Soviet Union participate in international stockpile efforts designed primarily for the benefit of less developed countries; the Soviets, however, have expressed little interest in such plans and even less willingness to participate in them. In 1976, however, the Soviets agreed to purchase grain on a regular basis from the United States for a five-year period. The amount to be purchased is about 7 million tons per year, with options for more if the United States has a good crop year.[9]

Some analysts have proposed barter deals between the United States and the Soviet Union, with Soviet oil and gas to be exchanged for United States grain, manufactured products, and capital investment in Soviet oil and gas fields. The maximum amount of oil that the United States could obtain from the Siberian oil fields, however, appears to be approximately 200,000 to 300,000 barrels per day, compared with present United States consumption levels of about 18 million barrels daily, about 40 percent of which is imported. Most estimates are that the production costs would be above the current OPEC posted price of $13.34 a barrel. Without United States government credits, therefore, such arrangements would clearly not be economically attractive to United States business.

United States grain surpluses constitute a potential weapon of considerable importance to this nation in its dealings with the Soviet Union. However, in the past the policy of detente produced a reluctance on the part of American officials to use economic leverage in our bilateral relations with the Soviets. If the new administration proves willing to use such leverage, it might have considerable impact on Soviet policy; in one of his earliest pronouncements on United States–Soviet relations, however, Secretary of State Vance renounced any attempt to link Soviet-American economic relations to Soviet behavior, and the prospects for the application of economic leverage against the USSR do not therefore appear bright.

2. Technology Transfers

Anthony Sutton has documented the role of Western technology in building the Soviet industrial base from the time of the Russian Revolution to the present.[10] These technological transfers are of more than historical interest. Today, Soviet commercial strategy is based on importing the most modern technology available from the Western industrial countries. Soviet buyers have scoured Western markets for the most advanced industrial processes, machinery, and equipment to meet their multifarious needs. The purchase of such technology by the Soviets in some instances has allowed them to leapfrog over intermediate stages of technological development into what Zbigniew Brzezinski has called the "technetronic age." United States exports of machinery and equipment to the Soviet Union increased from less than $50 million in 1970 to $547 million in 1975 (the last year for which complete statistics are available).[11] Other advanced technology has been made available to the Soviets by other sources such as Western Europe and Japan.[12]

While the utilization of imported technology requires initial domestic investment, the technology itself releases domestic resources for other projects such as capital formation and military production. Thus while two recent analysts estimate that the overall impact of Soviet technology purchases is resource demanding, they observe that "the long-term effect of Western technology transfers to the Soviet Union will probably be to strengthen the Soviet economy."[13]

The combination of massive technology transfers from the Western countries to the Soviets with resultant increases in Soviet indebtedness to the West poses a major foreign policy dilemma for the United States. Dr. Kissinger suggested in October 1976 that the West negotiate a common set of guidelines for OECD-country trade relations with the Soviet Union, lest the Soviet Union take advantage of anxious capitalists "willing to compete among themselves to sell Moscow the rope with which to hang them."[14] No action has been taken on this proposal to date by either the Ford or the Carter administrations. Instead of developing a coordinated policy on East-West trade to the advantage of the West, we have allowed the Soviets to use our desire to expand trade on liberal credit terms to their net advantage. A broadened "Jackson Amendment" approach, in which the United States ties expanded economic relations with the USSR to explicit changes in Soviet international behavior, ought to become a key element in United States national security policy in the decade ahead.

3. Soviet Maritime Policy

The growth of the Soviet merchant marine is underrated as a factor in international economic diplomacy. In the period 1946–1974, the Soviet merchant fleet moved from twenty-third to sixth place among the merchant fleets of the world. During the same time frame, the United States moved from first to eighth place. The Soviet Union now carries more than 7 percent of United States ocean-borne foreign commerce, and it anticipates carrying 15 percent or more within the next three years.[15] The Soviets have expanded their role in worldwide sea transportation by undercutting established shipping tariffs. In effect, the Soviets are seeking domination of the market by underselling the competition, with the clear possibility that prices will be increased should a monopoly or near-monopoly be obtained. It is ironic that virtually the entire Soviet merchant fleet has been built using Western technology. Anthony Sutton has evaluated forty-four types of Soviet maritime diesel engines, and in all but two cases he was able to identify the technology as of Western origin.[16] Sutton concluded that there is no such thing as a Soviet-designed marine diesel engine.

At the same time, the United States maritime fleet has continuously been downgraded, and here again our once substantial technological lead has been lost to our prime adversary.

FOREIGN AID

Traditionally, foreign aid has been divided into two categories: bilateral and multilateral. Bilateral aid is dispensed on a country-to-country basis and clearly provides the maximum leverage for the donor nation. Multilateral aid is dispersed through such lending institutions as the World Bank or the Inter-American Development Bank. Recently, a third form of foreign aid has become a major new factor in this equation: private bank lending directly to governments of the developing countries for general balance of payments and debt service financing. A broad new approach to foreign aid, of course, is embodied in the concerted demand of the LDCs for a New International Economic Order.

1. Bilateral Assistance

Bilateral foreign aid is held in disrepute by some observers precisely because it has considerable potential as an effective foreign policy tool. The United States, however, has used bilateral economic aid as an instrument of foreign policy less frequently than the USSR, which does so exclusively. In recent years, in particular, there has been little effort to maximize the foreign policy impact of such assistance, largely because of fear of offending developing nations. Attempts to develop a positive policy in this area have also been impeded by pious moralizing of the sort typified by the "Right to Food" resolution recently sponsored by Rep. Donald Fraser (D-Minn.) in the U.S. House of Representatives. Representative Fraser rejected the argument that the state of the United States economy did not permit a United States commitment to feed the world; the United States, he added, could not "forsake the responsibilities we share as members of the human family." Substantially increased assistance to food-poor nations, he noted, "would contribute to a less tension-filled atmosphere for international dialogue and negotiations."[17] On the other side, Rep. Edward Derwinski (R-Ill.) argued that despite the worthy objectives of the resolution, there was a danger of promising more than we can deliver. He reminded his colleagues that the final solution to the world's food problems depends primarily on the actions of the governments of those countries in need. Many of these countries, he observed, had adopted policies that discouraged full and efficient food production despite the potential that these nations possess in natural resources to feed their own people (e.g., restriction and rigid controls over farmers via government economic planning). Derwinski pointed out an important axiom that should be kept in mind by proponents of pious moralizing in foreign policy:

> The cause of food deficits are [sic] much more complex than the simple lack of food supplies. The United States has little or no control over many of these problems and should not assume a role it could not execute and responsibilities it cannot fulfill.[18]

The "Right to Food" resolution proposed by Representative Fraser clearly raises false expectations without setting forth a realistic policy that can be implemented in a complicated and complex world.

Occasionally, however, the Congress has attempted to direct bilateral foreign economic assistance in ways that would advance United States foreign policy objectives as Congress perceives them. A recent example was the attempt during 1976 to prohibit the administration from channeling more than $12 million in United States aid funds to Mozambique to offset the costs of her compliance with the UN embargo of Rhodesia. The State Department had proposed that bilateral assistance should be provided Mozambique because of that nation's economic difficulties. Conservative opposition, led by James Allen (D-Ala.) in the Senate and Philip Crane (R-Ill.) in the House, resulted in an eventual standoff. The prohibition was left in the appropriation legislation; however, funds appropriated earlier were still in the pipeline, and the administration was able to provide Mozambique with some assistance.

Contrasting vividly with the American reluctance to use the country's annual $3 billion in bilateral foreign aid for its own political advantage is the position of the Soviet Union. A recent report from Moscow noted:

> The Soviet Union has begun to make clear its policy of giving preferential treatment in foreign aid to those underdeveloped countries that embrace socialism and support Moscow's position in world affairs, and of denying help to those considered hostile.[19]

Moscow's leaders have categorically rejected Third World demands for a mandatory transfer of a fixed share of gross national product (now set at 0.7 percent in the pronouncements setting forth the objectives of the UN's Second Development Decade). The Soviets argue that the low state of development in the Third World is due to the depredations of Western states during the colonial period, and that the problem must be solved by the mandatory transfer of economic resources from the former colonial powers. Their approach to such matters demonstrates once again that the impact of "world public opinion" on Soviet policy is virtually nil. The Soviets use foreign aid policy to reward their friends, punish their enemies, and assist their own economy. These should be standard criteria for the foreign economic policy of the West as well.

2. Multilateral Assistance

Volumes have been written on the possible role of multilateral agencies in promoting the economic development of the world. One basic argument employed by those favoring a greater role for multilateral institutions has rested on the conviction that multilateral aid permits the recipient government to maintain its dignity and autonomy; the intermediate international institution acts as a buffer, and the individual donor countries do not control the distribution of funds.

These arguments have traditionally not commanded great support in the United States. Some members of Congress who at one time were supporters of multilateral institutions have recently come to oppose expanded United States support for their activities because of their lending policies. Rep. Henry Reuss (D-Wisc.) has, for example, expressed his displeasure at the World Bank for extending loans to Chile by voting against the appropriation for the International Development Association, the Bank's soft-loan affiliate. Despite such efforts to bend World Bank policies to United States desires—which incidentally have emanated from both the Left and the Right in Congress—the nature of multilateral institutions is such that there is only a limited range of opportunities for the United States to shape their programs in support of a positive foreign economic policy.

THE NEW INTERNATIONAL ECONOMIC ORDER

The basic concept of the New International Economic Order (NIEO) evolved in the wake of the first United Nations Conference on Trade and Development (UNCTAD) in 1964. Its basic premise is the assertion that the industrialized countries have for centuries "exploited" the countries of the underdeveloped world and now owe them indemnification as a matter of justice. This indemnification should include, at a minimum, the development of new terms of international trade which would benefit the less-developed countries (LDCs), substantially increased purchases of finished goods by the advanced nations from the LDCs, a general moratorium on the repayment of debts by the LDCs to the developed world, and greatly increased technology transfers from the multinational corporations to the LDCs.

The United States position on these demands remained firm throughout the negotiations that occurred at the Sixth Special Session at the UN and the Twenty-ninth General Assembly of the UN. At the Seventh Special Session of the UN, however, a series of counterproposals was put forth by the United States delegation. These have met with a mixed response from the LDCs, and discussions are continuing on a regular basis in Paris under the auspices of the Council on International Economic Cooperation.[20]

There is a lesson in the report filed by the congressional advisors to the 1976 UNCTAD IV meeting in Nairobi. The report notes that the United States and most Western nations do not accept the intellectual assumptions of the Manila Declaration, which restates the need for a NIEO:

> Although there was not great variance between the U.S. position and many items in the Manila Declaration, there were substantial differences on key agenda items. Nevertheless, four weeks of discussions should have allowed sufficient time for the differences to be accommodated.[21]

In other words, while the United States disagrees with the basic premises and with many of the specific proposed agenda items, it is prepared to be accommodating, while the LDCs were almost totally intransigent in their negotiating position. If agreement is to be reached in the Paris negotiations, the congressional advisors infer, the United States will have to accommodate itself almost totally to the LDCs.

It is this kind of thinking that is responsible, at least in part, for the fact that the United States rarely assumes a vigorous role in advancing its own interests in such forums. United States policymakers generally have failed to realize that the countries of the South (the LDCs) have already declared economic warfare on the West and are using every available opportunity to attack us for holding to our principles.

CONCLUSION

The legislative framework for implementing an effective economic policy is already in place. It includes such diverse laws as the Trading with the Enemy Act of 1916, the new administrative policies dealing with agricultural exports to the Soviet Union, the Ribicoff Amendment on the Arab boycott, the Export Administration Act, and other pieces of legislation. However, the actual implementation of a coordinated international economic policy requires that the diverse viewpoints of the various agencies of the government be reconciled. That this is a difficult task has been noted by others.[22] As Richard Erb has pointed out, the State Department has been reluctant to use economic leverage in support of United States foreign policy, while the Treasury Department in recent years has had fewer scruples in this area.

Because of the increased involvement of the government in the domestic economy, various parts of the private sector are able to bring the power of the government to bear on their side in disputes that would formerly have been considered to have an overriding "national security" aspect. Erb's conclusion that economic policy ought to be divorced from national security policy ignores the inevitable interrelationship of the two and the desirability of finding nonmilitary means of exerting influence in the world arena. Indeed, many United States decision makers, like Erb, tend to ignore the international economic dimensions of national security policy. Many, in fact, treat economic issues as annoying distractions from the "important" issues, i.e., those that are directly military or political in nature. As long as this is the case, the United States will suffer from missed opportunities that lead to a weaker American posture in all of our international relations.

The Soviets have no reluctance to use economic aid to their own advantage. Similarly, the Chinese foreign aid program has been carefully designed to suit their own strategic interests, principally in Africa.[23] Further, those nations that are trading with Taiwan, but would also like to trade with mainland China, are put at a disadvantage by the People's Republic of China (PRC) because of their Taiwan ties. Some company representatives have been denied visas or excluded from trade missions if their company has dealings with Taiwan.[24] Secretary Kissinger himself cited the leverage that United States dependence on Saudi Arabian oil provides the Arab countries in explaining his desire to sell Maverick missiles to that country. Testifying before the Senate Foreign Relations Committee, the secretary did not hesitate to point out the need for a cooperative relationship between the United States and Saudi Arabia. The Saudis, he noted, have become the largest single foreign suppliers of crude oil to the United States. In addition, Kissinger noted that within the OPEC states, the Saudis had consistently led the opposition to an oil price rise.

On the other hand, the record of American foreign policy is replete with missed opportunities to use economic means to support foreign policy objectives. The confusion within the State Department on such questions became clear during the Angolan situation in 1975–76. While Secretary Kissinger was formally eschewing economic warfare as a preferred tactic in the situation, his own department was pressing Gulf Oil Corporation to withhold its oil royalty payments from the anti–United States faction in the Angolan War. Later Gulf reinstituted payments to Angola and is today pumping oil both off the shore of Angola and from the Angolan enclave of Cabinda. If the United States had supported a separatist group in Cabinda and reorganized a new government there, we might have maintained at least indirect influence over the oil resources there and at the same time provided a base for the pro-Western faction of Angola to employ in their continuing struggle against the MLPA.

Concerning the transfer of technology to the East, the United States has lost the initiative. While it would be difficult to regain it, the task is by no means impossible. Similarly, the enormous leverage that the United States enjoys in world trade means that we might regain ground lost through political ineptitude by using food as a basic instrument of our national policy. An opportunity for the United States to employ its economic power in this way occurred in 1976, when the Treasury Department and the Federal Reserve Bank announced that the United States would support the Mexican peso. Following the decision of the Mexican government to let the peso float (which had the effect of a 40 percent devaluation), support was arranged for loans of up to $600 million to Mexico to shore up the peso on world currency markets. At the same time, the Fifth Session of the UN Law of the Seas Conference was closing in total disagreement, with the radical bloc in the Third World "turning the conference into an ideological battle between socialism and free enterprise."[25] Mexico was one of the leaders of those radical nations and was one of those most outspoken in its opposition to the United States position at the conference. It would have been relatively easy for the United States to convince the Mexican government that a $600 million loan entitles us to a friendlier and more cooperative attitude from her delegate at the Law of the Seas Conference than we were receiving.

From an examination of case studies and this series of current international economic issues, certain basic principles emerge:

1. United States foreign aid commitments should be inextricably linked to the United States national interest and to our national security.
2. The United States government should consistently attempt to protect United States private investment and United States private rights when negotiating in international meetings.
3. The use of economic strategy as an integral part of our national security policy must be endorsed at the highest decision-making levels in the United States government and coordinated with the Congress.

The opportunities for constructive action based on a coordinated policy accepted by both the legislative and executive branches would be greatly enhanced if as a people we began to understand the importance of economic options to United States national security policy.

NOTES

1. Richard D. Erb, *National Security and Economic Policies* (Washington, D.C.: American Enterprise Institute, 1976).

2. For an extensive survey of the literature on economic warfare, see Yuan-li Wu, *Economic Warfare* (Englewood Cliffs: Prentice-Hall, 1952) and Gunnar Adler-Karlson, *Western Economic Warfare: 1947–1967* (Stockholm: Almquest and Wiksell, 1968).

3. Robert Tucker, "A New International Order," *Commentary* 59, no. 2 (February 1975): 49.

4. Jerome Davis, "The Arab Use of Oil, October 1973–July 1974," *Cooperation and Conflict* 11 (1976): 63.

5. Interview in *Nation's Business* 64, no. 9 (September 1976): 32.

6. William Schneider, *Food, Foreign Policy and Raw Materials Cartels* (New York: Crane, Russak & Company, 1976). See also his "Agricultural Exports as an Instrument of Diplomacy," *Food Policy* 1 (November 1975).

7. For a detailed analysis see Samuel F. Clabaugh and Edwin J. Feulner, Jr., *Trading with the Communists* (Washington, D.C.: Center for Strategic and International Studies, 1968); and Feulner, "Recent Congressional Developments in Trading with Eastern Europe," in Grub and Holbik, *American-East European Trade* (Washington, D.C.: National Press, 1968).

8. Miles M. Costick, *The Economics of Détente and U.S.–Soviet Grain Trade* (Washington, D.C.: The Heritage Foundation, 1975).

9. See, for example, pt. III, "Foreign Economic Activities," in U.S., Congress, Joint Economic Committee, *Soviet Economy in a New Perspective,* Joint Committee Print (Washington, D.C.: Government Printing Office, 1976).

10. Anthony C. Sutton, *Western Technology and Soviet Economic Development,* 3 vols. (Stanford: Hoover Institution, 1968–73).

11. East-West Trade Board, *Fourth Quarterly Report,* 30 March 1976.

12. "Who's Leaking Technology to East Bloc Countries?" *Iron Age,* 23 August 1976, pp. 27–28.

13. John P. Hardt and George D. Holliday, "Western Technology and Economic Performance in the Eastern Countries," in U.S., Congress, House, Committee on International Relations, *Extension of the Export Administration Act of 1969, Hearings,* 94th Cong., 2d session, 1976.

14. Bernard Nossiter, "Soviet Bloc Debt: A Headache for the West," *Washington Post,* 17 October 1976; and C.L. Sulzberger, "Rope from the West," *New York Times,* 31 October 1976.

15. "Russia Now Knifes into U.S. Ocean Trade," *Business Week,* 4 October 1976, p. 34.

16. Costick, *Economics of Détente*, p. 95.

17. U.S., Congress, House, Representative Fraser speaking for the Right to Food Resolution, H Con. Res. 737, 94th Cong., 2d session, 21 September 1976, *Congressional Record* 122:10655.

18. Congressman Derwinski, ibid., 122:10649.

19. David K. Shipler, "Soviet Explains Aim of Its Foreign Aid," *New York Times*, 6 October 1976.

20. For an extended discussion of the development of the new international economic order, see Edwin J. Feulner, Jr., *Congress and the New International Economic Order* (Washington, D.C.: The Heritage Foundation, 1976).

21. U.S., Congress, House, Committee on International Relations, *Report of the Congressional Advisors to UNCTAD-IV*, 1976, p. 4.

22. See, for example, Erb, *National Security and Economic Policies*.

23. See Frank Ching, "China's Interest-Free Foreign Aid," *Wall Street Journal*, 12 November 1976.

24. Jacques Leslie, "U.S. Companies Punished by Chinese for Connection with Taiwan Trade Body," *Washington Post*, 26 September 1976.

25. *Wall Street Journal*, 20 September 1976.

Chapter Four

The Impetuous Vortex: Institutional Dimensions of United States National Security Policy

John Lehman

As every American president has learned to his distress, a democracy is not organized for the efficient conduct of foreign policy. Foreign policy is the art and science of applying common sense to one's actions vis-à-vis the external world. As such, it should be well within the capability of an enlightened and informed executive to formulate and carry out an efficient and even a wise foreign policy. In a democracy, however, the executive does not have the right to do so alone. The United States Constitution has been described as an invitation to the executive and the Congress jointly, and the Senate acting separately, to struggle for the privilege of directing American foreign policy. Power over foreign policy, moreover, is distributed among the branches of government in a manner purposely unspecific. The process by which this power sharing is carried out among the branches is a dynamic, everchanging one. If it is not constantly attended to, it can swiftly go awry, and it has done so often in the Republic's history. The attending must be done by all three branches and by the people. In foreign policy this is achieved by setting against the executive branch a legislative department that is in Madison's words, "everywhere extending the sphere of its activity and drawing all power into its impetuous vortex."

In the allocation of the foreign policy powers among the branches of the government, in fact, the Constitution embodies not one but two incompatible concepts of executive power, reflecting unreconciled differences among the drafters. One conception assumes that the executive exists solely to serve the legislature, wherein resides the will of the people;[1] the other assumes that the executive ought to be within generous limits autonomous and self-directory.[2] This dualism has enshrined a permanent struggle for power between the executive and legislative branches. All that the Constitution really does is to confer upon the president, in Article II, certain powers capable of affecting our foreign relations, and in Articles I and II certain other powers upon Congress as a whole.

The war and treaty powers, for example, have been unending sources of struggle between the branches. No constitutional solution will ever end this struggle because each branch has indisputable rights that overlap, or as Hamilton described it, "Joint Possession." Article II grants the president the executive power to take care that "the Laws be faithfully executed," and Article I grants Congress all legislative powers to "make all Laws which shall be necessary and proper for carrying into Execution . . . Powers vested by this Constitution in the Government of the United States, or in any Department or Officer thereof" (Article I, section 8). The president is endowed with the sole power of "Commander in Chief." Congress is directed "to raise and support Armies," to provide for disciplining the militia, "and for governing such Part of them as may be employed in the Service of the United States." No further guidance is given as to the content of these powers.[3]

Well, what do those words then mean? Do "legislative Powers" include the right to exercise a surveillance or superintendence of the executive, including the deployment and direction of military forces in the field? Does control of the purse strings include the right to refuse to raise armies or navies at all or to hamstring and inhibit the president in directing military operations undertaken as commander in chief? Does the power to advise and consent as to treaties include the right to abrogate "so far as the people and authorities of the United States are concerned," any treaty to which the United States is a party, or to abrogate or refuse to implement executive agreements?

Is "the executive Power" of that passive variety defined by Locke, or is it the power to act "according to discretion for the public good, without the prescription of the laws, and sometimes even against it" as exercised by Lincoln, Theodore and Franklin Roosevelt and others in times of crisis? Do the "laws" that the president must faithfully execute include treaties? Executive agreements? International law? Who should control the federal budget? What is the constitutional meaning of the word "war?"

Justice Holmes, in wry understatement, said of this dualism that "the great ordinances of the Constitution do not establish and divide fields of black and white."[4] Another theorist has waggishly characterized it as the kind of relationship marriage counselors describe as "antagonist-cooperative."[5] There can be no disputing the fact that a final and precise solution to the sharing of constitutional powers in foreign affairs is impossible to achieve. The framers have given us a system that a critic might justly characterize as contradictory, overlapping, and rife with unanswered questions.[6] One more favorably disposed, however, could, with equal justice, characterize it as a system of ingenious flexibility. Mr. Justice Brandeis indeed discerned perhaps the central virtue of this inefficiency in his dissenting opinion in *Myers* v. *United States*, wherein he said:

> the doctrine of the separation of powers was adopted by the Convention of 1787 not to promote efficiency but to preclude the exercise of arbitrary power. The purpose was not to avoid friction but by means of the inevitable friction incident to the distribution of governmental powers among three departments, to save the people from autocracy.[7]

The arbitrary power that Brandeis feared could occur as well in Congress as in the executive.

The other side of that coin, however, was noted by the English commentator Walter Bagehot, who observed that the great weakness of this built-in friction was not simply that it encouraged deadlocks between the president and Congress, but that it yielded no solution and no formula for finding one.[8] Some scholars, in culling nearly two centuries of constitutional interpretation, tradition, practice, and custom have found this dysfunction realized through the building into the structure and procedures of both branches an "unconscionable quantity of checks and balances" resulting in great difficulties for efficient policymaking.[9]

Other observers, however, have found in the historical evidence a validation of the "ingenious flexibility" provided by the overlapping powers. They stress the merits of a system that adapted readily to unforeseen military and diplomatic contingencies. They point to the amendment procedure as the evidence that the overlapping powers provided each generation with the opportunity—indeed the obligation —to adapt the document and its system to historical experience and contemporary problems.[10]

Bagehot, however, provides the best answers to his own strong objection. The Constitution, he said, would long ago have been brought to a bad end by the overlapping distribution of its powers were it not for the American genius for politics, our "moderation" in action, and our regard for law. "Sensible shareholders," I have heard a shrewd attorney say, "can work *any* deed of settlement; and so the men of Massachusetts could, I believe, work *any* Constitution."[11]

The grave rhetoric of constitutional crisis that inevitably attends the domestic struggle between the branches over foreign policy must therefore be taken with a grain of salt. To borrow a quip from Clinton Rossiter, the Constitution has always been the last refuge of the outargued politician. The executive will invariably refuse congressional demands for documents dealing with important policy issues, not on the grounds that they are politically embarrassing or administratively unwise, but because they are "unconstitutional." The exercise of power by the executive, similarly, is vigorously attacked as "unconstitutional" by critics who are far more concerned about the direction and substance of a specific policy than about the powers being exercised in pursuit of it. The more shrill the policy debate becomes, the more likely it will end in foreboding warnings of constitutional usurpation.

Sen. Richard Nixon in 1951 perceived such a usurpation of powers in actions by President Truman involving troop commitments, executive agreements, and executive privilege. In 1971, he also perceived a grave constitutional crisis developing over these same issues, but from exactly the opposite perspective.

In 1961, J. W. Fulbright, fearing the "localism and parochialism" of Congress, argued for the ceding of more powers in the conduct of foreign affairs by Congress to the executive. In 1971, he argued for the ceding of those same powers, but in the opposite direction.[12]

The Korean War, the Formosa Straits issue, the Bay of Pigs, and most recently, the Indochina War, gave wide currency to fears of constitutional usurpation by the executive. The repudiation of the League of Nations, the Neutrality Acts, the Connally Reservation, and the Rhodesian chrome amendment each in its time called forth grave commentaries concerning congressional interference with executive powers and responsibilities.

Partisanship, it must finally be noted, is another very important contributor to "constitutional crises." Its converse, bipartisanship in foreign policy, is not an American tradition. It came into being during World War II and was revivified by the early Cold War, and the attendant efforts of Democratic leaders, intellectuals, and sympathetic journalists to enlist Republican support for the postwar interventionism of the Truman administration. The assiduous cultivation of GOP foreign policy spokesmen by Secretaries Stettinius, Byrnes, and Marshall became an institution in itself.[13] As a word to be bowed to, it has a kind of beneficial power of its own, but the reality extends just so far as both parties arrive separately at the same perception of a problem, and often not that far.

The Republican party traditionally accepted a strong Hamiltonian conception of the executive role in foreign affairs. Wilson and Franklin Roosevelt were quite outside the Jeffersonian tradition that placed ultimate faith in Congress. The dynamics of partisan competition have, however, created strange patterns of constitutional allegiance, and even stranger constitutional arguments. The executive when in the hands of Democrats was suddenly revealed to the Republican opposition as inherently liberal-internationalist and even imperialistic, and the president himself as a high-handed usurper of congressional powers. The word "dictatorship" was prominently heard in Republican circles during the Wilson, Franklin Roosevelt, Truman, Kennedy, and Johnson administrations. During those same years the political, intellectual, and media leaders of Democratic persuasion spoke somberly of the reactionary nature of Congress, viewing it almost exclusively as a negative and obstructionist institution.[14]

During the Eisenhower, Nixon, and Ford administrations, however, an amazing transformation occurred. The Tafts, Dirksens, David Lawrences, and James Kilpatricks found undiscovered charms in a strong executive, while the Stevensons, Fulbrights, Commagers, and Schlesingers awoke to previously unsuspected constitutional dangers and executive usurpations.[15] And so it goes—the elected party leadership will support a president of the same party, and as the trend in

Congress has been to strengthen the party leadership at the expense of committee chairpersons, the support provided the executive by its party leadership, whether majority or minority, has grown stronger.[16] As noted above, the temptation to clothe one's partisan or policy arguments and attacks in the pin-striped suits of constitutional discourse is usually overwhelming. The serious student of these matters must therefore approach such debates with considerable skepticism.

ATTRIBUTES OF THE EXECUTIVE

While it is not necessary to agree with Washington that the transaction of business with foreign nations is altogether the province of the executive, it must be admitted that the nature of contemporary diplomacy, commerce, and war encourages development of an expansive view of executive power. Negotiation, conflict, crisis, and the practices of other nations do not readily adapt themselves to the peculiarities of legislative control.[17]

It is a fact of history that the expanded role of the federal government has occurred almost entirely in the executive branch. The process of expansion has been greatly accelerated during the last thirty years in response to military and strategic imperatives. The vast machinery of foreign and defense affairs is lodged in the executive branch. By contrast, since the founding of the Senate Committee on Foreign Relations in 1916, Congress can point only to the Congressional Research Service, the General Accounting Office, the Office of Technological Assessment, the Congressional Budget Office, and some considerable expansion of staff as signs of its response to emergent realities.

The personnel resources of the executive branch in quality and size are unmatched by any organization in the world. These legions of military and foreign and civil service personnel are of course employees of the federal government generally, but in the context of the struggle between the branches they are on the executive rolls. In terms of numbers, the resources of Congress are infinitesimally smaller.

In terms of expertise, the disparity is even greater. In the executive departments, the richness and sophistication in scientific, technological, military, diplomatic, statistical, medical, educational, geological, fiscal, legal, and sociological skills, including their most arcane branches, are truly awesome.

The continuity and stability of career services, staffed by people with countless experience in dealing with particular problems, provide an invaluable institutional wisdom in the conduct of foreign affairs totally absent in Congress, given the notoriously transient character of congressional staffs. The volume and complexity of international transactions, and the durability and complexity of substantive issues, make this expertise increasingly necessary just to stay in the game.[18] There is a temptation in Congress to oversimplify problems, and to be drawn, in Dean Acheson's words, "to courses high in debating appeal whose impracticalities are revealed only through considerable factual knowledge."[19]

The attributes of the bureaucracy are, however, a two-edged sword for the making of foreign policy. While the bureaucratic apparatus can be a great strength in carrying the day against Congress, in itself it constitutes a formidable domestic constraint on policy formulation. Chester Bowles once said that "getting the bureaucracy to accept new ideas is like carrying a double mattress up a narrow and winding stairway. It is a terrible job, and you exhaust yourself when you try it. But once you get the mattress up it is awfully hard for anyone else to get it down."[20] FDR himself once lamented: "You should go through the experience of trying to get any changes in the thinking, policy, and action of the career diplomats and then you'd know what a real problem was."[21]

The corollary attribute to executive expertise is intelligence acquisition, the established channels of which are an executive monopoly. The diplomatic, consular, military, electronic, photographic, and covert production of information on conditons that prevail in foreign countries flows to the executive, and only the executive has the capability to digest these daily volumes of raw data into rational and usable assessments. Congress possesses none of this information, save what it acquires secondhand from the executive or haphazardly from random direct sources. A significant dimension of such intelligence is the requirement that sources be protected from any disclosure whatsoever. The executive itself has never fully achieved such protection, but an open democratic assembly operates under far greater disabilities in providing it.

The greatest organic strength in the executive branch lies in administrative unity: in functional organization, hierarchical administration, unity of command, and internal discipline. These are the necessary attributes of problem solving, decision making, and policy execution. The orchestration and coordination of the complex military, diplomatic, and domestic moves necessary to deal with, e.g., a Cuban missile crisis, would be impossible without a single determining energy. The spontaneity and unpredictability of international affairs quite often requires prompt and even immediate response. The attributes of administrative unity enable the executive to plan and execute appropriate responses with dispatch.[22]

One hundred senators and four hundred thirty-five representatives, operating as individuals and/or as members of committees and subcommittees, policy caucuses, ad hoc ideologically based coalitions, and so forth, possess none of the attributes of administrative unity. The slow and open deliberations of a democratic legislature are attuned to the process of continuing compromise rather than the initiation of decisive action. In Congress controversy means delay, and missed opportunities.[23]

Another essential requirement for the successful conduct of foreign affairs is the ability to take a long-range view of situations, fashioning policy in light of long- and middle-range goals and effects. Success depends on identifying problems before they become crises and devising and executing preventive policies. While it is true that the entire United States government has been deficient in this regard, the executive is at least attuned to such a perspective; Congress cannot afford it. Public opinion, to which Congress must be directly responsive, tends to lag behind the facts of the international problems with which the executive must cope daily.[24] In the extreme, Congress has even been guilty of dealing with the future by legislating against the errors of the past.

One does not have to agree with Richard Neustadt that the presidency is the "sole crown-like symbol of the Union"[25] to accept the proposition that the executive branch has a national constituency and is responsible to "the whole people," to employ Woodrow Wilson's phrase. It is thus in a unique position to stand for the national interest as against the local and regional interests of congressional constituents and the special interests of organized lobbies. This fact is of special importance in foreign affairs.

Looked at in another way, it is a fact of life that there is virtually no political profit to be made in the serious pursuit of foreign affairs by a member of Congress. The role of critic after the fact, or of dramatic accusation, however, can generate useful publicity. And a latent American exasperation with "foreigners" has often exerted an obvious influence on congressional action, especially when international policy is competing with the political requirements generated by domestic and constituent concerns. Every member must stay close to these concerns. Only in the absence of opposition, interest, or consensus back home can a legislator be free to judge an international issue in terms of the larger national interest, and only then if he or she is free of the party whip, the pressure of a vital lobby, or of committee loyalties. Most regrettable of all, Congress is particularly vulnerable to powerful narrow interest lobbies, not merely the sordid black bag of the industry and labor lobbies, but the zealous forces of Common Cause, the Liberty Lobby, the Reserve Officers Association, the Greek-American societies, and the Sierra Club, each attempting to stampede vulnerable members to accept their own parochial view of the national interest.

Because, along with the vice-president, the president is the sole nationally elected government official, with the unique stature which that entails; the president brings to the executive branch a mighty psychological power, the force of symbolic personalized leadership. Whether a particular president's style is charismatic or not, the office provides an outlet for the universal human desire to personalize trust. The more abstruse, exotic, or dangerous the problem, the stronger the tendency to trust in one person. Lincoln or Roosevelt, for example, could never have acted with such independence of Congress had they lacked solid public support and personalized trust. Without this trust the executive branch is vastly weakened, as the administrations of Andrew Johnson, Herbert Hoover, Lyndon Johnson, and Richard Nixon have demonstrated.

While Woodrow Wilson may have exaggerated in saying that "inside the United States, the Senate is mostly despised,"[26] it is nevertheless true that the normal tedium of debate, incomprehensibility of procedure, and confusing array of elderly spokesmen or women vying for attention characteristic of the Senate is unlikely to arouse in the population an emotional allegiance to Congress. And it is indeed true that confronting a popular president and attempting to impose policy restraints upon such a president can be politically dangerous to a member. His or her constituency may easily confuse such opposition with obstruction of presidential efforts to deal effectively with national problems. The force of this personalization of trust is perhaps best understood in a period when it is absent, such as in the second Nixon administration.

This trust, and hence executive power, is greatly intensified by a general perception of national danger. "The circumstances that endanger the safety of nations are infinite," said Hamilton in the *Federalist* No. 23, "and for this reason no constitutional shackles can wisely be imposed on the power to which the care of it is committed."[27] While there have usually been voices of dissent during war and crisis, and "committees on conduct of the war" have occasionally been appointed, Congress has never been disposed during such periods to challenge executive actions seriously, even those of arguable constitutionality. Neutrality acts and war powers acts are a luxury of postwar periods only.

Indeed, the opinion of Congress during conflict and crisis has weighed in as often on the side of bellicosity and more forceful executive action as on the side of restraint and restrictions on the executive.[28]

The reasons are obvious enough. Popular opinion is always with the executive during a crisis, and woe unto the congressmen and women who lay themselves open to the charges of "stiffening the resolve of the enemy," "pulling the rug from under the president," or "abandoning our soldiers in the battle." Members of Congress will know that in moments of crisis, the executive will always have the drop on them, by having the president appeal over the head of Congress to the people.[29] Television and the press conference have made possible the strengthening of the president's bond with the public in a way that has no parallel for the 535 members of Congress. As far back as 1933 it was said that Roosevelt "has only to look toward a radio to bring Congress to terms."[30]

"Let him once win the admiration and confidence of the country," wrote Professor Woodrow Wilson, "and no other single force can withstand him, no combination of forces will easily overpower him. His position takes the imagination of the country. He is the representative of no constituency but of the whole people."[31]

ATTRIBUTES OF CONGRESS

The attributes and circumstances shaping congressional powers in foreign policy are less crisply identifiable and more difficult to catalog than those of the executive. Many of the deficiencies of Congress noted above—its multipolarity, divided authority, thinness of expertise, lack of intelligence information, inability to function secretly or to keep secrets, lack of continuity, and above all its localism and parochialism—are also the bases of its ultimate strength as a democratic institution.

The sanction of elections ties members inescapably to the will and mood of the people. Every member must be responsive to the constituency he or she represents. In the executive, only the president is elected. The powerful secretaries of state and defense, the service chiefs, and the director of the Central Intelligence Agency respond to no constituency but the president. While elected by the "whole people," the president serves three competing constituencies: the president's bureaucratic government constituency; the president's partisan constituency and the president's foreign constituency of allies and adversaries.[32]

Congress constitutes a vital part of the political matrix out of which the national consensus on foreign policy must be drawn. It alone is the institution capable of setting the parameters and boundaries of acceptable policy. In contrast to the initiating and executing functions requiring the particular virtues found in the executive, Congress alone is organically suited to shaping the broad flow of foreign affairs in direction, goals, and philosophy, and in so doing to mold popular understanding in support of wise policy.

Congress monitors, reviews, questions, criticizes, challenges, defines, modifies, approves, vetoes, and provides or withholds the appropriations for executive action. It stimulates executive action through both informal and legislative means and occasionally—usually with less happy results—mandates and initiates policies and operations against strong executive opposition.[33] Despite much rhetoric to the contrary, the activity and influence of Congress over foreign affairs are immense, and indeed probably greater than that of any other legislature in the world.[34]

Each of the virtues of the executive noted above has a reciprocal and checking counterpart among congressional attributes. Congressional freedom from the vast machinery of government allows a detachment from entrenched institutional viewpoints, a spontaneity of perception, and the opportunity to view forests rather than trees.

Unencumbered by armies of experts, the commonsense view of the congressional "nonprofessional" can temper the often narrow outlook of the executive. The arcane insights of specialists have often been accorded an attention and importance in foreign affairs far beyond their worth. The most important issues of foreign policy are not the proper preserve of the natural, technical, and political scientist, but are amenable to the widely shared insights and common wisdom found among members of Congress and other common people.

Congress, moreover, has a kind of expert talent not often found in the executive: virtuoso politicians long in the tooth. And there is, of course, the "congressional leadership." Presidents come and go, but the powerful chairpersons, whips, speakers, and majority/minority leaders appear nearly immortal. Not only do individuals physically hold their posts for as long as a quarter of a century or more, but when they pass from the scene, their understudies—of equal devotion to Congress and almost as long a term of service—assume the chair without missing a stroke of the gavel. They vary widely in education—and even wisdom— but are invariably the same in political cunning and the dark arts of maneuvering against the boys "downtown." There is no such thing as a "weakened" Congress in the way the term can be used accurately to describe a presidency. Because of seniority and the leadership, Congress—in the sense meant here—is always strong.

The corollary to the executive cult of the expert, as J. W. Fulbright has often reminded us, is the tyranny of secret information. The chaos of the classification system in the executive is legendary. While Executive Order 11652, issued 8 March 1972, has set in motion the process of rationalizing that system, it will take many years to accomplish the task.[35]

But virtually all "secrets" that are truly relevant to the responsibilities of Congress reach the interested members (and the press) with minimal delay in any case. Because of the very incontinency and openness of Congress, moreover, the public is usually guaranteed access to the most important intelligence and information not readily made available by the executive. The revelations attending the proceedings of the

Church and Pike committees in the Ninty-fourth Congress are cases in point.

The "high prerogative" people of the executive are always quick to remind us that Congress is incapable of acting with unity and dispatch as required by the pace of international events. But "in the legislature," as Hamilton has written,

> promptitude of decision is oftener an evil than a benefit. The differences of opinion, and the jarrings of parties in that department of the government, though they may sometimes obstruct salutary plans, yet often promote deliberating and circumspection, and serve to check excesses in the majority.[36]

It is such deliberation and circumspection that can often restrain unwise initiatives emanating from the executive about to act with unreasoned dispatch, e.g., in the proposed rescue of the French at Dien Bien Phu in 1954, or in rushing through an ill-advised SALT treaty. The deliberate skill and circumspect judgment of a Senator Russell, in handling a bitterly polarized and explosive issue during the investigative or legislative process, so that eventually a national consensus of gloriously broad generalities is arrived at, to which the wise and just then repair, is of incalculable value in a democracy.[37]

While it is unquestionably true that in foreign policy the executive in all important matters proposes, it remains equally true that in the same proportion Congress disposes. The activism of Congress in scrutinizing, and then substantially modifying, executive initiatives has increased apace with the increase in the latter. This congressional role has received much less scholarly and media attention than it deserves, because its methods, as Hamilton described them, "being at once more extensive and less susceptible of precise limits, . . . can, with the greater facility, mask, under complicated and indirect measures, the encroachments which it makes on the coordinate departments."[38] The executive gets all the headlines for initiating an Alliance for Progress or a Guam Doctrine or a new approach to East-West trade, but it is Congress that gives these policies substance, and, often, a far different texture, than intended by the executive. A recent observer has likened the process to the boss who pays off his employees and then gets them into a crap game in which he takes back all their money.[39]

After proposing grand policy schemes, the chief executive delegates responsibility for implementing them to subordinates. Their ability to protect and defend them from major congressional surgery, however, is quite limited. The isolationist legislation of the 1920s and 1930s, the violence annually wreaked on foreign aid, the long opposition to recognition of mainland China, the long-imposed restrictions on the use of East-West trade as a tool in managing Soviet-American relations, and the abrupt termination of assistance to pro-Western forces in Angola are well-known examples of the impact of Congress on executive initiatives. But less widely understood are the direct modifications of foreign policy by Congress acting in its role of prodder and goad on the executive. People tend to forget that it was Congress that forced unwanted policies upon Madison in the War of 1812, McKinley in the Spanish-American War, Truman on aid to Taiwan, and Nixon on Rhodesian chrome. Congressional influence has been significant also in dealing with structure, organization, and process in foreign affairs. The National Security Act of 1947 and the reorganization of the intelligence establishment, for example, were largely the result either of direct congressional initiatives or of active and equal participation by Congress with the executive branch in restructuring the nation's foreign policy machinery.

A closely related aspect of the active involvement of Congress in the policy process is the increasing disposition of the legislature, especially marked in the last twenty years, to oversee administrative detail and to superintend both the execution of policy and the performance and selection of personnel in the executive branch. This movement has included serious efforts even to "prescribe the mission of our troops in the field, in accordance with a foreign . . . policy of the United States which it is for Congress to set when it chooses to do so."[40]

A primary source of congressional strength in such efforts are the deeply entrenched bonds tying the executive bureaucracy to Congress. Every congressman and woman of seniority has cultivated numbers of career civil servants, military, foreign service, or intelligence officers throughout those agencies dealing with his or her areas of committee or constituent interest. The pattern of such symbiotic relationships typically stretches over three or more administrations. For the bureaucrats, the relationship yields benefits (or protection) for their agency or bureau office or perhaps their jobs. It can assist in their advancement within the system and possibly facilitate such matters as service academy appointments for favored constituents. The member of Congress, of course, may gain early access to needed information about problems or programs and an influence on the day-to-day implementation of policy. Nearly all of the chief political and permanent career officers of the executive are under constant pressure to do what the senior congressmen and women involved with the work of their agencies want them to do. They consult formally, informally, and even covertly, and their decisions on both policy and personnel are heavily influenced by those consultations.

The scrutiny, modification, and even initiation of policy by Congress provides another invaluable service. In subjecting executive proposals to the counsel and analysis of advisors owing no allegiance to the White House, an antidote is provided to the regal isolation of the presidency wherein all circumstances conspire to exclude criticism from the Oval Office. No one, as George Reedy has pointed out succinctly, has ever invited a president in person to "go soak his head," but that inestimable function can be and frequently has been bravely performed on the floors of Congress by Calhouns, Lodges, Brickers, Connallys, Rayburns, Jenners, Johnsons, Dirksens, Grosses, Hayeses, and Helmses, often with salutary effect.

The U.S. Congress is the only democratic legislature that sets the tenure service, pay, and benefits of every executive employee, enlarges, cuts, and radically modifies the executive budget, dictates administrative actions by line-item appropriating, and organizes, empowers, and delimits the very agencies of the executive branch themselves. And much of this is not even done by formal act or statute. The greatest influence is through committee action, telephone admonition, and bourbon in the back room.

THE CONSTRAINT OF THE PRESS

One facet of congressional interaction with the executive given scant attention in the professional literature is the symbiotic relationship between the media and Congress. One regularly makes the other an instrument of its dirty work. If reporters or commentators fail to get what they want from the State or Defense Department, they simply go to their friendly congressman or woman or committee staff and turn their requests into congressional reqests. In return, the member or staffer is provided a regular supply of inside information gleaned from the bureaucracy by the reporters or spoon-fed at "off-the-record" breakfast meetings with the secretary of state. These latter tidbits are generally of the sort calculated by the journalist to goad and gall the executive. Of such stuff are stories made. By its nature the media are powerful catalysts of conflict between the branches, and rarely if ever of harmony. Despite the conventional wisdom, television is not an unambiguous addition to presidential power. The harsh critics of the president, presenting evidence countering executive assertions, and the more sensational proceedings of congressional investigations, often receive considerably more air time than do the speeches of the president or the arguments of the president's principal foreign policy advisors, thus countering executive power. This was certainly the case during the Vietnam War.

CONSENSUS

It is by now almost too painful to use the word consensus in a serious treatise, so overworked and hackneyed has the term become in this post-Vietnam, post-Watergate era. But one must conclude from a review of the domestic constraints on United States foreign policy, outlined in this essay, that the establishment of a concensus in a democracy is absolutely necessary if the many checks, balances, and constraints are not to overwhelm and submerge any coherent policy initiatives. The term *consensus* here is limited to the acceptance by most members of Congress, the executive, and most importantly, the American people, of a common, conceptual framework for understanding of the world and the place of the United States in that world. Only through the development of such a common conceptual framework, and a wide agreement on its validity, can the niagara of daily events be given the kind of ordering necessary for coherent policy.

Prior to World War II it was sufficient to deal with policy issues on a fragmentary and individual basis; the functional involvement of the United States in world affairs was so low that it made no difference. World War II marked the involvement of the United States in global affairs on a massive and permanent scale, involving vast amounts of American resources directly influencing the lives of all of its people to such a degree that ad hoc and fragmented policy was no longer possible.

It was fortuitous that events in the period after World War II were of a simplicity and scale readily grasped by the American people and by their representatives in Congress. The postwar period was marked by the existence of an almost universally accepted conceptual framework for world events, known as the Cold War.

The concept was simple and easily understood: there was a large segment of the world under the control of a revolutionary and aggressive power; and there was another section of the world known as the "free world," whose high calling it was to "contain" the aggressive designs of the revolutionary power upon both the free world and the remaining portion of the world, then known as the "undeveloped world." The threat of world communism was a phenomenon whose existence no one doubted. The free world response, called the "containment" policy, was questioned only by those who argued that Western policy should transcend such passivity and "roll back" communism. In this universally accepted bipolar view of the world, the foreign policy process functioned with unprecedented smoothness. The executive branch and Congress shared a common conceptual framework, thus permitting a high level of dialogue along roughly parallel lines that focused on the means for carrying out policy based on goals that were not the subject of dispute. It is not to say that during this "golden age of bipartisanship" there was not considerably more conflict than both admirers and detractors of bipartisanship care to remember. The "great debate" over sending troops to Europe, and the bitterness between the legislature and the executive throughout Dean Acheson's tenure (especially during the Korean War), provide clear reminders that all was not harmony. It should not be forgotten that many of the ideas that led to policy during that period originated in Congress, such as the Surplus Agriculture Commodities Program, the International Development Association and the Arms Control and Disarmament Agency. A possible reason for the success and the longevity of this period of executive-legislative partnership was that the events of the world seemed to respond to American actions in ways that confirmed the validity of the underlying conceptual structure, thus legitimizing it and stimulating further action along the same lines.

The structure of the world politics, however, began to alter. Some time between the late 1950s and mid-1960s the conceptual framework appropriate to the period of the Cold War lost its functional conformity to the real world. American actions in the world no longer seemed to result in the consequences predicted by the framework. Unfortunately, the policy leaders in both branches of government failed to perceive the changing world structure. As a result, there was no modified or new framework for policy put forward. Policy formulation and decisions proceeded according to the established norms. In Cuba, the Dominican Republic, Guatemala, Chile, the Congo, Tanzania, and Indochina, American foreign policy proceeded along established channels that had less and less conformity with the real world. The policy consensus between Congress and the executive, and between the people and their government, began to disintegrate. The executive branch had completely lost faith in the old concept, but having no new one to put forward, and having a heavy vested interest in the momentum of established policy, it gritted its teeth and forged ahead. Congress had no new concept, but many voices decrying the old. The result was policy chaos in the late 1960s and early 1970s.

With the accession of the Nixon administration in 1969, a new conceptual framework was advanced for the first time since the 1946–47 period. Underlying the slogans of the Nixon doctrine, "Vietnamization," "the United States will no longer be the world's policeman," and "era of negotiation not confrontation," was the beginning of a coherent and comprehensive world outlook. Instead of the simple bipolar model of containment, the world was explained in terms of a model of diffuse power centers wherein American interests must be defended and pursued by adjusting policy to the balance of power. Overtures to mainland China, requests that United States allies shoulder more of the burdens of their own defense, and the pursuit of negotiations with the Soviet Union on the basis of mutual interest—this combination of policy initiatives exhibited an internal logic that was attractive to growing numbers of people, experts, and public alike. Congress naturally took a great deal longer to grasp this conceptual framework than did the unified executive branch. It is tragic that just as this consensus began to emerge fully and to gain acceptance in Congress and the media, it was obliterated by the devastation of the executive branch by the

Watergate affair. As a result the latter years of the Nixon and then Ford administrations were marked in the main by a lack of vigor in attempting to carry forward the full implications of the new policy consensus. Instead the administration seemed to cling evermore doggedly to one element of the larger policy, the detente relationship with the Soviet Union, as a shipwrecked sailor clings to a piece of wreckage.

The prospects for establishing a new consensus in the years of the first Carter administration are clouded. Constraints on the executive's freedom of action in foreign policy will coalesce in new forms as the Republican party assumes a new role as a small minority in both Houses of Congress, without allies in the executive branch but cooperating increasingly with conservative Democrats. Carter himself during his campaign closely adhered to positions that corresponded to widely held views in the American public. On the other hand, however, the foreign policy establishment of his administration has been staffed from a very narrow end of the spectrum in the Democratic party, by persons holding views considerably different from those of a large majority of Americans. There is a real possibility that the development of a new consensus in foreign policy will continue to elude us because of the wide gap in policy goals between the new foreign policy elite on the one hand and the views of the Republican minority, a substantial segment of the Democratic congressional delegation, and the public on the other.

In these circumstances it takes a considerable act of will to make optimistic forecasts about United States policy: As former Secretary of State Kissinger has said, "Our Government is in danger of progressively losing the ability to shape events, and a great nation that does not shape history eventually becomes its victim."

NOTES

1. See, for instance, [James Madison], "Letters of Helvidius: No. 1," in Alexander Hamilton and James Madison, *The Letters of Pacificus and Helvidius (1845) with the Letters of Americanus* (Delmar, N.Y.: Scholars' Facsimiles & Reprints, Inc., 1976).
2. See, for instance, [Alexander Hamilton], "Letters of Pacificus: No. 1," in ibid.
3. For varying interpretations see, inter alia, Louis Fisher, *The President and Congress: Power and Policy* (New York: The Free Press, 1972);

Louis Koenig, *The Presidency and the Crisis* (New York: Kings Crown Press, 1944); and Burton M. Sapin, *The Making of United States Foreign Policy* (New York: Published for the Brookings Institution by Frederick A. Praeger, 1966).

4. "The great ordinances of the Constitution do not establish and divide fields of black and white. Even the more specific of them are found to terminate in a penumbra shading gradually from one extreme to another. . . ." From the dissent of Mr. Justice Holmes in *Springer* v. *Philippine Islands,* cited in Robert Kramer and Herman Marcuse, "Executive Privilege: A Study of the Period 1953-1960," *George Washington Law Review* 29, no. 4 (April 1961): 623.

5. William Yandell Elliott, *United States Foreign Policy: Its Organization and Control,* Report of Woodrow Wilson Foundation: Study Group 1950-51 (New York: Columbia University Press, 1952), p. 44.

6. For a powerful argument to this effect, see Woodrow Wilson, *Congressional Government: A Study in American Politics* (New York: Meridian Books, 1956), pp. 28-31.

7. Myers v. United States, 272 U.S. 52 (1926).

8. Bagehot, as cited in Richard L. Tobin, "Who Makes Our Foreign Policy?" *Saturday Review,* 14 February 1970, p. 28.

9. Elliott, *United States Foreign Policy,* p. 63.

10. See for instance, William Anderson, "Intention of the Framers: A Note on Constitutional Interpretation," *American Political Science Review* 49, no. 2 (June 1955): 340.

11. Walter Bagehot, *The English Constitution,* The World's Classics (London: Oxford University Press, 1928), p. 202.

12. Arthur M. Schlesinger, Jr., "Congress and the Making of American Foreign Policy," *Foreign Affairs* 51 (October 1972): 107; see also J. William Fulbright, "United States Foreign Policy." Address delivered 29 June 1961, *Vital Speeches* 27 (1 August 1961): 616-19.

13. See David S. Broder, "The Limits of Being Bipartisan," *Washington Post,* 29 August 1973.

14. James MacGregor Burns, *Presidential Government: The Crucible of Leadership* (Boston: Houghton Mifflin, 1966), p. 313; Burton M. Sapin, *The Making of United States Foreign Policy* (Washington, D.C.: Brookings Institution, 1966), p. 54.

"Kennedy quoted with approval Woodrow Wilson's statement that 'the President is at liberty, both in law and conscience, to be as big a man as he can,' and said almost eagerly, that if the next President 'is the man the times demand,' he would discover 'that to be a big man in the White House inevitably brings cries of dictatorship.'" David S. Broder,

15. Schlesinger, "Congress and the Making of Foreign Policy," p. 105; John

C. Stennis and J. William Fulbright, *The Role of Congress in Foreign Policy* (Washington, D.C.: American Enterprise Institute for Public Policy Research, 1971), pp. 52-53; Henry Steele Commager, "Presidential Power: The Issue Analyzed," *New York Times Magazine*, 14 January 1971.

16. Burns, *Presidential Government*, p. 330.

17. As Walter Lippmann wrote, "In the final acts of state the issues are war and peace, security and solvency, order and insurrection. In these final acts the executive power cannot be exercised by the representative assembly." *Washington Post*, 25 June 1970.

18. George Kennan, *American Diplomacy: 1900-1950* (Chicago: University of Chicago Press, 1951), pp. 73-94. See also Richard E. Neustadt, "The Reality of Presidential Power," in Robert S. Hirschfield, *The Power of the Presidency* (New York: Atherton Press, 1968), p. 281.

19. Dean G. Acheson, *Present at the Creation: My Years in the State Department*, 1st ed. (New York: Norton, 1969), p. 600.

20. Arthur M. Schlesinger, Jr., *A Thousand Days* (London: Mayflower, 1967), p. 538.

21. Emmett John Hughes, *The Living Presidency* (New York: Coward, McCann & Geoghegan, 1973), p. 184.

22. As Walter Bagehot has observed: "The interlaced character of human affairs requires a single determining energy; a distinct force for each artificial compartment will make but a motley patchwork, if it live long enough to make anything." *The English Constitution*, p. 203.

23. For a useful development of this theme by a perceptive British observer, see Alastair Buchan, "Partners and Allies," *Foreign Affairs* 41 (July 1963): 621-37.

24. See the discussion in Clinton Rossiter, *The American Presidency* (New York: New American Library, 1956), pp. 15 ff.

25. Richard E. Neustadt, *Presidential Power: The Politics of Leadership* (New York: John Wiley & Sons, Inc., 1960), p. 270.

26. "Outside of the United States the Senate does not amount to a damn. And inside the United States, the Senate is mostly despised. They haven't had a thought down there in fifty years." Woodrow Wilson, quoted by John F. Kennedy in Hirschfield, *Power of the Presidency*, p. 131.

27. *The Federalist* 23, Mentor Books (New York: The New American Library of World Literature, Inc., 1961), p. 153.

28. "One need go back no further than the Cuban missile crisis to recall, as Robert Kennedy has told us, that the congressional leaders including Senators Russell and Fulbright, 'felt that the President should take more responsible action, a military attack or invasion and that the

blockade was far too weak a response.' " Schlesinger, "Making of Foreign Policy," p. 107.

29. See the discussion in Elliott, *United States Foreign Policy,* p. 65.

30. Hirschfield, *Power of the Presidency,* p. 223.

31. Cited in ibid., p. 243.

32. See Neustadt, *Presidential Power,* p. 270. For an opposing view see Burns, *Presidential Government,* p. 263. "Increased authority and scope have not made the Presidency a tyrannical institution; on the contrary, the office has become the main governmental bastion for the protection of individual liberty and the expansion of civil rights. The office represents the electorate at least as effectively and democratically as Congress. . . ."

33. See for instance James A. Robinson, *The Monroney Resolution: Congressional Initiative in Foreign Policy Making* (New York: Holt, 1959).

34. Holbert N. Carroll, "The Congress and National Security Policy," in David B. Truman, *The Congress and America's Future* (Englewood Cliffs, N.J.: Prentice-Hall, Inc., 1965), p. 152.

35. U.S., President, *Public Papers of the Presidents of the United States* (Washington, D.C.: Office of the *Federal Register,* National Archives and Records Service, 1953–), Richard M. Nixon, 1972, p. 401.

36. *The Federalist* 70, pp. 426–27.

37. For an example see Acheson, *Present at the Creation,* p. 526; and for another, Lyndon B. Johnson, *The Vantage Point* (New York: Holt, Rinehart and Winston, 1971), p. 451.

38. *The Federalist* 48, p. 310.

39. Samuel Stratton, "Weakness of the Presidency," in Hirschfield, *Power of the Presidency,* p. 301.

40. Professor Alexander Bickel, cited in Schlesinger, "Making of Foreign Policy," p. 106.

Chapter Five

The Military Dimension of United States National Security Policy

William Schneider, Jr.

INTRODUCTION

The defense function is indisputably the most fundamental function of the nation-state. Putting this rather simple notion in a more contemporary context, the defense function can be described as the only function of the central government that is truly "uncontrollable," in the sense that the aggregate amount of resources invested in the defense function is a result of threats that emerge from forces outside of the nation-state itself. International practice makes agreements between nations concluded under duress valid and binding in perpetuity, or at least as long as one of the parties has the power to enforce such an agreement. As a consequence, if a nation-state is to sustain its political and cultural identity, it must first of all provide for an adequate defense.

The problem of "How much is enough?" is one that is always difficult to answer, even for those with the best of intentions.[1] This paper will attempt to offer explicit proposals to strengthen the defense posture of the United States, and support such proposals by an analysis of the existing United States and Soviet defense postures. Regrettably, there is no single figure of merit that expresses the strengths or weaknesses, adequacy or inadequacy of a defense establishment. Rather, one must attempt to measure the disparate influences that affect the performance of military forces in a potential future conflict in order to emerge with an assessment. To this end, this paper will review and categorize the evidence on the United States and Soviet defense posture in three areas:

a. Doctrine: the body of thought that directs the employment of military forces
b. Inventories: the quantities and performance characteristics of military equipment available to the potential antagonists
c. Deployment of military forces: the geographic dispersion of forces

Too often, the analysis of the United States or Soviet defense posture reflects a static comparison of Order of Battle statistics or a sterile analysis of inventories of military equipment. The results are often misleading when an attempt is made 'to assess the potential performance of military forces in a conflict.

THE MILITARY THREAT TO THE UNITED STATES

The principal military threat to the United States are the armed forces of the Soviet Union. No other state possesses the combination of national drives and ambitions, ideology and military power sufficient to threaten directly the physical security of the United States. There are of course other nations which can exert a powerful regional influence as a consequence of their local military power (e.g., China in Northeast Asia). However, to threaten the United States requires of an adversary the ability to project military power well beyond its own borders. As a consequence, this discussion will not review in detail the military capabilities of other potential adversaries even though, in some circumstances, they must clearly be counted on the same side with (and at other times as opposed to) our principal adversary, the Soviet Union. The most direct threat to the United States occurs in the strategic nuclear environment because of the intercontinental properties of nuclear weapon delivery systems (ballistic missile and long-range aircraft). A secondary threat is posed by Soviet General Purpose Forces, that is, forces whether nuclear or nonnuclear that can be used at the theater level (e.g., Europe, Southeast Asia, West Africa, etc.) in a conflict with United States forces.

A. Strategic Forces

For many years, the Soviets have maintained a view of the problem of nuclear war that is fundamentally different from that of the United States. The Soviet formulation of the problem of nuclear war is Clausewitzian in origin; that is, it takes an instrumental view of nuclear war and, consequently, views nuclear conflict as a type of conflict that differs in degree but not in kind from other types of armed conflict.

The Soviets have never accepted United States concepts of mutual assured destruction whereby reciprocal deterrence is said to be maintained by the mutual ability to destroy each side's urban/industrial infrastructure. Soviet military doctrine emphasizes first, attacks on military installations, secondly, on war support industries (in Soviet parlance), and finally on counteradministration targets such as command centers. (The latter preference arises out of the Soviet belief that the destruction of the means of maintaining social organization and control is vital to the survival of a society.)[2]

Soviet doctrine has, in part, emerged from the lessons of World War II, where the Soviet armed forces were led by the victorious "artillery marshals." The dominance of the "artillery marshals" was sustained through most of the postwar period. There has been an emphasis on massive procurement and deployment of weapon systems of all types that is without parallel in any Western armed force. The doctrinal emphasis on mass is supported by a parallel emphasis on the notion of surprise and preemption. The Soviet view of military preparedness requires Soviet forces to be capable of conducting military operations by achieving tactical surprise. Moreover, the Soviets perceive that the side capable of striking a preemptive blow in a potential nuclear (or nonnuclear) conflict will almost certainly prevail. This doctrine is not so much a simple "first strike" doctrine as it is a doctrine that prepares Soviet forces to respond to short-term political warning when an attack from an adversary is "plausible." The Soviets distinguish between "detecting an attack" (for example, when large formations of missiles or aircraft are en route to their targets) and "anticipating" an attack. If Soviet war plans reflect their doctrine (which is, thus far, supported by their large-scale training maneuvers, their weapon inventories, and the character of their deployments), then one could expect the Soviets to be prepared to initiate a nuclear conflict only under circumstances where the deterioration in the international political environment had proceeded so far as to cause the Soviet leadership to believe that an attack on their forces or territory may be imminent. Table 1 shows the basic Soviet-American land-based strategic missile forces currently operational or in the process of being

TABLE 1
United States and Soviet ICBM Forces Under SALT
A. Soviet ICBMs[c]

SALT 1 Interim Agreement:

Type	SS-7: SS-8	SS-11	SS-13	SS-9	Total
Warheads/Missile	1	1[a]	1	1	
Throw Weight/Missile[b] (lbs.)	8,000	2,000	2,000	10–15,000	
1972–74 Deployment (Numbers)	209	1,012	60	288–313	1,600
Aggregate Throw Weight (lbs.)	1,600,000	2,000,000	100,000	3,000,000	6,000,000
Aggregate Warheads	209	1,012	60	288–313	1,600

New Systems:

Type	SS-17	SS-19	SS-16	SS-18	Total
Warheads/Missile	4	6	1	8	
Throw Weight/Missile[b] (lbs.)	5,000	7,000	2,000	15,000	
1980–83 Deployment (Numbers)	1,000–1,280	1,000–1,280	0–60	313	1,400–1,600[e]
Aggregate Throw Weight (lbs.)	5–6,000,000	7–9,000,000	0–100,000	4,700,000	10–14,000,000
Aggregate Warheads	4,000–5,000	6,000–7,700	0–60	12,500	6,600–8,400[d]

Interim Agreement and 1980:[e]

Type	Titan II	Minuteman II	Minuteman III	Total
Warheads/Missile	1	3		
Throw Weight/Missile[b] (lbs.)	8,000	2,500	2,500	
Deployment (numbers)	54	450	550	1,054
Aggregate Throw Weight (lbs.)	400,000	1,000,000	1,400,000	2,800,000
Aggregate Warheads	54	450	1,650	2,154

modernized in the wake of the Strategic Arms Limitation (SALT) Accords of 1972. It is these forces that are the backbone of the strategic deterrent and nuclear war-fighting capability of both the Soviet Union and the United States. The Soviet Union currently has nine major types of land-based intercontinental ballistic missiles deployed, some of which have several variants of each type.[3] The United States has a total of three types of land-based ICBMs including the Titan II—an obsolescent ICBM deployed in the early 1960s—and the more modern single-warhead solid-propellant Minuteman II, and the multiple-warhead (MIRV) solid-propellant Minuteman III.

Perhaps the most important long-term statistic shown in table 1 is the estimate of aggregate throw weight, the most important figure for characterizing the long-term growth capabilities of a ballistic missile force. The aggregate throw-weight estimates ranges between 10 and 14 million pounds compared to 2.8 million pounds for the United States. This figure is significant because the number of warheads that can be deployed on a ballistic missile is proportional to the throw weight of that ballistic missile. For example, if the 2,500-pound throw weight of the Minuteman III were, by a change in design or an increase in missile size, to increase to 5,000 pounds, then six of the current Minuteman III warheads could be accommodated on the same vehicle. For the strategic balance, this implies that the Soviet land-based ballistic missile throw weight ultimately confers upon them a potential advantage of 5 or 6 to 1 in aggregate warheads.[4]

The proximate cause of the asymmetry between the United States and the Soviet Union in terms of ballistic missile throw-weight advantage are the terms of the first round SALT accords ratified by the Congress in 1972. The SALT accords provided for a freeze on land-

---

SOURCE: William Schneider and Francis P. Hoeber, *Arms, Men, and Military Budgets: Issues for Fiscal Year 1978* (New York: Crane, Rusak and Co., Inc., 1977), pp. 29-30, 35.

a Some SS-11s are understood to have been deployed with "triplet" multiple reentry vehicles (MRVs). Since these are not independently targeted (that is, are not MIRVs), they are shown here.

b Throw-weight estimates are highly approximate. They may vary for a given missile, as there is a trade-off between throw weight and range; and some missiles may be given less throw weight (for example, by off-loading some MIRVs) in order to reach more distant targets. Estimates are for the maximum used load propelled in tests to intended ranges.

c The number of Soviet ICBMs in 1980 depends, among other things, on whether the old SS-7s and SS-8s are replaced with new ICBMs or, as is also permitted under the interim agreement as well as the Vladivostok guidelines, with SLBMs.

d The upper limit of aggregate Soviet warheads in the early 1980s is shown here as determined by the Vladivostok ceiling of 1,320 MIRVed missiles.

e The only change in United States forces from 1972 to 1980 is the completion in 1975 of the deployment of Minuteman III.

based ballistic missile deployments at the 1 July 1972 level and established a ceiling on Soviet nuclear-powered ballistic missile firing submarines (SSBN) constructed after 1964 of sixty-two submarines but left the United States with a freeze on its then current deployment of forty-one post-1964 SSBNs. The United States has not had the option of constructing either additional silos or modifying current silo dimensions to house substantially larger land-based ballistic missiles to offset the Soviet throw-weight advantage. As a consequence, the United States has had to emphasize the exploitation of advanced technology to maintain a significant lead in deliverable nuclear warheads. However, as one can note from the data presented in table 1, the United States advantage is a wasting asset as the Soviet Union catches up over time in the scientific and engineering skills required to improve their warhead design and production capability.

A similar asymmetry in deployed forces exists in the submarine force. As noted above, the Soviets are permitted an advantage of sixty-two deployed post-1964 SSBNs to only forty-one for the United States. The substantial momentum in the Soviet military R&D program, however, has permitted the Soviets to deploy a new class of submarine, the Delta class submarine (an early type, the Delta-I with twelve missile launching tubes, an advanced version, the Delta-II with sixteen launch tubes, and, most recently of all, the Delta-III with twenty tubes) that can accommodate the SSN-8, tested in late November and early December 1976 with a MIRV (Multiple Independently Targeted Reentry Vehicle) warhead package. The MIRVed version of the SSN-8 has a maximum range of 5,700 miles. The United States will not have a comparable system deployed until the early 1980s, when the Trident-I missile is deployed on modified SSBNs now carrying the 3,000-mile range Poseidon; the range of the Trident-I, however, will be only 4,000-plus miles. The new MIRV SS-NX-18 will have even greater range.

The Soviet strategic threat, however, is not constrained to only land- and sea-based ballistic missiles. The Soviets also deploy cruise missiles launched from both surface and subsurface naval vessels and from land-based manned bombers. The Soviets have had a persistent interest in cruise missiles for over two decades. Their deployment mode has emphasized relatively[5] short ranges from approximately 30 to approximately 400 miles based on low-altitude flight profiles. Over 5,000 cruise missiles of all types have been constructed by the Soviets since their deployments began in the mid-1950s.[6]

The Soviets have maintained a large manned bomber force as well. The Soviet Air Force does not exist as a monolithic organization such as is found in Western countries. Soviet air power is distributed among five functional groupings. For purposes of strategic forces, the relevant ones are the DA (*Dalniya Aviatsiya,* "Long Range Aviation"), which has the long-range aviation mission with strategic delivery systems. Aircraft currently assigned to DA include 95 TU-95 Bear Bombers, 40 aerial tanker aircraft, and 90 of the new (TU-26 Backfire B) supersonic bombers. The second element, AVMF (*Aviatsiya Voenno Morskava Flota,* "Naval Aviation"), provides land-based aircraft in support of naval reconnaissance and attack missions. The AVMF has a small quantity of long-range TU-95 bombers for maritime reconnaissance and strike roles, and a larger number of TU-16 (Badger) and TU-22 (Blinder) medium-range bombers. More recently Backfire A and B models are also being deployed to the AVMF. Most of the medium bombers, including approximately 800 TU-16 and TU-22 medium bombers and the bulk of the Backfire B production, are allocated to support the DA. The PVO-Stranny (*Protivo Vozduschniya Obarona Stranny,* the "Air Force of the Anti-aircraft Defense of the Homeland") provides for the strategic air and missile defense of the USSR.

The Soviet strategic forces span the continuum of types of delivery systems ranging from heavy payload intercontinental ballistic missiles, which pose a major direct threat to the United States, to low payload short-range cruise missiles and medium bombers, which have only a peripheral capability against targets in the United States. The Soviet emphasis on massive deployment of weapons of all types is amply recorded in the litany of systems they have deployed, particularly in the past decade, to augment their strategic nuclear capability. The manner in which these forces are organized and the character of their deployment suggests that Soviet forces are prepared to be employed as their military doctrine requires: to conduct military operations preemptively under the cover of surprise (assuming the prerequisites mentioned above are met).

The Soviet Union has passed through what its specialists describe as the first two stages of modern military development: nuclear weapons (fission and fusion) and long-range ballistic missiles. It has now entered the third stage of development embodying the preeminence of electronics and cybernetics. This implies that the Soviets will increasingly emphasize improvements in command and control and in the efficiency with which their massive forces can be used should circstances require it.[7] This may permit more of their forces, particularly those based at sea, to be on "alert," thereby increasing the threat to the United States.

B. General Purpose Forces

1. *Army and Air Force.* Many of the practices observed in Soviet strategic forces are writ large in the sphere of General Purpose Forces (GPF). The Eurasian land mass has been the traditional sphere of interest of Soviet diplomacy. As a consequence, their military deployments tend to reflect this interest. The Soviet GPF deployments in Eastern Europe and the western part of the USSR, both ground and air forces, are massive by Western standards. Again, these forces tend to reflect the Soviet interest in massive deployments, the ability to conduct warfare of all types including chemical, nuclear, and conventional conflict, and the maintenance of the ability to gain tactical surprise and to preempt anticipated attacks.

In recent years, the Soviets have focused their effort on improving the capability of their GPF, particularly those deployed in the vicinity of the European theater. (Contrary to frequent assertions, the Sino-Soviet border is not a major burden on Soviet resources. Approximately 25 percent or less of Soviet forces are engaged there, and they trend not to be Soviet first-line forces; those are allocated for service in Eastern Europe and in particular East Germany.)[8] In many cases Soviet efforts to improve their capability in Europe are being undertaken without explicit changes in the Order of Battle. That is, new divisions are not being raised and deployed to Eastern Europe. Rather, there is occurring a relentless upgrading of the capability of Soviet forces in Eastern Europe in several ways. First, an additional tank battalion is being deployed with each motorized rifle division currently deployed in Eastern Europe. This has resulted in a 15 to 20 percent increase in manpower per division and an increase of tanks in a motorized rifle division from an average of 188 per division in the late 1960s to 266 tanks per motorized rifle division in 1976. In the past year, the Soviets have reinforced the GSFG (Group of Soviet Forces in Germany) with advanced river-crossing equipment, including K-61 heavy amphibious vehicles, PTS-M heavy amphibious vehicles and GSP ferries. In addition, heavy bridging equipment has been provided to the sixteen bridging regiments of the GSFG. This development reflects the Soviet intention to reduce the amount of warning time any mobilization would give to their NATO adversaries. This may have been done in response to the limitations (in the form of required advance notification) on military maneuvers negotiated in the agreement on the Conference on Security and Cooperation in Europe (CSCE, the "Helsinki" conference). Heretofore, a favored clandestine Soviet mobilization device had been to conduct "maneuvers," as they did for a six-week period in advance of the Soviet invasion of Czechoslovakia. At the present time, the NATO allies would have a very limited opportunity to observe the deployment of vital Soviet river-crossing units from the western USSR because these units are already in place at the border regions on the NATO central front between East and West Germany. Table 2 below summarizes Soviet ground force and Frontal Aviation (*Frontoviya Aviatsiya*), the Soviet air arm designed to provide tactical air support to Soviet ground units in the European theater.

If nothing else, the statistics displayed in table 2 reveal a single-minded Soviet obsession with massive procurement. The deployment of 36,000 tanks west of the Ural mountains in Soviet hands and an additional 15,000 tanks in the hands of Soviet Warsaw Pact allies suggests a set of attitudes about the character of a future war that is often not widely appreciated in the West. Similarly, the 3,800 tactical aircraft assigned to the FA are currently undergoing modernization, being replaced by newer and more capable aircraft with range-payload characteristics similar to those of the United States and the other NATO nations.

These forces are driven by a tactical doctrine that emphasizes a modern form of blitzkrieg warfare that implies massive suppressive artillery, air, and short-range ballistic missile fire to permit echeloned Soviet armored columns to breach NATO defenses, encircle the defenders, and drive westward to destroy the ability of the NATO forces to marshal their superior resources for a counterattack. The post-

TABLE 2
Soviet and Non-Soviet Warsaw Pact Forces[a]
Committed to the European Theater (1975)

Military District	Troops[b]	Tanks[c]	Combat Aircraft[d]	Divisions Motorized Rifle	Armored	Airborne
Soviet Forces						
Leningrad	85,000[e]	1,700	200 (13th FAA)	6	1	1
Baltic	92,000	2,000	300 (30th FAA)	6	1	3
Byelorussian	115,000	2,500	300 (1st FAA)	7	1	2
Carpathian	90,000	2,000	350 (57th FAA)	7	0	3
Kiev	83,000	2,900	100 (17th FAA)	4	0	6
Moscow[i]	55,000	1,500	200 (FAA No. N.A.)	4	1	2
Odessa	75,000	1,100	250 (15th FAA)	6	1	0
North Caucasus	49,000	1,200	None[f]	6	0	0
Transcaucasus	120,000	2,100	300 (34th FAA)	10	1	1
Volga	30,000[g]	N.A.	None	2	1	1
Ural	30,000	N.A.	None	4	0	2
Group of Soviet Forces in Germany	168,000	7,000[h]	1,100 (16th FAA)	10	0	10
Central Army Group (Czechoslovakia)	54,000	4,500	100	3	0	2
Northern Army Group (Poland)	20,000	4,000[i]	350 (37th FAA)	0	0	2
Southern Army Group (Hungary)	40,000	3,900	275	4	0	2
Total (Soviet)	1,106,000	36,400	3,825	79	7	37
East Germany	112,000	2,000	330	4	0	2
Czechoslovakia	155,000	3,100	450	5	1/3	5
Poland	240,000	4,100	785	8	1	5
Hungary	90,000	1,500	108	5	0	1
Bulgaria	120,000	2,200	253	8	0	1 2/3
Romania	141,000	2,070	254	8	1/3	2
Total (Non-Soviet)	858,000	14,970	2,180	38	1 2/3	16 2/3

SOURCES: *The Military Balance 1975-1976* (London: International Institute for Strategic Studies, 1975). R. Meller, *International Defense Review* (Geneva), vol. 8, no. 2 (April 1975). O. von Pivka, *The Armies of Europe Today* (London: Osprey, 1973).

a Only the divisions allocated for the European theater of operations are included (123 divisions). The balance located in the Central Asian, Siberian, Transbaikal, and Far Eastern Military Districts (43 divisions, including two deployed in Mongolia) are not included. Some controversy exists as to the role of the 23 divisions deployed in the three Southern Military Districts. This study allocates all of them to the European mission because of the inadequacy of overland transportation to other theaters.

b Soviet forces are deployed at three levels of readiness, designated by Soviet authorities as Category I, II, or III. Forces maintained at less than Category I levels of readiness will lack a full complement of troops and mobility equipment. The definitions of the categories are as follows:

> Category I: Three-fourths to full strength, with complete equipment. This category includes all Soviet divisions deployed in Eastern Europe, one-third of the divisions in the Soviet Far East (three military districts), and one-third of those deployed in European USSR.
> Category II: One-half to three-fourths strength, with complete fighting vehicles. This category includes one-third of Soviet divisions deployed in the three Far Eastern Military Districts, and one-third of those deployed in the European USSR.
> Category III: One-third strength with complete fighting vehicles. This category includes the remaining one-third of the divisions deployed in the three Far Eastern Military Districts and the European USSR.

The most significant difference between the highest level of readiness (Category I) and the remaining Categories (II and III) is that the latter levels lack their full complement of trucks, particularly for the Motorized Rifle Divisions, which are dependent on such transportation. When the American-built Kama River truck plant is completed in the USSR, all Category II and III divisions will be capable of being brought to full readiness.

c At full strength, there are 325 main battle tanks per Soviet armored division, and 200 to 266 MBTs per Motorized Rifle Division. In Soviet Category I divisions in Eastern Europe, MBT strength has been increased by one third per division (from 30 tanks per battalion in 1970 to 40 tanks in 1975). In addition, there are 70,000 other tanks mothballed at depots in the Central USSR. The tanks are mostly of World War II vintage, primarily the famous T-34 and JS-11 types. The fact that T-34 tanks were efficiently employed by East German forces during the invasion of Czechoslovakia in 1968 (despite the fact that they have vast numbers of T-54/55 and T-62s available) indicates that this vast Soviet tank inventory of nearly 120,000 units cannot be totally overlooked. To emphasize the manic intensity of the Soviet defense establishment for holding on to obsolescent if not obsolete equipment, an Israeli armor officer reported to the author during a recent visit to the Golan Heights that the Syrians employed several World War II-captured German Pzkw. IVs sold to them by the Soviets during the 1967 war. These tanks were sold without engines to be used as fixed gun emplacements. One wonders what the Soviets did with the engines.

d This category consists only of aircraft assigned to Frontal Aviation Armies (FAA). It excludes the 2,000 aircraft assigned to the *PVO Stranny* (*Protivo Vozduschniya Obarona Stranny*, the Air Force of the Antiaircraft Defense of the Homeland), which deals exclusively with the strategic air defense mission. Also excluded are aircraft of the DA (*Dalniya Aviatsiya*, Long Range Aviation), AVMF (*Aviatsiya Voenno Morskava Flota*, Naval Aviation), and VTA (*Voenno Transportnaya Aviatsiya*, Air Transport Aviation). An FAA typically has two fighter-bomber divisions and three interceptor divisions. Each division is composed of three (or more) regiments of 40 operational and 15 reserve aircraft each. The most important FAA, the 16th deployed in East Germany, has additional reconnaissance and air transport regiments attached as well. Some FAAs in low priority districts will have far fewer aircraft, although the general scheme of organization will be similar.

e This figure includes 2,000 Naval Infantry troops (Marines) deployed at Murmansk earmarked for amphibious assault against northern Norway.

f If 150 combat aircraft of the 6th FAA deployed in the Turkestan Military District are included, then the total number of aircraft should be increased by that amount.

g These divisions constitute the strategic reserve for forces assigned to the European theater. Unlike the United States, which employs an individual replacement system when casualties occur, the Soviets wait until a combat unit is annihilated, and then withdraw whatever forces remain and put in an entire new unit.

h Approximately 60 percent of the tanks in the GSFG are T-62s. Approximately 1,000 have been added since 1972, but none of the older T-54/55s have been withdrawn. Deployment of a new tank, the T-64 (and a variant, the T-72) is also under way. It is similar to the T-62 except for a new gun (122 mm on the T-64/72; 115 mm for the T-62) and a three-man crew. It also

Vietnam disenchantment with military forces has taken its most dev-astating toll in the capabilities of United States General Purpose Forces. United States GPF have undergone a gradual erosion in strength in Europe from 412,000 deployed in 1962 to approximately 300,000 today. There are, moreover, massive deficiencies in terms of equipment shortages, deferred maintenance, and inadequate funding of operations to sustain high levels of readiness.[9]

(2) *Navy.* No less severe in terms of the attrition and capability to conduct military operations has been the deterioration in the capability of the Navy as a consequence of budgetary stringency. The most direct reflection of this is in the number of naval ships and aircraft deployed.

Since 1964, there has been a 50 percent reduction in ships in com-mission, a 31 percent reduction in the number of aircraft deployed with the fleet, and a 23 percent reduction in manpower assigned to the Navy. (See table 3.) The decline in United States forces is reflected

TABLE 3
United States Navy General Purpose Force Deployments
1964-76

	Ships	Aircraft	Personnel (in thousands)
1964	883	5,014	654
1970	722	4,544	669
1976	443	3,480	504
Reduction (Percent)	50	31	23

SOURCE: US Navy Comptroller, *Budget and Forces Summary,* November 1975, and earlier editions.

in the ability of the United States to deploy its fleet to important forward theaters of the world compared to the Soviets. In 1974, the last year for which complete unclassified data is available, the num-ber of Soviet surface ships deployed worldwide exceeded that of the United States. The disparity reflects the increasing ability of the

employs an automatic loader and combustible casing ammunition. The United States may have a similar tank ready for deployment in the early 1980s (the XM-1), if it does not decide to buy the West German Leopard II. Otherwise, the United States will have to rely on the 1958-design M-60 series now in service.

i Consists of 40 percent T-62-type tanks. There is no sign that Warsaw Pact forces are being supplied with the T-64/72. The Soviets initiated troop trials with a new tank, the T-80, in late 1977; it is similar to the F64/72 series, but has a new type of armor.

TABLE 4
United States–Soviet Naval Deployment, 1974
A. Average Numbers of Soviet Surface Ships Deployed in 1974

	Mediter-ranean	Atlantic	Pacific	Indian	Total
Helicopter Carriers	a	a	0	a	1
Cruisers and Frigates	5	2	1	1	9
Destroyers and Escorts	6	1	0	3	10
Amphibious Ships	2	1	0	1	4
Support Ships	22	24	14	14	74
Total	35	28	15	19	98

a Less than one.

B. Average Number of U.S. Navy Surface Ships Deployed in 1974

	Mediter-ranean	Pacific	Indian	Total
Aircraft Carriers	2	3	0	5
Helicopter Carriers	1	1	0	2
Cruisers and Frigates	4	5	0	9
Destroyers and Escorts	12	18	2	32
Amphibious Ships	4	7	0	11
Support Ships	10	20	1	31
Total	33	54	3	90

SOURCE: U.S. Congress, Senate Committee on Armed Services, *Hearings on Fiscal Year 1976 Authorization,* 94th Congress, 1st Session, 1975, p. 763.

Soviets to sustain relatively lengthy operational deployments outside of their coastal waters, the traditional province of the Soviet Navy until the mid-1960s. The two summary tables presented in table 4 show the distribution of interest as between theaters of operation on the part of the Soviet Navy. Only in the Pacific theater, where the United States has an extensive basing infrastructure, was the United States able to sustain a greater number of deployed naval vessels. The Soviets with basing facilities in ice-free ports only in Vladivostok and on the Kamchatka Peninsula could not sustain an extensive deployment without a further upgrading of their maritime capability. Moreover, because of the character of the Soviet Navy with its emphasis on cruise missile attack, the Pacific is an inhospitable region for their deployments in the absence of a better basing structure.[10]

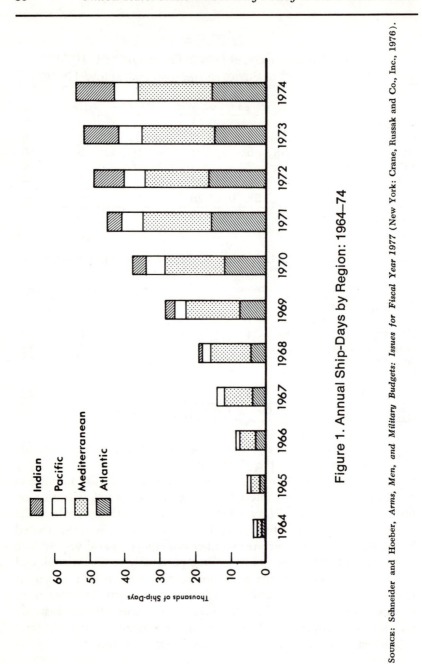

Figure 1. Annual Ship-Days by Region: 1964–74

Source: Schneider and Hoeber, *Arms, Men, and Military Budgets: Issues for Fiscal Year 1977* (New York: Crane, Russak and Co., Inc., 1976).

The modernization of the Soviet Navy that has taken place since the mid-1960s has also been reflected in the dramatic increase in the number of ship-days (i.e., days at sea per ship) carried out by the Soviet Navy. Figure 1 shows the monotonic increase in the number of ship-days that has taken place since 1964.

The trend observed in Figure 1 reflects not so much the number of Soviet vessels as it does the change in character of these vessels. Since 1964, the Soviets have changed from a coastal navy to a deep-water navy, albeit one with a different mission from that of the United States Navy.

The threat posed by Soviet General Purpose Forces represents a major threat to the ability of the United States to support its foreign policy objectives in areas of the world where those interests may clash with those of the Soviet Union. Although the Soviets' focus remains on Western Europe, the increasing capability of the Soviets to deploy their forces on a worldwide basis can pose an important peripheral threat to the interests of the United States. The inattention of the United States to changes in the General Purpose Force threat in Europe has tended to weaken the credibility of the United States non-nuclear deterrent in the theater, thereby running all of the political risks such a loss of credibility implies. The long-simmering controversy over the significance of the modernization of Soviet naval forces has simply reinforced the unwillingness of policymakers to come to grips with the cumulative effects of the changes in the Soviet military posture.

THE UNITED STATES RESPONSE
TO THE SOVIET THREAT

As noted earlier, there are some important differences between United States and Soviet doctrine that have serious implications for a future military conflict. Doctrinal preferences are often far more important than merely different means of attaining the same end. In fact, they often reflect different ends. This is particularly true with respect to strategic forces, where the United States is predominantly oriented toward achieving deterrence by threatening the Soviet leadership with a potential loss of an important fraction of their civilian population and industrial infrastructure. While the Soviets retain a residual capacity to inflict vast civil destruction, the focus of their doctrine and consequently of their military forces is on other targets. The Soviets are primarily interested in destroying the military capability of an adversary and destroying the adversary regime's capacity for exercising control over its population and resources. Without any empirical basis for confidence that the Soviets share our point of view, we too easily have assumed that the Soviet leadership is deterred by a potential threat to the survival of an important fraction (20 to 35 percent) of its urban population and industrial infrastructure (⅔ to ¾).[11] This misplaced "miror imaging" of Soviet preferences has led the United States down a specialized path in its procurement decisions, research and development choices, military force structure, and arms control policy. For many years in the postwar period, the doctrinal disparity was blurred by the sheer military advantage the United States possessed. In an era of diminishing military advantage for the United States, the force of these doctrinal disparities becomes far more important. The United States no longer can afford the luxury of ignoring the doctrinal differences with the Soviets if it is to effectively and credibly deal with unanticipated Soviet military threats.

In the fiscal year 1977, the United States expended on the defense function approximately 10 percent less in constant dollar terms than was expended on this function in fiscal year 1964, the last pre-Vietnam year. Despite the substantial public turmoil over defense expenditures, in every measure by which the burden of government expenditures is commonly measured the burden of defense expenditures is lower now than it has been since the fiscal year 1950. This diminished level of investment of real resources in the defense function is reflected in the adverse changes in the strategic balance between the United States and the Soviet Union both with respect to Strategic and General Purpose Forces. Although there are many things that can be done to improve the efficiency of forces and the effective use of funds invested in defense, mere management changes cannot be expected to overcome the effects of disinvestment in defense; more resources are required if the cumulative effects of a decade of inadequate defense funding are to be offset.

Since 1969, the United States has been intensely engaged in a series of arms control negotiations that cover the spectrum of the major modern means of waging war. The Strategic Arms Limitation discussions in Geneva have been successful in achieving a substantial degree of agreement between the United States and the Soviet Union. However, the results have left the United States in at least a temporary disadvantage in terms of the major aggregates of strategic nuclear power. A separate but parallel set of negotiations has been proceeding for five years in Vienna, known as the Conference on Mutual and Balanced Force Reductions in Europe (MBFR). With objectives in certain ways similar to the Strategic Arms Limitation discussions, these multilateral negotiations have focused upon reducing the level of forces deployed along NATO's central front in a way that would not diminish the security of either side. The formidable obstacles to this agreement include such problems as the geographic asymmetry in United States and Soviet deployments: the Soviets may withdraw their forces 400 miles over land into Soviet territory, whereas if United States forces are required to be returned to the continental United States, a redeployment of over 4,000 miles would be required to bring them back in the case of an emergency. Another significant arms control effort is proceeding in an attempt to extend the ban on underground nuclear tests, now limited to detonations above 150 kilotons of TNT equivalent yield, through a Comprehensive Test Ban (CTB) that would prohibit all nuclear explosions in any environment. The collective purpose of these arms control negotiations is to find a means of maintaining United States security interests without continuing to bear the high costs that both sides incur in maintaining a substantial defense establishment. As is often the case, however, the practice of arms control, for ideological, institutional, and technical reasons, varies substantially from the theory of arms control. As a consequence, the character of United States arms control measures has served to place long-range United States security interests in jeopardy without providing offsetting, cost-reducing or war-risk limiting elements to arms control results.

POLICY PROPOSALS FOR THE FUTURE
1. Resources
The United States needs to recoup the attrition its forces have suffered as a consequence of a decade of disinvestment in defense. Increasing

constant dollar (i.e., real resources) outlays for defense by 10 percent per annum through FY 83 and 5 percent per annum through FY 88 would mitigate, but not wholly offset, disparities in important areas of Soviet-American military competition. Increases of this magnitude would neither have a disequilibrating effect on the economy nor a distorting effect on the industrial base, but would permit United States military forces to reduce the potential disadvantage they must now contend with. This proposed increase in defense effort would result in outlays of $133 billion (in FY 77 constant dollars) in FY 79 (the fiscal year now being reviewed by the Congress) or about $10 billion less than the Carter administration proposes to spend.

2. Stabilization of Personnel Costs

Personnel costs now account for over half of the costs of the Department of Defense. The fraction has increased from 42 percent in FY 64, due to the Nixon administration's decision to make military pay scales comparable to those in the civilian sector and to the higher direct costs of relying entirely on volunteers to fill the ranks of the armed services (or to induce volunteers in services that do not directly rely on conscription). As a result, we have gone from a low direct cost–high turnover conscript armed force to a high cost–high turnover volunteer force. There are alternatives to conscription that can reduce manpower costs, however, and these should be exploited. Specifically, these entail manipulating enlistment and retention policy to maximize the length of the first term of enlistment where cost is lowest and productivity is high, and exercising a highly selective retention policy to minimize the retirement liability imposed by career soldiers.[12]

3. Arms Control Posture

The United States arms control posture, particularly with respect to strategic forces, is seriously in need of revision. The Interim Agreement on Offensive Arms (SALT I) expired in October 1977 after being in force since 1972. It has been suggested that SALT I "did something worth doing badly (limiting offensive arms), but did something *not* worth doing too well (limiting defensive arms)." The first round SALT agreement from the United States perspective has been counterproductive in that it has provided an "envelope" within which the Soviets could engage in a vast program of modernization of their strategic forces, while the wistful hope of a "permanent" agreement has delayed making decisions about offsetting improvements in United States strategic forces to maintain the military balance in strategic nuclear arms. We first must develop a taste for the notion that no agreement may, in some circumstances, be better than any agreement that we happen to be able to negotiate. This posture implies a higher set of standards than we have applied to date concerning the quality of agreements we are willing to accept. Future SALT agreements should be symmetric in the limitation of a relevant index of strategic force capability (e.g., ballistic missile throw weight rather than strategic delivery vehicles as was done in the Vladivostok accords); they should be verifiable at high levels of confidence; they should not attempt to include systems that might adversely affect United States alliance systems (e.g., Forward Based Systems, whether they are aircraft, cruise missiles, or submarine-launched ballistic missiles), and they should be negotiated in a manner which places all elements of the behavior required by the parties under the agreement in the text of the agreement rather than in ancillary documents that we are unwilling or unable to enforce.[13]

4. The United States Theater Posture in Europe

The central reality of European diplomacy is the existence of the massive direct Soviet military threat to Western Europe. This posture is supported by a forward deployment of massive quantities of troops and materiel, and by a military doctrine that emphasizes surprise and preemption as a central element of its tactical operations. The United States (and NATO) posture reflects more the salad days of undisputed United States military (nuclear) superiority than it does a clear recognition of the increase in Soviet military power in Central Europe. Complacency is reflected in a "business-as-usual" attitude toward widespread shortages of materiel, the maldeployment of NATO military forces on the central front, and the inadequate combat power (in both attack and defense modes) of United States and NATO forces in the presence of the current Soviet posture in Europe. What is required is the following:

    a. A change in the force structure of United States and NATO forces to put more combat power in forward positions and to thereby exploit the superior NATO resource base for supporting military forces

    b. Greater attention to providing United States forces with the equipment needed to offset the Soviet buildup in Central Europe, including more close air support aircraft (the A-10), more high-performance air-superiority aircraft (i.e., the F-15), a modernized tactical nuclear force to replace the existing limited-utility force, much of which dates from as early as the mid-1950s, and additional armored vehicles (tanks and APCs) and artillery

These changes will not entirely reverse the cumulative process of erosion of NATO's strength that has taken place over the past decade, but it will encourage a change in the perception of the United States both within NATO and the Warsaw Pact to the effect that the decay in the United States military posture is not irreversible.

5. Modernization

Although most of the polemics associated with defense have focused on the procurement of new weapon systems, such procurement accounts for less than one-third of defense expenditures. Independent of the procurement choices particular analysts would favor, there is little doubt that if a function-by-function review of the United States defense posture were made, there would be evidence of a substantial shortfall in modernization, not only to take advantage of the cost-reducing modern technology that has become available for many military functions, but more importantly, to keep pace with the change in the military threat posed to the United States by the growth in Soviet military power. The question of modernization is necessarily linked with the issue of providing more resources to the defense function, even though it is unquestionably feasible to extract greater efficiency (and wisdom) in procurement practices and choices. The need for additional resources to support modernization is essential and will remain so for several years even if substantially greater resources are invested. The following objectives for modernization are perhaps the most urgent:

    a. Strategic force survivability (Trident I, the MX ICBM, and
       the B-1 manned bomber to reduce the vulnerability of ex-
       isting strategic forces to preemptive attacks, antisubmarine
       advances, and air defense improvements). Defense historians
       may mark the Carter administration's cancellation of B-1
       procurement as one of the greatest defense policy errors of
       the decade.
    b. Strategic force flexibility and discrimination capability (im-
       proved accuracy with lower warhead yield, long-range air-
       and submarine-launched cruise missiles).
    c. General Purpose Force mobility (a new utility helicopter,
       UTTAS, and a new short takeoff and landing transport air-
       craft, greater emphasis on mechanized infantry and armored
       divisions, and reduced emphasis on light infantry divisions).
    d. Improved strategic and field air defense (SAM-D surface-
       to-air missile system, the F-15 aircraft, and the AWACS
       airborne radar and control system).
    e. Improved naval forces, particularly in their ability to sustain
       long forward deployments with an autonomous self-defense
       capability and a greater "surge" capability to deploy and
       sustain additional military forces in a crisis. Such a capabil-
       ity cannot be supported with either a 400- or 500-ship navy
       or with the present level of attack carriers (12). A rebuild-
       ing of the Navy is needed to restore its ability to support
       United States foreign policy objectives through the projec-
       tion of military power.[14]

6. The Industrial and Mobilization Base

During the past decade of disinvestment in defense, there has been a
slow but significant deterioration in the industrial base that supports
the mobilization capability of the United States. This was dramatically brought to the attention of the American public in 1973, when
urgent Israeli needs for tanks to replace battlefield losses eliminated
more than two years of United States production in a matter of weeks.
United States forces in Europe still do not have their required number
of tanks, and United States armored forces remain more than 1,500
tanks understrength. Building an industrial mobilization base to support United States requirements during a conflict is not something that
can be "turned on" in a matter of weeks; there has been a genuine

degradation of capacity that requires the urgent attention of the Carter administration if we are to avoid a circumstance where we cannot meet the military needs of our own forces or of those of an ally in a time of crisis. The mobilization requirements of the United States need to be systematically reviewed if we are to be adequately prepared.

NOTES

1. After seven years of recommending reductions in United States defense expenditures, The Brookings Institution has reversed its position: "defense spending will have to increase in real terms for at least the next five years." See *Setting National Priorities: The Next Ten Years* (Washington, D.C.: The Brookings Institution, 1976), p. 127.

2. The most important recent Soviet works on doctrine are the three editions of Sokolvskig's *Voennaya Strategiva (Military Strategy)* (last edition: 1968).The five editions of *Marksizm-Leninizm o Voyne i Armii (Marxism-Leninism on War and the Army)* (last edition: 1968) present the prevailing ideological dogma on military affairs. The two editions of *Metodologicheskie Problemy Voennoy Teorii Prakitiki* (last edition: 1969) are by the young military intellectuals of the Lenin Military Political Academy. There are also a number of monographs and collected works: P.A. Kurochkin (ed.), *Osnovy motodiki Voenno-Nauchnogo Issledovaniya (Fundamentals of Military-Scientific Investigation)*, 1969; S.N. Kozlov, et al. (eds.), *O. Sovetskoy Voennoy Nauke (On Soviet Military Science)*, 1964; N.A. Lomov, *Sovetskaya Voennaya Doktrina (Soviet Military Doctrine)*, 1963; M.V. Popov, *Sushehnost Zakonov Vooruzhennoy Bor'by (The Essence of the Laws of Armed Struggle)*, 1964; N.P. Prokop'ev, *O Voyne i Armii (On War and the Army)*, 1965; N.V. Pukhovskij, *O Mire i Voyne (On Peace and War)*, 1965; E.I. Rybkin, *Voyna i Politika (War and Politics)*, 1959; I.A. Seleznev, *Voyna i Ideologicheskaya Bor'ba (War and the Ideological Struggle)*, 1964; A.A. Sidorenko°, *Nastuplenie (The Offensive)*, 1970; P.V. Sokolov, *Voenno-Ekonomicheskiye Voprosy v Kurse Politekonomii (Military-Economic Problems in a Political Economy Course)*, 1968; P.I. Trifonenkov, *Ob osnovnykh Zakonakh khonda i iskhoda sovremennoy voyny (On the Fundamental Laws about the Course and Outcome of Contemporary War)*, 1962; S.A. Tyushkevich, *Neobhodimost' i sluchaynost v voyne (Necessity and Chance in War)*, 1962; M.S. Shifman, *Voyna i Ekonomika (War and Economics)*, 1964; V.S. Yarovikov (ed.)°, *Problemy Revolyutsii v voennom dele (The Problems of the Revolution in Military Affairs)*, 1965. An asterisk indicates that the document has also been published in the U.S. Air Force translation series in *Soviet Military Thought* (Washington, GPO). The Lenin Military Academy publishes *Kommunist Yooruzhennykhsil;* *Voennyi Vestnik* is published by

the Frunze Academy, and a classified journal (*Voennaya Mysl'*) is published by the Military Science Administration under the General Staff. The three journals are the most important forums for discussion and dissemination of Soviet doctrine.

3. For example, the SS-9 was believed to be deployed in four versions: one was a single 25-megaton warhead, one with a triplet (3 warhead) multiple warhead of 5 megatons per warhead, a FOBS (Fractional Orbital Bombardment System) payload, and a fourth with a warhead for depressed trajectory delivery. The SS-9 is being replaced by the SS-18 of which at least two variants have been identified: a single re-entry (RV) payload of N 50 megatons, and a second version with a 5–8 MIRV payload.

4. Other factors such as warhead miniaturization, designated target array, anticipated type of attack (i.e., surface or air burst) and other doctrinal and technical considerations will determine the actual warhead mix.

5. Statement of Roy Mason, U.K. Minister of Defense, May 1976.

6. The capabilities of a cruise missile are particularly difficult ones for the analyst of a Soviet threat. The range of a cruise missile is difficult to estimate because of the wide variation that can be imparted to cruise missile range by altering the altitude with which the cruise missile flies, the amount of payload it carries, the efficiency of the propulsion system (a jet engine), and aerodynamic properties of the cruise missile itself. As a consequence, some United States analysts have estimated that Soviet cruise missiles, particularly the longer range cruise missiles, may have a range, when flown at optimum cruise altitudes, of 2,000 miles or more; this is a source of concern for the United States because of the lack of antiaircraft defenses in the United States which would permit virtual "free entry" to a cruise missile operating at relatively high altitudes, and the proximity of the U.S. MVA (manufacturing value added) and urban population centers adjacent to the coastline. Thus, the Soviets have a natural advantage in cruise missile deployments that the United States can only offset by building substantially more capable cruise missiles than are required by the Soviets. Soviet interest is sustained; witness the recent increase in the production rate of the C-class nuclear-powered cruise missile submarine from three per year to two per month (twenty-four per year).

7. For a useful discusion of Soviet doctrine, see J.J. Holst, "Comparative U.S. and Soviet Deployments, Doctrine, and Arms Limitation," in M.A. Kaplan (ed.), *SALT: Problems and Prospects* (Morristown: General Learning Press, 1973), pp. 68–75. The Soviet employment of a TU-114 (MOSS) airborne warning and control aircraft in the 1971 Indo-Pakistan war to vector Indian fighters and bombers against Pakistan emphasizes the Soviet commitment to adopting the computer to its military

forces. A similar (though more capable) aircraft, the E3A (AWACS) aircraft is now being deployed with United States forces.

8. In the past three years, only one additional Soviet division has been deployed to the Sino-Soviet border area, a motorized rifle division sent to Mongolia in 1976. Only 15 of the 45 divisions deployed on the Sino-Soviet border are Category 1 divisions (full operational readiness) whereas all the Soviet divisions (31) in Eastern Europe are Category 1 divisions.

9. According to testimony of the then-Army Chief of Staff, Gen. Frederick Weyand, before the Senate Committee on the budget in 1975, the U.S. Army alone suffers from $11 billion in deficiencies in equipment and deferred maintenance.

10. Soviet naval vessels are built with minimum reload capability. As a consequence, the Soviet Navy has often been described as a "first strike" navy because of its inability to reload after its initial salvo due to the absence of ammunition storage facilities on board Soviet vessels. Soviet naval vessels tend to be heavily armed by comparison with their United States counterparts, but with little "staying" power. Without an adequate basing structure (as in the Pacific), the Soviets are required to be heavily dependent on support vessels. Moreover, given the lack of adequate capabilities for underway replenishment of Soviet cruise missiles, they are dependent upon a basing structure for reload. The now famous Soviet base in Somalia was designed primarily for this purpose.

11. We apparently also assume Soviet civil defense preparation, particularly that initiated since 1972, has no effect on the survival of the Soviet civilian population and industrial infrastructure. A recent *New York Times* interview with the retiring U.S. Air Force Assistant Chief of Staff for Intelligence, Maj. Gen. George Keegan, tends to undermine this comfortable assumption. (*The New York Times*, 2 January 1977).

12. Unlike the remainder of the federal government, DOD retirement is a direct annual charge to the defense budget. Unless changed by statute, DOD retirement will be $11 billion in FY 80. For a comprehensive discussion of alternatives, see S.L. Canby and R.A. Butler, "The Military Manpower Question," in Schneider and Hoeber, *Arms, Men and Military Budgets: Issues for Fiscal Year 1978* (New York: Crane, Russak & Company, Inc., 1977), pp. 183-214.

13. With but a few exceptions, Soviet violations of the United States understanding of the terms of the SALT I accords came through violation of the terms of appended documents on "agreed understandings" and unilateral asertions (both submitted to the Congress nevertheless) of expected behavior.

14. For a discussion of Naval force level alternatives see D.S. Zalkeim, *U.S. Naval Force Alternatives,* U.S. Congressional Budget Office, March 26, 1976; A.M. Bowen, *U.S. Naval Expansion Program: An Analysis of the Cost of Expanding the Navy from 500 to 600 Ships,* Congressional Research Service, Library of Congress, April, 1976, and D. Kassing, "General Purpose Forces: Navy and Marine Corps," in Schneider and Hoeber, *Arms, Men and Military Budgets, Issues for Fiscal Year 1978* (New York: Crane, Russak & Company, Inc., 1977), pp. 107–137.

Chapter Six

The Rules of the Game: Why the West is Down and the East is Up*

Robert Conquest

By far the most striking, though also the most neglected, fact about the current conduct of international relations between the Soviet bloc and the West is to be found in the conditions under which they are pursued—the "rules of the game."

These are, in effect, summed up by saying that in almost every field the West is allowed defensive action only, while the Russians are permitted both offense and defense. And it is, of course, particularly difficult to win a campaign of any sort, in any sense, if the counteroffensive is forbidden you from the start and you have made this clear to your opponents.

What we find is that the Russians are on the whole permitted, without rebuff or rebuttal, speech, maneuver, and action of types the West has denied itself. Taken together, they give the Kremlin a built-in advantage that might prove decisive in the critical years ahead, and that is quite unnecessary. There exists, in fact, what amounts to an unspoken agreement that the West shall not exploit Soviet weaknesses, while the USSR remains free to exploit those of the West.[1] Do I exaggerate? Let us look at the facts.

One of the fundamental new rules is that while the Soviet rulers may express their true aims, and declare their total hostility to the West

*Originally prepared for the Strategic Studies Center of Stanford Research Institute, in connection with a study sponsored by the Advanced Research Projects Agency, Department of Defense, and revised for delivery as part of the Capitol Hill lecture series sponsored by the Department of Politics of Catholic University.

and all it stands for, our own spokesmen must not reply in kind, under pain of being accused of fomenting Cold War.

Soviet pronouncements, up to and including formal speeches by Brezhnev in person, have constantly and consistently defined detente as "a method of struggle"; they have stressed that it can in no way abate the "ideological" conflict; and they have insisted that it must never be taken as affecting Soviet support for the "class struggle" of the international proletariat (i.e., Communist action everywhere) and for "national liberation" movements in the Third World. Needless to say, detente, or the currently nameless but otherwise similar policy that succeeded it, is not to be interpreted as granting the West equivalent rights. The "ideological struggle" is to be conducted by freely operating Communist parties and presses in Western Europe and the United States, but by the total suppression of Western-orientated ideas in the Communist bloc. The CPSU party secretaries in charge of ideology, and of relations with foreign countries—in particular Boris Pomonarev and Mikhail Suslov—attend the congresses of Communist parties in the West, making speeches and giving general guidance or advice to them in their struggle for power. There are no legal parties representing Western views in the Communist bloc, of course. But it would be regarded as quite unacceptable for a Western Socialist statesman, for example, to attend a congress of exiled Hungarian or Polish Social Democrats or of underground ones within the countries concerned.

It would be tedious to rehearse yet again the many instances in which the Soviet position has been presented by Brezhnev in person, in the Party program; by Suslov; by Pomonarev. Gromyko himself, in direct charge of foreign operations, has formulated it in terms of the utmost clarity, and his words alone should suffice to prevent any misunderstanding:

> The Communist Party subordinates all of its theoretical and practical activity in the sphere of international relations to the task of strengthening the positions of socialism, and the interests of further developing and deepening the world revolutionary process. Directed towards strengthening peace and the security of the peoples, imbued with a spirit of solidarity with revolutionary, progressive forces throughout the world, Soviet foreign policy constitutes one of the chief factors of the class struggle in the international arena.[2]

Dmitri Ustinov put the point ex cathedra in his address, representing the Party in the most formal manner possible, on the occasion of the celebrations of the anniversary of the Revolution, on 6 November 1976: detente, he stated flatly, does not mean any Soviet abandonment of full support for revolutionary movements in the non-Communist world.

In the minds of many in the West such perfectly clear pronouncements (which have been, moreover, impeccably fulfilled in practice) are paid little attention. Instead, as Hugh Seton-Watson, professor of Russian History at the University of London, has ironically remarked, "What 200,000 Communist Party officials, from Brezhnev down to the secretaries of party branches in factories or collective farms, tell their subjects is all camouflage: the real views of the Soviet leaders are what some nice guy from the Soviet delegation at the U.N. said over a quiet drink, or what an itinerant Midwestern scientist heard from some friendly academician in Novosibirsk."

At any rate, for the West detente is *not* seen as a method of struggle. It is seen as a method of peaceful agreement. The two opposed concepts have resulted in an extravagant asymmetry.

It is not appropriate to cover here the pluses and minuses of SALT, and of Vladivostok, though even in these it is possible—to put it mildly —to recognize a tendency to grant the Soviets the right to higher weapon levels than the United States. The same principle applies to a considerable degree for such things as Soviet surveillance, reconnaissance, and incursion, including especially MIG-25 high-altitude reconnaissance, and to naval reconnaissance considerably more active and intrusive than anything the West permits itself. The North Sea oil rigs, for example, are continually subjected to very close aircraft observation. Large-scale Soviet military exercises, both by land and sea, involving a concentration of large forces in sensitive areas such as the Baltic, the Barents Sea, and the Caucasus, and amounting to an ostentatious pressure quite unparalleled by any similar allied maneuvers, are a regular feature of the world scene.

The enormously disproportionate investment in armament behind all this, a barely tolerable strain on the Soviet economy, could only be undertaken as the result of an exceedingly powerful political motivation. In a general sense, it could justly be argued that the immensely expensive Soviet missile arm, and even the missile-carrying submarine fleet, might (on a mutual deterrence view) be in principle defensive. But the continual effort to obtain not equality but superiority largely destroys this argument even in this field. And when it comes to the immense effort put into the blue water fleet, we are in the presence of a clearly expansionist policy. As in the time of William II in Germany, the construction by a great Eurasian land power of a vast surface fleet is overtly and solely part of a desire for expansion overseas.

The political potential of even a fairly small Soviet squadron, particularly with helicopter-landing vessels, operating (for example) in the Indian Ocean, can be seen when we consider that in the early sixties quite small detachments of British marines from ships in the area were called in to put down military rebellions against Nyerere in what was then Tanganyika, Kenyatta in Kenya, and Obote in Uganda. Nowadays, once installed, a pro-Soviet regime could in most circumstances be maintained indefinitely by similar means; in addition, there are other possible uses for such troops in disturbances under neutral or hostile regimes in the area. Under the present rules Soviet fleets already operate everywhere. But the mere idea of an American squadron visiting Finland or Rumania is hardly thinkable. Even minor and brief appearances of small American naval forces on the Black Sea coast of Turkey, a NATO ally, are regarded by some as bold and dubious.

In principle, the Soviet preponderance in conventional forces in Europe cannot be translated into action without full-scale war. In practice, things are not so easy. Not only are there prospects of a political neutralization of at least part of NATO by the action of local Communist parties, but the general willpower of the West is subject to a certain erosion. And, not only in Europe but also in other areas, mere military power can, without actually being used, constitute a pressure of its own—it can, as it were, be "leaned" against the prospective victim.

Soviet foreign policy combines the military threat with political pressure. And even when military moves proper are made, this is at least in part not just for simple strategic reasons, but as part of the main politico-military game. As Colonel G.F.R. Henderson remarks in his *Stonewall Jackson*: "The motive power which ruled the enemy's politics as well as his armies was always his real objective. . . . Every blow struck in the Valley campaign, from Kernstown to Cross Keys, was struck at Lincoln and his Cabinet."

The attempt to master Portugal by direct revolutionary action now seems to have failed. This leaves possibilities in Italy, and to a lesser degree France on the one hand, and the rather different perspective raised by Greco-Turkish antagonism on the other. Developments in Spain remain uncertain. This leaves, in effect, the Italian case as the one where we may best trace the possibility of a political break in the West.

It is correct for the Soviet Union to impose orthodoxy by armed force onto an errant Communist state, as the case of Czechoslovakia made clear; but the idea of an American, or a NATO, intervention against an Italy that had changed sides is unthinkable. It was possible for American spokesmen to say it is all right if the Italian Communists enter the government, though a more sensible attitude now seems to prevail. Can we imagine similar Soviet permission to even a Social Democratic membership in the Polish government?

For one important rule, needless to say, is that while the Communists may encourage those in the West wishing to change our political and economic system, we on our side shrink from encouraging, or even excusing, the leaders of antitotalitarian thought in or from the USSR, so that (an extreme and isolated case perhaps, but even one such case is too many) President Ford would not see Solzhenitsyn. The Carter administration has been a notable improvement in this sphere. But it still seems susceptible to the domestic pressures put upon it by those who imagine that the Soviet Union would make agreements in the sphere of armaments and elsewhere only with states that waive any general challenge to the whole totalitarian idea (while leaving Moscow free to mount the opposite challenge to Western democracy!).

More generally, one notes that in return for worthless assurances we are required to provide modern technology to our opponent, in case its military effort should fall behind ours, and, when it has overstrained its economy by inordinate arms investment and has no food, to provide the necessary rations to see that no beating of rockets into plough-shares shall be necessary. The rule governing the exchange of benefits is that the West must provide tangibles, while the USSR is only expected to make promises and gestures. To take a minor example, the arrangements for the exchange of technical information between the USSR and the United States resulted in the sending to Russia of a large body of useful scholarly papers, recompensed by material which came much later, was of considerably lesser bulk, and was negligible in substantive content. We have even reached the state in which the American intelligence services notoriously dispose of factual material highly damaging to the USSR's reputation but which they are not allowed to release on "detente" grounds, while, of course, any American secret material tending to harm the reputation of the United States is freely extracted from them and published, to the delectation of American liberals and Soviet Communists alike.

The Helsinki Agreement, of course, marked a special crux in this asymmetrical relationship. A number of the smaller European NATO nations in particular, though also the French and Germans,[3] had long urged that the essential test of Soviet hostility to the West was to be found in the total suppression in the USSR of all Western-style thought, and the monopoly imposition there of the view that irreconcilable struggle against all we stand for is the basic fact of world politics.

Basket Three on the free movement of ideas and of people was thus seen as central to anything resembling a lasting and stable peace. And, since the West has no other political demands, it was thought that any concession to the Russians in other fields could best be matched in this sphere. We are demanding, after all, no more than we already grant. Indeed, Basket Three only prescribed a very modest beginning in these matters, by no means paralleling the almost complete liberty of movement of Communists and of Communist ideas in the West.

Even this miniscule attempt to obtain a quid pro quo resulted in nothing but a Soviet signature, which brought no actual results whatever. There have been voices in the West strongly deploring this, for example that of Mrs. Margaret Thatcher, but there has been no serious attempt to insist on the fulfillment of Soviet promises—on the contrary, it seems to be taken for granted that the Russians can hardly be expected by reasonable people to carry out such obligations.[4]

The Helsinki Agreement was supposed to inaugurate a whole new epoch of peace and cooperation in Europe, and so in the world. If its provisions had been carried out by the Soviet bloc, it would indeed have done this. We would today be seeing, under the sections on the free exchange of information, the open sale of democratic Western newspapers in Moscow, just as Communist papers are available in New York and London. Under the human rights sections, we would be seeing in the USSR and its satellites what the agreement referred to as "the effective exercise of civil, political, economic, social, cultural and other rights and freedoms all of which derive from the inherent dignity of the human person and are essential for his free and full development."

To these propositions the representative of the Soviet Union "solemnly"—such was the phrase employed—bound his country. It has done virtually nothing to carry out its pledges.

More than one imprisoned Soviet dissident has pleaded that the Soviet acceptance of the Helsinki Agreement and the UN Declaration of Human Rights should mean their immediate release, only to have their interrogator say, "That isn't for us. That's for blacks"—that is, of course, for blacks as long as they remain unsovietized.

As it is—and this we are told by the unanimous voice of the Soviet dissenters—things would be even worse in the Soviet Union if it were not for the vigilant eyes with which Soviet excesses are watched by some in the West. Ironically enough, it is because the Russians wish not to irrevocably destroy their entire reputation even among the most hardened dupes in the West, and because they want to use certain elements in the West for their own political purposes, that they are showing what is for them comparative restraint. They have not shot dissenters—they employ only such techniques as starvation rations and psychiatric torture. But as to granting positive rights—no.

Thus an agreement with the Soviet Union is not worth the paper it is written on unless we have some sanction to induce them to carry out their obligations. Their Helsinki obligations are absolutely clear, as are their obligations under the UN Declaration of Human Rights—and they have taken no steps whatsoever to fulfill them. Once again, we gave them something that they wanted—a legitimization of their conquests in Eastern Europe—in exchange for an assorted batch of smiles and promises.

Those who are skeptical of Soviet goodwill have once again been proved absolutely right, and those sanguine folk who held that the Russian signature on these high-minded documents inaugurated a new age of peace have proved to be suckers. But, let us repeat, a few lessons are drawn from this. And this failure to react is gloomy evidence of a huge deterioration in the political sense, and the political will, of the West.

The policies that came to be known as detente were never envisaged in terms of unilateral surrender. While agreement was to be sought in various fields, and a general moderating of the international acerbities was expected to ensue, it was envisaged that any Soviet departures from these principles should be met with by a firm attitude on the part of the United States and its allies. If (as many of us believe) the whole concept of detente involved a misunderstanding of the nature and depth of basic Soviet motivations, it seems equally true that they also involve a misunderstanding of the nature of Western politics. Political action by the United States depends very much on the power of public support at home. But when the public has been told over a period of years that the Russians are no longer to be regarded as truly hostile, but rather as partners, or prospective partners, in an amicable world community, and it is then asked to support firm action in a crisis, it is naturally confused and unprepared, as was seen in Angola.

The isolationist, or semi-isolationist mood, prevalent in American political and media circles after the Vietnam debacle, naturally had a deleterious effect on the whole non-Communist position. The outcry that action over Angola would mean "getting bogged down in another Vietnam"—a phrase also used of the prospects of any trouble in Panama —was indicative enough. Needless to say, neither situation had any resemblance, or even any potential resemblance, to Vietnam. An Israeli statesman is said to have remarked that he was surprised no American had expressed the fear that the Israeli stay—an hour or so—at Entebbe airport might "get them bogged down in another Vietnam."

However, the point is not the literal applicability of thoughtless slogans so much as the general mood they reveal. It showed that major political forces were prepared to write off important areas to the Russians. It is possible that firm political leadership would have produced, or would produce, a clearer stand among the electorate as a whole; but that was not forthcoming.

In the first place, why was this? Partly, indeed, because the West is full of politicians and publicists willing and eager to sustain the Soviet charge that their own countries are the greatest villains on the world scene, and responsible in particular for everything that is still imperfect in the excolonial (and, indeed, never-colonial) territories of the Third World.

They are assisted by the fact that under current circumstances it is difficult to find a small accomplice, as the Russians have found Cuba, to carry out some pro-Western operation, though heart may be taken from the Moroccan-French operation, which denied Soviet puppets control of Zaire. Nor, again, would it be easy for the United States to organize such a move in an adequately clandestine fashion. Not only would a free press be around, inquisitive to the nth degree, but, on the record, one might suppose that high-minded officials in American government circles might feel it their duty to betray their country's plans (with an altruism fortified by the fact that previous leaks have gone unpunished or virtually unpunished, which in the Soviet case would certainly have led to summary execution, preceded by intensive interrogation in the Lubyanka, thus fulfilling the condition that there is always one rule for the Russians and another for the Westerners).

The suicide of the executive in the United States had a natural, though possibly not inevitable, effect on the country's political will power in international affairs. Up until the early part of 1974, detente appeared to be generally interpreted in a much harder fashion (except perhaps for the SALT agreements). It was possible to carry out the bombing of Hanoi without provoking any effective response from the major Communist powers. And the Vietnam settlement, though far from ideal, would have been tenable but for the collapse of the presidency. Mr. Nixon's progressive loss of grip, and final removal, led to continually greater emphasis on the more Kissingerite, or softer, concepts of detente. Even so, the Communist probing attacks in the South Vietnamese mountains early in 1975 were very tentative, and only when American air force intervention, expected by both sides, was not forthcoming did the plan for the final offensive, involving the transfer of virtually the whole North Vietnamese army to the area, seem feasible to the High Command in Hanoi. Thus, the potential of firmer Western policies is, or was, recognized even by our opponents. Is there any reasonable possibility of a revival of our political will? As was shown in the (so far) brief and exceptional UN career of Daniel P. Moynihan, the Western public remains ready to be told that it is in the right, and that its interests will be defended. That brief career alone markedly strengthened the moral nerve of America and, conversely, the years of accepting accusations of guilt and repudiations of the domestic principle from all sides weakens the Western willpower. I would argue this was the essential—or an essential—fallacy of Kissingerism. It is no good assuring your public that the Russians are really amiable detente-fodder, while on the other hand seeking to maintain the possibility of giving them strong rebuffs when they lapse. Angola showed, amongst other things, that the congressional-media establishment was quite incapable of rousing itself from its deep dream of peace at such short notice. Kissinger blamed the Congress, but his entire policy—including the junking of Moynihan—had contributed greatly to that mood. And how much has it since changed?

Angola seems to have established in the American political mind yet another rule: that the United States will not regard Western intervention against aggression as justifiable except in the case of (perhaps) Israel, of Western Europe, and of the arc from Japan to Australia. The idea that American interests would be unaffected if all of Africa and southern Asia became a Soviet dependency is odd enough. More troubling still is the widespread feeling that even the territories America still feels obliged to defend may be subject to revision. If Africa is written off, why not Israel? Why not Italy?

The extent of the disaster in Angola has not perhaps been sufficiently appreciated. As the first major Soviet expansionist effort outside their traditional sphere, at least since Khrushchev's Cuban adventure, it was entered into in a very careful and tentative fashion by the USSR. The use of Cuban puppet troops and a limited number of Soviet military advisers, with no overt commitment, evidently represented an enterprise that, if countered by even a minimal display of force, could have readily been abandoned without loss of face. As one European commentator put it, a single obsolescent American aircraft carrier with one engine out of action would probably have been sufficient.

The whole operation, in fact, seems to have been undertaken with misgivings, and there are plausible reports of opposition to it within the Politburo. However, it was undertatken: and that alone is enough to show the strength of the current expansionist mood in Moscow.

The success of the whole maneuver immensely increased the dangers to the West for several reasons. In increasing order of seriousness these may be listed. First, a major source of important raw materials has been thrown away. Second, the Russians are now in a position to support and maintain a smoldering border war against South Africa, in which all the political advantages on the world scale are theirs. Third, the more adventurist elements in the Kremlin have been proved right, and those who urge a comparative prudence are discredited. And fourth, a signal was given to all of Africa, and in principle to the whole Third World, that political forces supported by the Soviet Union have good prospects while those supported by the West are liable to be abandoned. Not only are pro-Communist elements greatly encouraged, but, even more important, the much larger group of the waverers, the undecided, received the signal that it is best to go along with the likely winners: and even pro-Western forces begin to feel that they will have little choice but to accommodate with the enemy unless the trend is radically reversed. It is true that through various subsequent events—in particular, continuing anti-Soviet resistance and the Soviet error of trying to subvert Zaire—the Russians lost some of their advantage; but they still hold their bridgehead, ready for further action on the lines suggested.

Outside Europe the political contest throughout the globe remains a matter of our attitudes to the Third World as a whole, the largest and potentially the most explosive arena of "ideological struggle." It is here that the double standard is most strikingly, most unnecessarily, and most disastrously illustrated.

The "rules of the game" include nowadays the curious convention, in the United Nations and international forums in general, by which the Communist countries, and the more militant representatives of the Third World, attack the Western record, while representatives of the West do not answer back. This is an extraordinary change since the early fifties, when Labour and Conservative, Democratic and Republican delegates alike freely counterattacked the Soviet Union's hypocritical "anti-imperialism" (and exposed internal terrors like the forced labor camp system, and so on). It is clear that current passive tactics—interrupted only by the brief United Nations career of Moynihan—are misconceived in several ways.

It has become fashionable to speak of the fundamental problem of international politics as being the need to narrow the divergences between the richer and poorer countries—what is often referred to as the North-South relationship. This is sometimes treated as an antagonism, or potential antagonism, which might lead to a vast world jacquerie.

That such a problem exists in some sense is clear enough. That it is the major problem of world politics, properly speaking, is a proposition that loses much of its credibility when the following facts are recalled: first, that the Third World wish to become prosperous is not to be solved by the moral danegeld methods now largely accepted on both sides (and that many Third World leaders, when it comes to the point, have enough sense not to cut off their noses in order to spite their faces, or to slaughter the available golden geese); and, secondly, that any political and military threat to the West (or to the East, for that matter) from this source is quite chimerical unless as a minor weight in the scales in the Soviet-Western conflict.

Before the war, and even in the first postwar decade, it was generally assumed even in the more backward parts of the world that political democracy was the most advanced form of the state. Countries that remained wholly or partly dictatorships nevertheless tended to believe that this was due to the temporary circumstance of that backwardness, and to aspire in principle to a more democratic condition. Turkey was a prime example, with its constant yet never total intervention by the army in its politics and its equally constant return to a limited parliamentarianism. But where Turkey was a model it is now an exception. The new dictatorships, military or otherwise, rarely apologize and assert the temporary nature of their rule. On the contrary, and to some degree relying on the justificatory jargon of Leninism, they represent the one-party state as in itself desirable and superior to "bourgeois democracy."

What is worse is that under the new "rules" Western democracies have let the position go by default. They fail, in the international forums, in public speeches at home, and also in their direct relations with the Third World, forthrightly to maintain the superiority of Western political systems, compared with the fashionable "one-party democracies" beloved by the USSR and by local gunmen.

To take a typical case, during Moynihan's foray at the UN the British representative, Mr. Ivor Richard, went out of his way to insult our ally, as he had never insulted our enemies, with snide talk of cowboy tactics. But Richard not only made no attempt to defend Western libertarian principles; he even described them as merely a "particular brand of political theology"—a real, total, and typical surrender of our position. With inane piety he defended the General Assembly as a "democratic institution"—whereas, of course, it is (in Solzhenitsyn's formulation) not a United Nations at all in any real sense, but merely a United Governments, the great majority elected by no one. A number of the representatives of former colonial territories have no legitimacy except their claim to have led the anti-imperialist struggle. In fact, as Conor Cruise O'Brien has pointed out (in the *New York Review of Books*), in many cases—and in particular when it comes to the most vociferous "anti-imperialists"—the struggle that brought the successor regimes to power was not to get rid of the British, who were leaving anyway, but to seize control of the new state from a variety of indigenous rivals. In this sphere, as elsewhere, sometimes by default, but sometimes in active collaboration, the West has accepted the terminology of its enemies. "National liberation" is freely used to describe movements whose aim is to impose their own gang rule.

Now in the first place, such abject tactics encourage even reasonably well meaning rulers in the direction of "one-party democracy," since there is little feeling that anyone on our side cares one way or the other. They do not even hear incisive exposure of the barbarian regressiveness of Marxism-Leninism, so easy to state, so largely neglected. When they actively attack, they are treated in the fashion formerly advocated in "liberal" circles—though now largely abandoned—for coping with the tantrums of infants: that is, allowing them to go on, and making no attempt sharply to pull them up. This is of course (as is realized by the better elements in those countries themselves) grossly patronizing. Nor could anything be more calculated to make the tantrums ever worse and more destructive.

I chanced to be present at a colloquium at the Smithsonian Institution in Washington at the time of the furor over Moynihan. The Italian ambassador to the United Nations was the speaker, and he gave, on this theme, the patronizing and hostile line then taken about Dr. Moynihan by various Western Europeans. Feeling that it was easier for myself than for Americans present to come to Moynihan's defense, I put his case very strongly, and in particular said that the Third World countries would in the long run prefer being treated frankly, and as adults. Among those present was a distinguished Nepalese, himself a former ambassador to the UN, who intervened firmly with a series of observations on the theme, "I must agree with my British colleague."

Yet all sorts of specially fabricated anti-Western notions, like "neo-colonialism," are now freely bandied about without rebuttal. Generally speaking, as in this case, the prefix "neo" in fact means "non," signifying merely that colonial rule has actually ended, but pretending that it has not, on the grounds, usually, that the successor state is pro-Western, or at least insufficiently anti-Western, in that trade with the West goes on (even that Western investment takes place), and that Westerners are physically present in such territories as teachers, experts, merchants, and so forth.

The foreign aid policies of the West too are largely involved, in the Western political mind itself, with the concept dictated by the communists and accepted for want of counterargument by much of the Third World, that Western wealth is disgraceful, and that it is the duty of the Western powers not only to send vast sums to the Third World, but to receive kicks and abuse in exchange. This too is associated with "imperialism," "colonialism," and so forth, conventionally accepted as crimes committed by the former Western imperial powers whose role is to confess and to atone for as far as possible (full atonement being impossible). Yet it is perfectly well known to many Third Worlders that colonial rule was beneficent rather than not. There is no reason to deny that, like all other complex phenomena, it had a negative side —and that in particular, as local national feeling gradually developed, the mere rule of foreigners became in itself unacceptable. It was, indeed, always an imperial principle, at least since the middle of the last century, that power would eventually have to be transferred to the local population, as Macaulay's famous memorandum made clear in the case of India; Kipling himself takes it for granted that his "pro-consuls" are training "Power that must their power displace."

But how often nowadays does one hear the British or the French saying a good word of any sort for their country's record, either absolutely or, in particular, compared to Soviet colonialism, or even to the former empire's current condition? This has to be left, in fact, to such persons as the spokesmen of the Indian opposition parties prior to the recent election, who pointed out publicly the superior liberties they enjoyed under the Raj.

Even more ridiculous is the failure to rebut the entirely erroneous concept, Leninist in origin, of the "exploitative" essence of Western colonialism. In Lenin's view, still orthodox, the whole point of imperialism was the export of capital to the backward countries where, owing to the low wage rates, "super-profits" would be made. In no sense was this a true account of the economic development of the colonial territories. There was no great capital investment. In fact British investment abroad involved virtually no net outflow of capital at all. The French colonies imported more than they exported. And where there was major investment, it did not produce superprofits; the Rand mines, for example, gave an average annual return of not over 4.1 percent.

There are other fallacies in the Marxist account of imperialism: for example, the thesis that "finance capital," in the form of the great banks, was particularly keen on colonial expansion (they were not). Yet the whole conception is now more or less accepted, and anyone who points out that the trade balance between Britain and India, for example, was virtually unaffected by independence, or produces any of the other facts that spoil the simple horror picture, is regarded as a dangerous eccentric. And, of course, it would be worse still for anyone who turned attention to Russia's colonies, as yet unliberated—and perhaps even quoted Chekhov's remark (omitted from the Soviet edition of the *Collected Works*), that while both the Russians and the British had annexed foreign territory, the Russians had not, and the British had, given the inhabitants much in exchange.

As against the Western attitude, can one imagine Third World dictators saying that their own type of state was not, or was not approaching, a form ideally suited to their country? As for the Communist opponents, they have never in any circumstances conceded that any Western type of state is, in principle, legitimate at all.

Yet there are few Western countries that adequately counter the verbal aggressions of the Communist states on these issues as (again) the first postwar Labour Government in Great Britain and its contemporaries in the West used to do. When it comes to Third World attacks on the West for colonialism, neocolonialism and so forth, the Western tactic has been to ignore them. It is argued that the Third World attitude in these matters is largely symbolical and rhetorical, and that words can never hurt us. Not only the most extravagant abuse, but even disgraceful activities such as the 1976 "Nonaligned" Conference (with its unconditional support for a North Korea it had the impudence to accept as also "nonaligned") are overlooked.

Of course it is true, or was originally true, that much Third World abuse of the West is ritualistic. Yet, what this abject calculation fails to comprehend is that, in the end, to surrender the symbol is also to surrender the substance. This central error or miscalculation is what throws the game, as in other spheres, to the USSR. It is in part a product of this attitude, at once fawning and patronizing, that we appear to find also in fashionable attitudes to foreign aid. It has long since been pointed out (in particular, of course, by Professor Peter Bauer of the London School of Economics, but by other economists of equal prominence like Professor Harry Johnson of the University of Chicago) that the whole conception that the advanced countries should simply hand cash over to the underdeveloped countries in order to promote economic growth contains a profound fallacy. In the first place, of course, in a number of countries (described by Bauer as "kleptocracies") the greater part of such funds disappears into the pockets of the bureaucrats. In others it is diverted into ideologically conceived and economically worthless schemes. It may even be the case that major projects that on the face of it look promising even to Westerners possessing a keen economic eye may contain the seeds of disaster. For example, the Aswan High Dam, of which so much was expected, already seems to have as its main results the accumulation of the vital Nile silt where it is not wanted, the lowering of the water table, and the spread of bilharzia.

The Western "capitalist" countries owe their prosperity to the political system, and the entire culture, which rendered it possible. And they should, *and do not*, say so—again leaving the field to those attracted to a one-party pseudosocialism favorable to the Soviet Union. The backward countries will not in fact achieve anything unless and until they have to some degree absorbed Western principles. Nor should it be thought that this is simple. If the world's farmers operated like those of Britain or the United States, there would be no question of food shortages, even for a much larger population than the world has at present. Satellite photographs astonishingly illustrate the effect of politics and culture. It might have been expected that Israeli frontiers, or the United States–Mexican border, should be clearly visible. But it is even the case that a clear-cut line divides the wholly comparable territories of Montana and Saskatchewan (the latter having a government moderately discouraging to private enterprise): it is even possible to trace the Texas–New Mexico line, Texas having a rather better system of agricultural bank loans. More directly to our point, a large green area is visible in the Sahel: it proves to belong to a French consortium that has not overgrazed the land. This latter problem—to farm livestock economically rather than on a fetishist basis, to secure the optimum rather than the maximum number of cattle—is absolutely crucial to African development (just as destruction of the goat, effected in Israel but nowhere else in the Middle East, is vital for that area). But both involve a very great change in cultural attitudes, not easily to be effected, yet constituting the main problem. The interest of the USSR, in conjunction with indoctrinated local bureaucrats, is to abort such progress. We, in our own interest—and that of the Third World itself—should, and do not, make the issue clear in a forthright fashion.

Bauer argues that the way to bring the underdeveloped countries to the levels of prosperity achieved in the West is not by handouts, which at best put them in a parasitical relationship to the advanced country, but by policies that would tend to encourage them in the creation of economies of the advanced type. Those Third World countries that see this, even in the absence of positive encouragement from the West (in particular South Korea, Singapore, Hong Kong, and Taiwan), have in fact prospered. When Western money comes freely in the form of investment, that, and that only, is a sign that the economies are, or will be, viable. They get little public or political reclame even in the West. It is the agrogorod-crazy Nyerere who wins the applause.

All in all, the notion that the West is fulfilling its economic duty by merely passing money over is absurd. Foreign aid, in this primitive sense, is of little genuine help to the backward countries, and its main effect is to give Western liberals a warm glow of satisfaction at their own generosity. But—just as in many high-minded, plausible, and well-funded expenditures at home—pouring money into rat holes does no one any lasting good. (Occasions of immediate humanitarian need—famine in the Sahel or flood in the Sundarbans—are another matter; here instant purchase and supply of food and equipment is indeed both right and sensible.) But generally, in this broad area of policy, the West has once more accepted rules incompatible with good sense, with its own interests, and with economic progress—and hence, in the long run, with world peace.

Moreover, it has accepted rules of political—though not only of political—conduct in relations with the Third World that quite gratuitously concede the invalid notion that the USSR is without the taint of imperialism and is the legitimate ally and sponsor of all Third World claims and ambitions. When one adds that this position has been reached in spite of the fact that the Western countries pay out in aid to these areas sums almost comically in excess of the trickle of Soviet alms, one can only shake one's head.

None of this is to deny that relationships with the Third World are of major importance—and particularly in the larger context of East-West relationships. On the contrary, Soviet domination of Africa and southern Asia would—one would say "obviously," but there are those who do not see it[5]—be an enormous advantage economically, strategically, and politically to Moscow. And if we are to return to sound principles in foreign policy, this applies equally to our relations with both spheres—to the Soviet bloc as it manifests itself in the Third World, and to the Third World in its own right. As has often been pointed out, it is better to be hated than despised. But, generally speaking those who hate us as a matter of principle are not a majority of the Third World. And those who now despise us, or who hate us only because they despise us, are more likely to side with a bulldog than with a jellyfish. The UN in particular is a forum in which our good sense, and our attachment to our principles, is continually being put to the test before the world public, and equally continually found wanting.

It is quite usual these days to have the issue of Puerto Rican liberation raised by a Third World–Communist grouping against the United States, but not Estonia against the USSR. Rather similarly the United Kingdom is regularly taxed with the vicious imperialism by which it retains Gibraltar and the Falkland Islands with no reference to (for example) the Georgian SSR. The fact that free elections invariably show the United States and United Kingdom territories unwilling to give up the American or British connection is simply ignored, as is the fact that no true election takes place in the Soviet colonies. The 2 November 1976 elections showed the parties urging Puerto Rican independence gaining 5 percent of the vote on that island; but that will make no difference nor, on present form, will the fact be strongly emphasized in international meetings by the United States. Similarly, in spite of a determined British attempt to get the Gibraltarians to accept some sort of arrangement with Spain, the voters there returned a huge majority for the status quo. When it comes to the Falkland Islands, Argentina has admitted the British affections of the population but said flatly that in this case self-determination must be ignored. Britain has failed to rebuff this nonsense before the "uncommitted" nations who heard and subscribed to it.

What one asks for is the firm rebuttal of anti-Western slanders—not just occasionally, but every time, as a matter both of principle and of practical politics; the equally forceful exposure of Soviet hypocrisy on the colonial issue, for example with chapter and verse about the Baltic states every time they attack us as imperialists; and so on. A clear and frank maintenance of our position vis-à-vis the Third World itself is part and parcel of the same attitude. Nor is it true that it is necessarily a losing tactic even in the short run. As Dr. Moynihan pointed out in a formal letter to the secretary of state, though it had been alleged that his tactics would lose African and other Third World votes for American proposals in the United Nations, in fact (whether as a result of his style or not) the United States had done rather better than usual. The contrary assumption was, then, a purely a priori one.

In sum, then, the rules of the international game concerning relations between the West and those Third World countries traditionally regarded in Moscow, since Lenin's time, as potential auxiliaries of the Communists in the struggle for world power, are as follows: (a) the West is to blame for their backwardness, (b) they are entitled to set up and maintain political orders similar to those of the Soviet Union, and guaranteed to prevent economic progress, (c) the West must in no way intervene, even with advice against such counterproductive policies, let alone insist on a measure of political friendship as a condition, but merely offset local failure by paying out large sums unconditionally, (d) the USSR has no imperialist record, is to be regarded as a natural support for the Third World countries, and is entitled to intervene, with mercenaries if necessary, to ensure the defeat of pro-Western elements in contested areas. And these rules, moreover, have so far been more or less accepted by the West itself.

This affects policy in three important fields. In the first place, it gives the Russians the argument, and provides them—to their immense advantage—with a world reputation they in no way deserve. Second, it encourages or appeases those circles in the West most warmly devoted to hostility to their own culture, thus undermining the political will of the democracies.

Thus in every area in which the Russians are sponsoring anti-Western movements—in every sphere in which the West and the Kremlin are in contact—the West has waived its case. Strategically, the currently accepted rules of the game concede, or tend to concede, Soviet expansionism, while accepting that no part of the Soviet empire can be detached. Politically, they encourage everywhere, and in every way, attitudes hostile to the democratic culture.

Let us imagine the opposite scenario to what we have described as actually existing on the world scene. During troubles, in say, Albania, the French Foreign Legion goes in and brings a pro-Western group to power. The president of the United States makes continual speeches to the effect that communism will not be tolerated in the West, but Western ideas must be freely admitted to the Communist countries. His representatives, at the highest level, are sent to attend meetings of dissidents in the Eastern European area, bringing the official greetings of the Western rulers, with encouragement to continue the struggle until the political and social order is overthrown. Huge American naval maneuvers take place on the seas off Murmansk, Sevastopol, and Vladivostok. Western airplanes buzz Soviet installations in the Barents and Okhotsk seas. Meanwhile, in Italy, the government installed by the American invasion in 1968 remains in power without recourse to elections.

What is wrong with this picture? It is, of course, merely a dramatization, a mirror image. There are some things the West's own system precludes it from doing. There are, nevertheless, plenty of areas where it surrenders symbol and substance for no reason at all.

And on what basis? Not to cause offense? Not to hold up negotiation? We have already pointed out that such tactics are fallacious in
dealing with countries for whose support we and the Kremlin are competing. When it comes to the USSR itself, let us remind ourselves of the
essentials that the most amiable and optimistic tactics will not change.

The Soviet Union will not fulfill its obligations, however solemnly
undertaken, unless it is made disadvantageous for it not to do so. So
long as the Russians can get what they want in the way of trade, in
the way of recognition of their conquests, in the way of noninterference with their expansionism, without having to make any concessions
in exchange, they will go on doing so. They will make no improvements on the absolutely vital human rights issue unless we vigilantly
insist on it as a quid pro quo for any concession we make in other
fields.

The Soviet leaders are hostile in principle to all that we stand for.
There is nothing secret about this. They state it quite openly in their
public speeches in Moscow, in their worldwide propaganda, in their
indoctrination of their own populations. They attack us and our society
continually. They build up vast armaments and attack us for our lesser
effort. They rule scores of subject peoples and attack us as imperialists.
Nor is this constant and virulent hostility difficult to understand. The
average Westerner has a perfectly clear mind on this subject.

Such are the facts. Are we to ignore them? Some people seem to
think so.

They think that peace is best served by pretending that all is well
when it is not; by saying that the Soviet leaders are other than they are,
and that their aims and practices are quite different from what we
know them to be; by avoiding the "provocation" of maintaining and
pressing our own principles; by accepting rules of the game equivalent
to an Olympic decision under which Western, but not Soviet, athletes
must run under the handicap of heavy ball and chain.

Only, it seems, by a conscious reversal of present attitudes can the
situation be restored. This would involve Western governments that
are ready, and known to be ready, to take action in Angola-type crises.
It would involve a refusal to let the Russians carry out their unilateral
military pressures. And, perhaps more important yet, it would involve
the insistence, in all public international forums, on the superiority of

the Western political process; the carrying of the argument to the Russians, with appropriate denunciation of their crimes and weaknesses to an extent not yet envisaged; and a warning to the Third World that hostility to the West will not be rewarded—at least not by the West itself.

NOTES

1. This was written before President Carter's letter to Academician Sakharov, which was thought to mark the beginning of a new United States approach to these matters. Sounder principles did indeed seem to be accepted in 1977, but after a few months they appeared to have been overlaid or compromised to some degree by supposedly tactical or particular considerations, as before, though not by any means abandoned. The centrality of the point that Soviet persecution of Russian democrats is the real litmus paper of their intent toward democrats outside their present power—that is, toward ourselves—does not seem to have been adequately appreciated; a full consistency of understanding, both principled and pragmatic, is still a hope rather than a reality.

2. *The Foreign Policy of the Soviet Union* (Moscow, 1975).

3. The Schmidt regime in the Federal Republic of Germany lately appears to be having some second thoughts about actively holding the Soviets to account on the Helsinki agreement, for reasons which are not yet clear.

4. Much of the criticism, both in the United States and abroad, of the Carter administration's human rights campaign is instructive in this connection.

5. For another view, see Chapter Twelve by Anthony Harrigan.

Chapter Seven

The United States and Western Europe: Security Questions, Old and New

Colin S. Gray

Dramatic policy initiatives of a declaratory kind have an unfortunate habit of rebounding embarrassingly upon their authors. Looking to the 1980s, the United States requires a policy of substance rather than style and gesture vis-à-vis Western Europe. One proclaimed "year of Europe" each decade in American foreign policy is probably one too many. Dr. Kissinger's "year of Europe," 1973,[1] was to demonstrate all too clearly the limits of alliance cohesion, as most NATO-European countries pursued policies of unilateral salvation in the face of the oil embargo that succeeded the October War.

A prerequisite for sensible American policy formulation is the recognition that European security comprises a set of conditions or, if focused, a set of long-enduring questions, and not a short list of problems that can be solved. If careful study, clear thinking, or even bold new (largely declaratory) policy initiatives on the part of Americans could transform the European security condition in a benign direction, such a transformation would have been accomplished long ago. However, although the dominant activist style in American foreign policy tends to be ill-fitted to coping with enduring questions, as opposed to problems that can be tackled (with task forces, basic policy reviews, and the like) in short order, an attitude of passive acquiescence over developments in, and concerning, Europe is not appropriate for the years immediately ahead. These opening paragraphs have sought to point to the limits of prospective policy achievement. Most of this paper is constructive by intent: to identify the proper role of political architecture on the grand scale and, more particularly, to identify some of the practical ways in which the security condition of Western Europe might be improved in the short to medium terms.

GEOPOLITICS

The Soviet Union is a European power that cannot help but be profoundly interested in political developments in the European peninsula. That obvious statement is as important as it is close to being trite. Barring dramatic changes in the character of the Soviet political system (and even those might not suffice) or the fragmentation of the Soviet state, both the shadow and the substance of Soviet military power is going to threaten Western Europe for the foreseeable future. The mood of East-West political relations will fluctuate from periods of greater relaxation to greater tenseness, but built into the structure of European politics is the fact that Western Europeans must share a continent with a first-class military superpower. Over the medium to long term, Western Europeans have three core choices in designing their security condition vis-à-vis Soviet power: (1) they can attempt to protract the existing security structure—whereby American conventional, theater nuclear, and strategic nuclear power is engaged very actively in order to achieve a local balance (with compensating links to the central balance); (2) they can attempt, slowly but steadily, to provide more and more for themselves the military muscle and political organization needed to maintain a standoff; or (3) they can acquiesce in (they would hope, a relatively benign form of) a Soviet hegemony.

Those somewhat stark choices, 1 through 3, do beg some important questions. For a prominent example, it is asumed that the Soviet Union has ambitions to control the destiny of all of Europe, if not (necessarily) impose costly occupation regimes.[2] This assumption is not beyond challenge. It might be argued that over the long term the Soviet Union is far more worried about its eastern than its western flank, and that the quasi-imperial structure sustained in Eastern Europe speaks neither to aggressive ambitions (a springboard to the West), nor even to very serious defensive fears (a security glacis).

Instead, so the argument might proceed, the Eastern European security structure of the Soviet Union is a bequest from recent history that cannot be dismantled. Domination (in different ways and in differing degrees from country to country) of Eastern Europe imposes an order, a stability, and a predictability for which Soviet officials can discern no attractive substitutes. Following this fairly benign interpretation of Soviet motives still further, Soviet officials might well reason that the dismantlement of their empire in Eastern Europe would almost certainly lead to a total or very near total American military withdrawal from the continent—and the dominant influence in Europe from the Atlantic to the Pripet Marshes would be what?—Germany (West and East, and possibly reunited).

The above argument is almost certainly in error, but it does warrant characterization as a plausible fallacy that is not devoid of policy relevance for the United States and Western Europe—given the number of people who endorse some variant of it. Many people on both sides of the Atlantic do believe (or at least suspect) that the Soviet Union really harbors no ambitions inimical to Western Europe. Historical accident and a cycle of mutual misperception, in this view, produced the essentially frozen politicomilitary condition of the Europe of the 1950s, 1960s, and 1970s. The existing military structures fuel suspicions on both sides; as a result, neither side dares to dismantle its military structure, and the residual anxiety and fear is such that they cannot engage in mutual dismantlement. Would that this line of argument were true (or, at least, were backed far more substantially by persuasive evidence)!

A more reasonable interpretation of "the Soviet problem" for Western Europeans cannot deny that there is *some* truth in the above theme of argument. Accident of history did bring the Soviet army into Central Europe; for reasons of ideology that cannot lightly be dismissed, and on the basis of some historical evidence (the Allied intervention against the new Soviet republic is very much a live memory, as are Soviet suspicions that the Western democracies in the 1930s might not have been averse to allowing Hitler a free hand in the East), Soviet officials are both obliged to, and do, define Western societies as being basically antagonistic; also, it is a fact that an Eastern Europe freed of Soviet tutelage could well have major effects upon the strength of disruptive (from the point of view of the Soviet state) forces active within Soviet society. However, there is good reason to believe that the Soviet Union deems Eastern Europe to be not merely a burden and a political embarrassment, but also an essential forward stage for the projection of military power in useful ways and to politically productive ends.[3] Soviet officials do believe, as they are compelled to, that they are committed to a long-term life-and-death struggle with the United States. In company with Henry Kissinger, and indeed anybody who has devoted any time to historical reflection, Soviet officials believe that the power of states, relative to each other, alters over time. Ideology and realpolitik point to the same conclusion. Soviet ideology posits a permanent struggle between antagonistic social systems, while realpolitik reminds Soviet officials that there are (still) only two superpowers, and that Western Europe remains the principal "prize" in their rivalry. For Soviet officials to "acquire" that prize, however, without in the process destroying it, and for them to control and exploit it, without in so doing infecting Soviet society with fatal contradictions, would—admittedly—be difficult.

Atavistic though it may sound to those Americans who bask in the contemplation of the challenge of "new international orders" or fundamental (and spurious) foreign policy "choices," as portrayed in such organs of responsible opinion as *Foreign Policy* and *Foreign Affairs*,[4] the balance of the evidence—direct and to be inferred—is to the effect that Soviet foreign policy ambitions are brutal, old-fashioned, and distinctly outside the mainstream of American post-Vietnam liberal thinking. "Keeping the Soviet Union out" of Western Europe is a much simplified formulation, and it may distract from the more probable character of threats to Western European security, but it does have the elemental nature of advertising the principal and permanent source of Western European security anxieties.

The geopolitics of European security pose fundamental problems both for the near term and the long term. For the near term, there is the persisting problem that the United States, the major security producer for the West, is geographically far removed from the area in principal contention. Because the United States is a power in Europe, as opposed to being a European power, the strength of the American commitment to the physical security of Europeans is always subject to question. This would matter less were either the locally deployed (and readily mobilizable) NATO force structure a very robust one, or were the nuclear-weapon resources of the alliance divided more evenly between American and NATO-European provision. It is, of course, true to claim that the United States has vital interests in Europe (and *vital* interests usually are defined as interests worth fighting for),[5] but those interests are (a) notably less vital than the interests of Western Europeans; (b) probably perceived by Soviet officials as being less vital than the interests of the Soviet Union as a regional power; and (c) clearly less vital than would be the case were American territory directly involved.

Geography impinges upon NATO's strategic problems in almost all respects. Some examples: NATO lacks depth for defensive maneuver (even if France is fully engaged on NATO's part);[6] NATO's seaborne and overland lines of communication (LOC) would be increasingly restricted as a Pact offensive progressively uncovered the West German North Sea ports, and then the Dutch and Belgian ports; and there is the fact of psychological, as well as physical, geography. To Americans, NATO-Europe is an ocean away. Considerable effort is required to maintain a plausible connection between the defense of Europe and the possible employment of American strategic nuclear forces.

Some security questions are better raised by extraofficial analysts than they are by governments. Predictions by American officials of *eventual* American military disengagement from the continent of Europe would, almost certainly, be misunderstood and would create needless, disruptive and dysfunctional anxieties. However, it is disturbing that the prevalent NATO-European attitude continues to be one of adherence to the maxim that "sufficient unto the day is the evil thereof." Western Europe is not noticeably closer to the creation of a cohesive regional politicomilitary entity than it was ten years ago. This lack of progress may well reflect some not inconsiderable official wisdom. In other words, serious NATO-European planning (as opposed to fitful discussions) directed toward such an end might well serve to accelerate American disengagement: either because real progress might remove the perceived need for much of the local American military effort, or because the process of defense-community creation could easily prove to be abrasive of United States/NATO-

European relations. Policymakers live in a succession of short terms. At the present time NATO-Europe, in its disunited condition, requires the full panoply of American political-military support. No prudent official in Europe is going to risk that supportive panoply in the interest of embarking upon a process of defense-community construction that may not be needed until the year 2000.

Notwithstanding the caveats registered above, it would be entirely appropriate for American foreign- and defense-policy analysts (as opposed to officials) to ask of their European colleagues just what they envisaged for the long-term security architecture of Western Europe. Once one steps outside the existing security structure, major and relatively novel problems emerge. First, could the United States withdraw the vast majority of its ground and tactical air forces from NATO's Central Front without, as a consequence, severely attenuating the credibility of promised contingent theater and strategic nuclear action? Just as an orderly retreat is among the most difficult of military operations to effect,[7] so a process of orderly peacetime phase-down of forward military commitments would be exceedingly difficult to control. Second, would a European political-defense community be dominated by West Germany? No matter how orderly a process of American devolution of security tasks upon a new Western European entity might be, Americans (and Europeans) would have to consider the possible costs of the substantial Europeanization of Europe's security structure in terms of Soviet perceptions, and the likely Soviet threshold of tolerance of political events and trends on the borders of its empire. Every system of "order" requires guardians. While the Soviet Union would undoubtedly view with favor a Western Europe that comprised a loose alliance of states, shorn of any very credible American security connection, it is difficult to imagine Soviet officials waxing enthusiastic over, or even being very tolerant of, West German guardianship in NATO-Europe—with West Germany serving substantially and functionally as the successor state to the United States.[8]

Many historians have noted, plausibly, that European history for more than one hundred years has had as its focus the problem of accomodating Germany in a reasonably stable balance-of-power system. The "German problem," in all its complexity, was resolved for the foreseeable future in 1955 when West Germany entered NATO and

East Germany joined the newly formed Warsaw Pact (in January 1956). Notwithstanding the rise of the Soviet Union to first-class superpower status, many critical elements of the long-familiar German problem remain outstanding—complicated by the de facto World War II settlement. Stated fairly brutally, "the German problem" is not a cause for concern in the late 1970s, precisely because of the (joint and separate) superpower domination of the structure of security in Europe. Any radical alteration in European security arrangements could see the rapid and very dangerous reemergence of "the German problem." Undisciplined by the large-scale presence of American and Soviet forces, Germans—East and West—would have a disturbingly wide range of choice of policy options for the organization of their separate, *or collective,* futures. In short, there is a multi-tiered structure of security problems in Europe. On the surface, the East-West conflict continues to freeze political developments on the continent (East European–West European connections are, in good part, policed by the Soviet Union; while Western Europe fears to engage in very serious collective political experiment lest the American security connection be damaged). However, lurking beneath the Cold War division lines are the problems of the relations between the two Germanies, the relations between Germany (or the Germanies) and its neighbors, and the host of interstate issues in Eastern Europe that Soviet hegemony has suppressed since 1945.

This section has raised questions of long-term significance that policymakers are able to ignore day by day. Perhaps the most important geopolitical fact is that no matter what course European security arangements take, the Soviet Union will forever be in Europe as the greatest regional power—and the United States *may* not be. Both for the short and the long term, major policy challenges for American and NATO-European officials are (a) to design a character of American security connection with which Americans can be content, and (b) to ensure that any diminution in the security produced for Western Europe by the United States is matched by an increase in a local European capacity for collective action. The "trans-Atlantic bargain" between the United States and NATO-Europe requires that NATO-Europeans do, and be believed to be doing, enough for their own defense, in order to persuade the American public that NATO is in fact a collective security enterprise.[9] Barring the occurrence of some mobilizing security shock, which is always possible, it is predictable that the balance is shifting more and more to the Soviet advantage, and the United States might lack the military means/political will to function as an effective regional guardian in Europe.

INSECURITY IN EUROPE

A professional defense analyst, in considering the sources of insecurity in Europe, is tempted to focus narrowly upon the dangers latent in the order of battle of the Warsaw Pact. However, relevant though Soviet military options and choices are to very many questions pertaining to political developments in Western Europe, other, less dramatic, dangers probably are more likely to have policy relevance for Western governments over the next decade. For example, chronic domestic economic (Great Britain and Italy) and/or political (Italy) problems threaten to undermine the community of values that the Atlantic Alliance has, thus far, represented. In addition, critical problems of political succession (to dictatorships that stood outside the mainstream of European political-economic life) remain to be finally resolved in a convincing fashion in Spain and in Portugal. Possibly the only comfort NATO countries can draw from the prospects of Communist participation in government in Western Europe is that the Soviet Union has been as ambivalent to that development as they have themselves. From the Soviet point of view, on balance, Giscard d'Estaing in the last French election was a known proposition whose general policy line was deemed compatible and constructive given the general line of Soviet policy; François Mitterand, on the other hand, was largely an unknown proposition and was not favored substantially for that reason. Soviet ambivalence towards far-left political parties and electoral coalitions in Western Europe would appear to be genuine and not contrived (for fear of embarrassing local communists). A more extreme example of the conservative Soviet approach to foreign leaders and parties was the quite explicit preference registered for Richard Nixon over George McGovern in the 1972 American presidential election.

Whether or not economic and political instability in some Western countries is easily exploitable by the Soviet Union, the potential of such instability for damage to trans-Atlantic relations in particular, and to NATO cohesiveness more generally, does need to be underscored. It happens to be a fact, even though very many NATO-Europeans resist its registration, that the trans-Atlantic bargain that is at the core of the American commitment to NATO-Europe requires Western Europe to provide the American public with evidence that the enterprise is worthwhile. It may be foolish, given the objective American stake in denying Western Europe to the Soviet political, economic, and military system, but it is distinctly possible that if one or two NATO governments took on substantial Communist coloration, the enthusiasm of the American electorate for NATO security connections would wane very rapidly. Although it is true that West-West issues often seem to have a greater immediate policy salience than do East-West issues for NATO governments, there are changes—actual and impending—in the military balances (and imbalances) relevant to European security, which are urgently in need of policy attention. The Carter administration appears to be far less concerned, for the short term at least, with negotiating strategy adjustments with its NATO allies intended to improve the prospects for keeping Soviet military power out of Western Europe, than it is with the economic health of NATO members and with domestic political developments in, say, Italy and Spain (and, eventually, Yugoslavia). Economic malaise, inflation, political instability—these are actual, real problems of 1978: stopping the 2nd Guards Tank Army on the North German plain is seen by relatively few people as a very real problem for 1978.

It has to be admitted, even by defense analysts who are charged with worrying about such things, that the likelihood of the Soviet Union exercising any of its military options against 'Western Europe does seem, at present, to be remote. However, Western understanding of Soviet motives and risk calculations could be seriously in error—it is a matter of the most elementary prudence for NATO to deny the Soviet Union any military options in Europe that might appear to Soviet officials to be of a "low-risk" kind.[10] Skeptics in the West are fond of posing the question, "But why would the Soviet Union want to attack Western Europe?" The answer, of course, is that under almost any circumstances the Soviet Union would not want to launch such an attack. Nonetheless, military posture should not be designed to be relevant for periods of low anxiety and danger—rather does it have to be able to perform adequately in those rare moments of acute stress, when nonmilitary policy alternatives manifestly are incapable of solving problems that officials are convinced need prompt resolution. Also, it is probably a profound error to attempt to delve into Soviet intentions. Military capabilities do not speak for themselves entirely, but they do provide some tangible evidence of the range of military use options that a potential adversary deems worth acquiring.

Expert Western commentators on the Soviet military are agreed that simple explanations of Soviet defense behavior almost certainly are in error. But they also agree that (a) Soviet officials perceive no offensive military threat in NATO's order of battle in Europe; and that (b) Soviet military capabilities clearly directed against Western Europe are vastly excessive save with reference to the prospective needs of forward campaigning.[11] In other words, whatever one's judgment concerning Soviet political intentions, it is difficult not to be impressed by the scale and character of Soviet military preparations. The sensible American and NATO-European policy response is first, to adopt an agnostic stance on political questions, and second, to act on the basis of the principle that military power needs to be balanced on its own terms (even if that military power does not seem clearly to be related to rational foreign policy ends).

The United States defense budget for FY 1979 does register a noticeable increase in resource allocation for NATO-oriented conventional military missions, but this increase is more than offset by the pace of Soviet modernization.

Broadly speaking, there are two camps among Westerners who contemplate the purpose of NATO's military structure. The first camp is that which maintains that the NATO forces are in place in order (1) to provide evidence of alliance commitment, and (2) to guarantee to an attacker a major war.[12] This orientation holds that NATO need not, and indeed probably should not, prepare to defend Western Europe. NATO's order of battle, in this view, simply conveys the message that (1) any attack westward will be opposed by large forces, and that (2) a large war will ensue. This camp is prepared to indulge those soldiers and defense analysts who worry about the technical and doctrinal details of conducting a war—but those details are not held to be important. The second camp holds that NATO can and should attempt to defeat an attacker. To endeavor to give reality to a rational defense design for NATO *may* contribute little or nothing to desired deterrent effect—but it might just be critically important should war occur (for reasons that none could predict with conviction or confidence).

There are more and less sophisticated variants of the views of the two broad camps specified above. Relative disinterest in the details of the military balance may relate to a belief that large-scale warfare for stakes as high as those that must be involved in Europe could not be controlled for long beneath predetermined thresholds (of geography and weapons). Alternatively, it may be believed that deterrent effect is maximized if a potential adversary is compelled to contemplate a seamless web, a continuity of violence in the event that he joins battle with NATO forces. Unfortunately for the plausibility of this point of view, it is very comon knowledge that there is no seamless web of violence. Escalation to the use of theater nuclear and strategic nuclear forces requires positive acts of will by an American president.

The Carter administration, in thinking about the military sources of insecurity in, and relating to, Europe, needs to take detailed and very serious account of the following set of facts and considerations:

(1) There is an enduring mismatch between American and Soviet strategic ideas. For example, Soviet and American officials do not share a common appreciation of the concept of *escalation* (which is critically important, given NATO's commitment to flexible response). In the Soviet view, the level of violence appropriate to a particular conflict is determined by the political issues in dispute—the idea of orchestrating geographical or weapon constraints, as a near-autonomous venture, is alien to the Soviet context. (This is not to say that Western escalation theory does not have its merits—only that the putative adversary gives no evidence of recognizing them.)[13]

(2) The Schlesinger doctrine of limited strategic options (LSOs) has much to recommend it,[14] but its credibility in deterrence and effectiveness in action depend vitally upon the overall state of the strategic balance. It is not at all clear that American strategic forces will be essentially equivalent to the strategic forces of the Soviet Union in the 1980s—moreover, even essential equivalence may be inadequate if

the superpowers place essentially nonequivalent foreign policy obligations on their forces. Geography intrudes here, yet again. If the
United States were to initiate *strategic* nuclear action in an attempt to
restore deterrence, in the context of an evolving military disaster in
Europe, what character of Soviet response should be anticipated? It
is quite possible, indeed probable, that the Soviet Union would enjoy
escalation dominance. Soviet officials could respond to American LSOs,
in the early 1980s, by taking out all save 150–200 of the American
ICBM force . . . and what then?[15] In other words, it is entirely misleading, and possibly fatal, for NATO governments to accede to a
strategy that, on its bottom line, calls for American strategic nuclear
intervention, unless the state of the strategic balance is such that
American strategic nuclear action is both credible and is likely to lead
to a much improved outcome.

(3) Soviet and Warsaw Pact allied military capabilities have greatly been improved, across the board, over the past decade. This improvement has been described in great detail elsewhere, particularly by John
Erickson, and will not be repeated here.[16] However, the important point
to recognize is that in the same time period the strategic nuclear back-
drop to NATO has been losing much, if not all, of its relevance, the
military threat in the theater has become far more severe. Soviet
divisions in the four "groups of forces" in Eastern Europe (Germany—
twenty divisions; Northern, Poland—two to three divisions; Central,
Czechoslovakia—five divisions; Southern, Hungary—four divisions)
have had their equipment holdings and manpower upgraded, and the
quality in all categories of equipment has been improved. In numerical terms, the Soviet Union could launch westward on very short
notice (four to eight days) close to forty divisions (including selected
Eastern European formations), following a process of very swift re-
groupment, with rapid reinforcement by nearly thirty divisions from
the three most western of the military districts of the Soviet Union
(Baltic, Byelorussian, and Carpathian); plus an additional thirty-two,
or more, a few weeks later, from the Kiev, Leningrad, and Odessa
military districts. In short, the Warsaw Pact could throw the better
part of one hundred divisions against Western Europe in the space
of a few weeks. Until recently, NATO assumed that it would receive
twenty-three days' warning of a Warsaw Pact mobilization; that esti-

mate has now been amended to four days. (The four-day figure is not a prediction; rather, it is an acknowledgment that the Pact could launch a forty-division attack following four days of mobilization.) Soviet military science stresses surprise, deception, and speed in attack.[17]

A MILITARY FOCUS

NATO's military problems flow from many sources. In summary form, the more debilitating include the following: the conviction of very many politicians and officials that war is close to an impossibility in Europe; the fact that NATO genuinely is an alliance of fourteen and a half unevenly motivated states—wherein national considerations (particularly where jobs are concerned) almost invariably overwhelm consideration of the effectiveness of the common defense; and, finally, an unwillingness/inability to accept the military-political logic that is inherent in Soviet military posture and Soviet military science. Apart from the question of the timing of nuclear use, the character of the Soviet military threat to Western Europe is not really very much in doubt. Having devoted massive preemptive attention to the paralyzing of NATO's command, control, and communications (C^3), and to NATO's nuclear stockpile and means of nuclear delivery, the Soviet Union would move its armored forces as rapidly as possible with as great a degree of surprise as could be achieved. How well the Soviets would fare is a question that none can answer with high confidence. Critically important is the question of warning time and the use that NATO makes of that time.

To deny victory to the Soviet Union in Europe, NATO needs the ability to roll with the first punch, stabilize a defensible line, mobilize, and then restore the status quo ante. Leaving aside the many persuasive (and competing) arguments over NATO's competence or lack of competence in particular fields, certain facts do have to be recorded. There is no dispute that for at least the first month of a war in Europe, the balance of military resources that could be committed to battle must, overwhelmingly, favor the Warsaw Pact. The four groups of Soviet armies in Eastern Europe, plus the forces (more or less) readily deployable from the European USSR, comprise a total force in excess of ninety divisions (plus some, very uncertain, fraction of the fifty to sixty division-equivalents maintained by Warsaw Pact allies).[18] The difficulty of knowing just what to count on the Soviet side is matched by uncertainty with respect to NATO's order of battle. France is in the political organization of NATO—yet remains outside its military command structure. The Dutch and Belgian corps are critically important to the integrity of NATO's forward order of battle, but those divisions are deployed in peacetime *at home*, and would need to be moved into West Germany on short notice.

On both political and military grounds, the farther forward NATO can stabilize its main line of resistance, the better. Notwithstanding the difficulty of securing adequate, *unambiguous*, warning of an attack, the optimal period for NATO to exert itself to the utmost in an effort to halt an offensive is within the first few days. Because of the need to concentrate and move very rapidly—in order to provide minimal warning and to reduce the time period wherein armor is heavily concentrated for breakthrough attempts in narrow sectors (about four kilometers per division)[19]—the Soviet attack timetable is almost certain to make very little allowance for major interruption. If NATO could draw down sufficient firepower onto Warsaw Pact second-echelon forces before they could complete their passage of the attack corridors, the offensive would be likely to falter through heavy attrition and traffic jams.[20]

There is only one way to *guarantee* that a Warsaw Pact offensive would fail, and that would be to launch theater nuclear strikes within the first few hours of an attack, before the enemy has moved much armor through the attack corridors. If the strikes were heavy enough (though clearly battlefield-dedicated), the Warsaw Pact offensive would halt before it properly was begun. Soviet planners recognize this potentially fatal vulnerability and appear to hope to be able to move their forces sufficiently rapidly that they would outrun NATO's nuclear-release decision lead time. Alternatively, they might hope so to cripple NATO's command, control, and communications—and theater nuclear posture—in a massive, preemptive nuclear-conventional attack, that NATO could not launch an immediate and effective nuclear riposte, even if it so desired. (NATO-assigned ballistic-missile-carrying submarines *could* launch such an attack, but it seems improbable that an American president would order strikes by the strategic forces—even in tactical roles—at the very outset of a war, whether or not the Soviets had initiated nuclear use.)

NATO's prospects for stemming a purely conventional blitzkrieg do not look very promising. A great danger, that seems inadequately to be appreciated by officials and politicians, is that NATO would trade space that it cannot afford to lose for time that it could not put to very effective use. The immediate shock power of Soviet armor is likely to be so severe—given some measure of tactical surprise—that NATO may never recover from the initial punch (just as NATO's C³ may never recover from their initial pounding).[21] Moreover, the cumulative weight of a hypothetical attack will be such that NATO would not be granted any substantial respite for many months. Behind the ninety-five divisions in Eastern Europe and the European USSR (of which grand total more than fifty are Category 1), the forces of differing quality of Warsaw Pact allies, and the divisions deployed elsewhere in the Soviet Union (approximately seventy-three, very few of which are immediately combat-ready), lies the medium-term Soviet mobilization potential. (According to John Erickson, "the total pool of reserve manpower is . . . probably on the order of twenty million men, half of whom have at least twelve months service with operational units": the "immediate reserve," a proportion of which would be needed to flesh out Category 2 and 3 formations, comprises close to 5,700,000.)[22]

Some analysts in the West have identified new, precision-guided, conventional weaponry as a great equalizer for NATO. Indeed, one commentator has asked whether or not the tank-heavy Soviet forces are obsolete in the face of antitank guided weapons.[23] The Soviet defense establishment has asked itself the same question, and has—thus far at least—confirmed its devotion to the armored fighting vehicle (for which there is no substitute if one seeks to seize ground in a short space of time).[24] On balance, Soviet confidence in their ability to launch and sustain an armored offensive in the face of precision-guided munitions (PGMs) is probably well founded. Most PGMs can be defeated by fairly elementary countermeasures (technological and tactical), and most PGMs do not work at all well in bad weather, at night, or in urban areas. Of course, NATO's ATGWs will take a heavy toll of Soviet armor, but it is difficult to have confidence in NATO's ability to take such a sufficiently high toll as to arrest the momentum of an offensive. The Soviet armed forces simply resign themselves to taking high casualties.

Enhanced-radiation weapons (the so-called neutron bomb) could be extremely useful for the attrition of the crews of armored fighting vehicles (while imposing next to no unwanted collateral damage), but it is improbable that NATO will deploy enough of them for delivery by removable platforms, or will devise a tactical doctrine that might maximize their potential enough for one to claim that the CR weapon is (*another*) great equalizer. Wars are not won or lost by single technical developments.

For reasons well beyond the pale of military analysis, deterrence may hold firm in Europe. However, the new administration should be made aware of three closely related facts that bear very directly upon the strategic environment of American–West European relations:

(1) The Soviet Union has the capability to wage a conventional campaign in Europe, with excellent chances of success.

(2) The Soviet Union has a growing superiority in theater-nuclear strike systems (NATO has no answer to the new MIRVed SS-20).[25]

(3) The Soviet Union is striving to attain a politically useful measure of strategic superiority. It seems more likely than not that for much of the 1980s (say 1982–89) the Soviet Union will enjoy a very substantial advantage in silo-killing potential—while Soviet domestic war-survival programs (admittedly of uncertain effectiveness) may give Soviet leaders a confidence in an acute crisis unmatched on the part of the United States.

In the event, through bad management and/or bad luck, the Soviet advantages listed above may not translate into victory. However, those advantages are not theoretical—whatever the political intention of Soviet leaders may be, the strategic situation of NATO is deteriorating in all major, measurable, respects.

WHAT IS TO BE DONE?

With respect to the political evolution of Western Europe, the United States can seek to make haste only very slowly. The United States cannot impose a grand (re-)design for security in Europe. On the other hand, the United States is at liberty to decline to pay security costs that others, more directly involved, are capable of meeting. Clearly, the Carter administration needs to be aware that there are at least two major sets of policy questions for the United States vis-à-vis Western Europe. For the short term, the adverse trend in all of the pertinent military balances needs to be reversed, and NATO strategy is in urgent need of overhaul. Throwing more money at NATO's defense problems will accomplish nothing of value if the men and equipment purchased are set to the accomplishment of the wrong missions. For the long term, the United States should endeavor to *encourage* its European allies to create a collective political authority, as the prerequisite for a defense community, that could go a good part of the way toward providing an in-theater balance to Soviet power and influence. At the risk of undue repetition, the Carter administration should be reminded of the geostrategic reality of (in-)security in Europe. In the words of a distinguished West German defense commentator: "The Soviet Union is the only European power which has the means to wage a war of aggression on the Continent and to win it —under favorable circumstances—against any possible coalition of other European countries."[26] Long-range planning in foreign policy is believed in by nobody outside the academic community. However, a proper respect for history (there are few genuinely novel security problems) and a clear recognition of important constants should enable one to identify major problems long in advance of their appearance. For example, as this chapter has sought to argue, there is certain to be a very difficult (even dangerous) period wherein Western Europe attempts to effect a transition from very heavy reliance upon explicit and substantial, tangible, American military commitments for its security, to a condition of security (near-)autarky.

In summary form, embracing a range of political-military questions, the following comprises this author's short list of recommendations for the future:

(1) Essential equivalence (at least) must be preserved in strategic nuclear forces. No strategic nuclear compensation can be sought for possible deficiencies in NATO's local defenses, unless Soviet leaders can be induced to believe that the United States would initiate limited strategic strikes. Flexible targeting plans alone are insufficient.

(2) NATO should be encouraged to put its strategic ideas in order. MC 14/3 offers a potentially fatal mismatch in operational practices vis-à-vis what may be inferred concerning Soviet plans and style. NATO needs an excellent *forward* defense, if it is to have a serious defense at all—and its political leaders should understand that the late use of theater nuclear weapons would probably be worse than not firing them at all.

(3) (A trite but very important point) Political consultation with NATO allies should be taken seriously by Washington. There are, of course, some very real problems in this area. As a superpower with global responsibilities, the United States cannot, and will not, permit a process of consultation to approach the level of joint policymaking on any save a narrow range of Europe-relevant issues. However, European officials, by and large, recognize the practicable limits of consultation.

(4) Given the permanence of Soviet power in Europe, the character of enduring Soviet political ambitions, and the geography of the NATO alliance, NATO Europeans should be encouraged to begin thinking through their long-term security requirements and options. As a fairly low-key strategy, American officials should emphasize the nonmilitary interests of the United States in Europe. Such a long-term campaign of emphasis should be beneficial to all interested observers (Western Europeans, Soviet, and Chinese officials, and the American public) of American–Western European relations. This could be characterized as long-term damage-limitation.

(5) The discussions on mutual and balanced force reductions (MBFR) in Europe, that have been in intermittent session since 30 October 1973, are profoundly unimportant. NATO has no leverage worthy of note that might induce the Soviet Union to agree to a package of reduction measures that would genuinely reduce the potential offensive punch of Soviet armor in Central Europe. (To simplify, it is the scale of the Soviet *tank* park that is the critical source of military insecurity in Europe.)[27] Because of the geostrategic asymmetries between East and West, in and bearing upon Europe, it will be difficult to design an agreement that does not yield the Soviet Union some advantage. If the Carter administration were to kill MBFR, there would be very few, if any, mourners in NATO. Token

agreement certainly is possible, but that agreement probably could only be defended on the basis of its political symbolic value (it would not be an arms-control success).

NOTES

1. See Henry A. Kissinger, "A New Atlantic Charter," *Survival* 15 (July/ August 1973): 188–92.
2. An excellent recent collection of essays on the subject of Soviet policy in, and toward, Europe is Richard Pipes, ed., *Soviet Strategy in Europe* (New York: Crane, Russak & Company, 1976), particularly pp. 23–24.
3. Careful discussions of Soviet attitudes toward the utility of military power are Ken Booth, *The Military Instrument in Soviet Foreign Policy, 1917–1972* (London: Royal United Services Institute for Defence Studies, 1973); and R.J. Vincent, *Military Power and Political Influence: The Soviet Union and Western Europe* (London: International Institute for Strategic Studies, Autumn 1975).
4. See Stanley Hoffmann, "Choices," *Foreign Policy*, no. 12 (Fall 1973), pp. 3–42; and Seyom Brown, "The Changing Essence of Power," *Foreign Affairs* 51 (January 1973): 286–99.
5. See Colin S. Gray, *The United States and Security in Europe*, HI-1979-DP (Croton-on-Hudson, N.Y.: Hudson Institute, 20 February 1974).
6. Whether or not French ports, territory, and airspace would be available to NATO in the event of war in Europe remains a matter for conjecture. In recent years there has been a distinct "warming" of France toward NATO's military missions, but that "warming" trend falls short of an unequivocal commitment to stand "shoulder to shoulder."
7. By way of illustration, the Wehrmacht demonstrated in 1943–45 how an orderly retreat should be conducted (with relatively few exceptions —recovery from the Allied breakout from the Normandy perimeter being one of those exceptions); while South Vietnam in the spring of 1975 demonstrated how *not* to conduct a fighting retreat.
8. Of all the possible "outbreak of war" scenarios that could be written for the next quarter century, Soviet intervention in West Germany for profoundly defensive reasons—in response to "domestic" political developments in that country that Soviet leaders deemed unduly threatening—is among the most plausible.
9. A work of enduring value is Harlan Cleveland, *NATO: The Transatlantic Bargain* (New York: Harper and Row, 1970). The author was United States ambassador to NATO from 1965 until 1969.

10. See the pertinent comments in John Erickson, "Soviet Military Posture and Policy in Europe," in Pipes, ed., *Soviet Strategy in Europe*, particularly pp. 206–207.

11. It is important for readers to recognize that genuinely "expert Western commentators" on the Soviet military are exceedingly thin on the ground. If one-tenth of the resources that the American political science profession devotes to (wastes upon) the "behavioral" study of the American electorate, were committed to the study of a serious real-world problem—i.e., the functions of the Soviet military establishment, in *Soviet* appreciation—the American government might have avoided some of its more egregious foreign policy errors of the past decade. Academic freedom, unfortunately, all too often translates into the freedom to indulge in trivial enquiry!

12. This "guaranteeing a major war" or requiring an attack of "major proportions" is a theme which, for example, permeates Kenneth Hunt, *The Alliance and Europe: Part II: Defence with Fewer Men*, Adelphi Paper no. 98 (London: International Institute for Strategic Studies, 1973).

13. See John Erickson, *Soviet-Warsaw Pact Force Levels*, USSI Report 76-2 (Washington, D.C.: United States Strategic Institute, 1976), p. 69.

14. For a generally friendly exposition, see Lynn E. Davis, *Limited Nuclear Options: Deterrence and the New American Doctrine*, Adelphi Paper no. 121 (London: International Institute for Strategic Studies, 1975).

15. For detailed support of this possibility, see Colin S. Gray, *The Future of Land-Based Missile Forces*, Adelphi Paper no. 140 (London: International Institute for Strategic Studies, Winter 1977).

16. See Erickson, *Soviet-Warsaw Pact Force Levels*.

17. An excellent dissection of Soviet military science, as it appeared in print at least, is Joseph D. Douglass, Jr., *The Soviet Theater Nuclear Offensive*, Studies in Communist Affairs, vol. 1 (Washington, D.C.: U.S. Government Printing Office, 1976).

18. A useful brief summary is *The Military Balance, 1977–1978* (London: International Institute for Strategic Studies, 1977), pp. 102–10.

19. John Erickson, "Soviet Breakthrough Operations: Resources and Restraints," *RUSI Journal* 121 (September 1976): 75.

20. Note the discussion in Douglass, *The Soviet Theater Nuclear Offensive*, particularly pp. 5, 75–81.

21. The concept of "shock power" is developed at length in Steven Canby, *The Alliance and Europe: Part IV: Military Doctrine and Technology*, Adelphi Paper no. 109 (London: International Institute for Strategic Studies, 1975).

22. Erickson, *Soviet-Warsaw Pact Force Levels*, p. 17.

23. E.B. Atkeson, "Is the Soviet Army Obsolete?" *Army* (May 1974), pp. 10–16. On balance, Colonel Atkeson judged that it is obsolete. A similar point of view pervades Jeffrey Record, *Sizing Up the Soviet Army* (Washington, D.C.: Brookings Institution, 1975).

24. An outstanding Western analysis of the Soviet debate over the viability of the armored offensive is Phillip A. Karber, "The Soviet Anti-Tank Debate," *Survival* 18 (May/June 1976): 105–11. Also see Erickson, "Soviet Breakthrough Operations: Resources and Restraints."

25. For many years it has been customary to presume a NATO advantage on the order of 2:1 in the field of theater-nuclear warheads. This 7,000–3,500 relationship was never much more than a "back of the envelope" guess. It does seem probable (though *evidence* is lacking) that NATO retains a commanding lead in low (1–10 kilotons) and very low (up to 1 kiloton) yield options in its nuclear stockpile, but the scale of the gross NATO advantage almost certainly is nowhere near 2:1 as of early 1978. Since the 2:1 ratio first gained uncritical currency, (1) a new generation of Soviet ground-attack aircraft has entered front-line service with Soviet frontal aviation, (2) the nuclear-capable tactical missile holdings of the Soviet ground forces have been expanded, and (3) a new generation of intermediate- (at least) range ballistic missiles is being deployed—the MIRVed SS-20, and (4) self-propelled, nuclear-capable artillery has been introduced. The relatively high yields (so Western analysts *believe*—they do not know) of Soviet theater-dedicated warheads is not necessarily a source of Soviet disadvantage. The Soviet concept of theater-nuclear warfare differs quite markedly from that authoritative to NATO. See Douglass, *The Soviet Theater Nuclear Offensive.*

26. Lothar Ruehl, "The Negotiations on Force Reductions in Central Europe," *NATO Review* 24 (September-October, 1976): 19.

27. The total Soviet tank park is approximately 80,000 strong, of which 40,000 are in the active inventory. Warsaw Pact tank holdings in North-Central Europe total approximately 19,000—of which 11,000 are in the hands of Soviet formations.

Chapter Eight

United States Policy in the Middle East*

Stephen P. Gibert

Four years after the Yom Kippur War and the accompanying oil embargo, the United States still does not have an agreed-upon comprehensive strategy for dealing with either the Arab-Israeli conflict or with the oil countries of the Persian Gulf. To be sure, the flimsy edifice which Secretary of State Kissinger built through his celebrated "shuttle diplomacy" somehow still stands erect on the sands of the Sinai. It is true also that the supply of oil is flowing and in constant dollar terms the price of oil (although clearly headed upward again) is not much higher than it was in early 1974. Finally, Soviet influence over developments in the Middle East appears to be less than it has been for some twenty years.

On the surface, therefore, it would appear that things are going swimmingly. And considering that two of the Nixon-Ford administration's alleged accomplishments—achieving a peace agreement in Vietnam and establishing "detente" with the Soviet Union—are proving to be, to put it mildly, rather hollow victories, it is not surprising that the present favorable situation in the Middle East is still pointed to as one of the proudest accomplishments of former Secretary Kissinger. Without, however, in any way denigrating the contributions Dr. Kissinger made to bringing about a more hopeful state of affairs, it is nevertheless clear that American policy in the Middle East is now no more coherent than it was prior to the disasters of 1973. Indeed, even stronger criticism is warranted in that the breathing period of the last

*Editor's note: This chapter was completed in March 1977, eight months prior to Prime Minister Anwar Sadat's visit to Israel in November 1977. See the author's postscript at the end of this chapter for a brief comment on this event.

several years has been and is being frittered away. One reason for this regrettable situation is the relative intractability of the problems concerned—problems that would confound even the wisest policies. A second and perhaps equally compelling factor is that in no area is United States foreign policy so intertwined with American domestic politics than is the case with the Middle East.

Nevertheless, these are explanations and not excuses for failure. Praise for the Sinai Agreements, ritualistic reaffirmations of United States support for United Nations Resolution 242 and arms for the Shah of Iran do not a policy make. Given its strategic location at the crossroads of three continents (a geopolitical factor whose importance has been reduced but not eliminated by technological change), its potential for catalyzing superpower confrontation, and its dominant position in the world oil market, the Middle East should claim priority attention from the Carter administration. It is hoped that this essay will contribute in a modest way to clarifying the issues that confront the American policymakers with regard to the two major Middle East problems: coping with the Arab-Israeli conflict, and dealing with the energy issue and the related issue of arms transfers to the oil countries of the Persian Gulf. Finally, future United States policy must be formulated in full recognition that Soviet efforts to replace Western influence in the Middle East with that of Moscow are likely to continue unabated, irrespective of current hopes for detente.

THE ARAB-ISRAELI CONFLICT

The Arab-Israeli dispute would not impinge strongly upon United States national security were it not for the fact that both the United States and the Soviet Union have chosen (albeit for different reasons) to convert what would be a relatively minor regional quarrel into an international political problem of momentous consequence, and had the Arabs not successfully linked the availability of oil with settlement of the Arab-Israeli situation to Arab satisfaction. Without the interven-vention of outside powers, it is at least conceivable that the Arabs and Israelis would have learned, as the result of several inconclusive wars, that neither could impose its will by force on the other. The Arabs would have suffered successive defeats by the Israeli armed forces. But the Israelis would not have been able to alter the fundamental power relationships that are rooted in the geopolitical, demographic, and ideological aspects of the struggle. Even crushing Israeli military victories over the Arabs, accordingly, probably would have proved inconclusive in the long run.

The most critical feature of the Arab-Israeli conflict is that it is not a "normal" dispute. That is, the dispute involves "intractable" differences between the two sides: the fundamental unwillingness of the more militant Arabs—especially the Palestinians—to accept the existence of the Israeli state, and the distrust with which Tel Aviv greets Arab statements signifying their acceptance of Israel's right to exist that are notably unaccompanied by actions that would give that acceptance meaning. Thus, while these Arabs speak of the return of conquered lands, Israelis see this as the first step in an "unraveling of the past." Israel would like to tie the boundaries question to other issues, such as transit of the Suez and Red Sea and an end to the economic blockade. The Arabs reject such linkage. Israel would moreover like to attempt a settlement with Egypt first, but this is resisted by the Arabs. Israel would like to be referred to by the Arabs as "Israel," not the "Zionist enemy." Arab leaders insist that Israel accept the Palestinians as legitimate negotiating partners; Israelis view PLO leaders as "terrorists." To these differences are added an irreconcilable desire by two different peoples to occupy the same physical space; complete satisfaction of one set of claims cannot be accomplished by compromise but only by elimination of the other.

Past Arab-Israeli problems add to the present difficulties in seeking a just peace. In essence, the October 1973 conflict was a violent upsurge in an ongoing thirty years war. As a result, one cannot now imagine Arabs and Jews referring to each other as "cousins" as they could in 1947; a generation of murderous raids and brutal retaliations has scarred both sides. Additionally, both Arabs and Israelis are the victims, not only of their recent history, but of decisions taken long ago which set into motion irreconcilable claims by opposing religiously based nationalisms.[1] In such a context, trivial questions, such as whether persons can travel both to Israel and Arab countries on the same passport, take on an exaggerated importance; the Israelis insist that the Arabs indicate their intention of moving toward acceptance of Israel by rescinding such irritants. This the Arabs will not do, justifying their refusal on the grounds that a continued state of war exists with Israel.

The most important particular issue between Israel and the Arab states is the Arab demand for the return of lands seized by Israel in the 1967 war and Israel's refusal to agree to this except as part of a general settlement. Even if this were forthcoming, Israel has not agreed to return all the conquered lands, since Tel Aviv maintains that to do so would compromise its security to an unacceptable degree. The Israeli government maintains: "The extra territory gained in 1967 spells a substantial degree of security, as was amply demonstrated in the War of October 1973. Retention of at least part of this territory is an absolute precondition for Israel's future security. . . ."[2]

Israel and the Confrontation Arab States Before the 1973 War

Egypt, since it is the strongest of the Arab countries adjacent to Israel, is decisive in determining overall Arab-Israeli relations. It was Egypt that initiated the 1967 Six Day War and the 1970 War of Attrition; it was Egypt's Sadat who planned the October 1973 conflict and whose developing relationship with Saudi Arabia's King Faisal helped bring about the oil embargo; it is Egypt that controls the Suez Canal and is the largest Arab state and that has long been a target for Soviet influence. If Israel could have come to terms with Egypt between 1967 and 1973 there would have been no Yom Kippur War.[3] The irony of this situation is that there are no really insoluble problems in Israeli-Egyptian relations. Israel, of course, has occupied Egyptian territory up to the Suez Canal since 1967. This additional territory affords Israel the possibility of a military defense in depth; however, even if Israel retreated back to the 1967 border with Egypt the situation would be militarily manageable. Accordingly, Israel would like to separate Egypt from the Arab problem generally; a separate peace might have been possible between Israel and Egypt had Israel returned the territory seized from Egypt in the 1967 war. The Israelis, however, would not withdraw without a peace treaty, nor would Israel agree to total withdrawal, but only to "secure" borders.[4] Israel also insisted upon freedom of passage through the Suez and the Strait of Tiran, retention of Jerusalem, and a solution to the refugee problem that involved the settlement of the refugees primarily in Arab, not Israeli, territory.

The Egyptian government was opposed to a formal peace treaty or even direct Egyptian-Israeli negotiations, and demanded total Israeli withdrawal from all (not just Egyptian) occupied Arab territories. The Egyptian position was vague on the refugee issue and settlement of the refugees; Egypt would permit Israeli passage through the Strait of Tiran but insisted that Cairo had the right to deny any country passage through Suez. Negotiations continued through 1971 but no progress was made in reconciling the Israeli position of making particular concessions versus the Egyptian position that Israel accept a "general settlement" that included total Israeli withdrawal from Egyptian and other Arab territory.

The Syrian-Israeli situation has long been characterized by extreme hostility. Unlike Egypt, which does appear interested in an eventual peaceful settlement, Syria (at least until recently) has shown far less evidence of sincerely wanting peace with Israel. With a record of instability (Syria has averaged a new government about every sixteen months since World War II) and a declared aim of total destruction of Israel, Syria would not undertake any negotiations with Tel Aviv. After the pro-Soviet extreme wing of the Ba'ath party was ousted by the present government in 1970, there seemed to be some possibility that Syria would modify its stand on Israel. The expulsion of the fedayeen from Jordan in the fall of 1970, however, had led to their establishment in Syria and Lebanon. Terrorist raids led to Israeli-Syrian fighting, with serious clashes occurring in November 1972 and January 1973, resulting in a Syrian call for an Arab resumption of full-scale warfare against Israel.

Unlike the case with Egypt, neither the border situation nor the terrain facilitate an Israeli-Syrian settlement. The distances from the border to Tel Aviv and Damascus are so short as to make the capitals of both Syria and Israel highly vulnerable. Furthermore, control of the Golan Heights area would confer substantial military advantages on the controlling power. Unlike the case with the Egyptian-Israeli border, therefore, there is little "room" for Israeli withdrawals without placing its national security in severe jeopardy.[5]

In July 1973, Egypt and Syria announced that they had arrived at a common policy toward Israel. Undoubtedly this "common policy" called for coordination for the October 1973 war. Syria also accepted

United Nations Resolution 242 as the basis of Syria's policy toward Israel. Such an acceptance was important because it meant the agreement by Syria to Sadat's plan that the goal of the war was essentially political. That is, by agreeing for the first time that the aim was not the destruction of Israel but the rectification of borders, Syria made possible the limited-war strategy devised by Sadat.

The most complex problem in the area is the triangular one involving Israel, Jordan, and the Palestinian Arabs. This is, first, because of the border situation, with West Bank Palestine extending to within a few miles of the Mediterranean seacoast; second, because of the essential artificiality of the borders of Jordan and any independent Palestinian state that might be created; and finally, because of the dangers posed by Palestinian extremists to both Israel and Jordan. In spite of the agreement among the Arabs reached in Rabat in September 1974 that the Palestine Liberation Organization (PLO) will represent the Palestinians in negotiations with Israel,[6] factional disputes among the various Palestinian organizations will undoubtedly continue and sporadic acts of violence will occur.

The Palestinian organizations have hitherto made no secret of their refusal to consider any compromise involving the continued existence of Israel. Though their leaders no longer speak in public of "driving the Jews into the sea," their program of a secular but Arab state of Palestine, in which "Palestinian" Jews would find their place as a religious minority, and non-Palestinian Jews and their descendants would leave, would mean the end of Israeli statehood. Even the most "moderate" Palestinian solution—that of a truncated Israel, within the original United Nations 1947 partition borders—is obviously wholly unacceptable to Israel. And it is not certain that even this settlement would be aceptable to the Palestinians.[7]

Jordan would prefer to come to terms with Israel. Without the Palestinian refugee problem, there is little doubt that Israel and Jordan could agree on borders and a peaceful settlement between the two countries could be devised.

Lebanon, although bordering on Israel, is not considered a "confrontation" state since Lebanon has repeatedly avoided conflict with Israel. Prior to the 1973 war, the only issue between Israel and Lebanon was the use of Lebanese territory by terrorists as a base from which to launch raids into Israel. Israeli retaliation naturally placed a great strain on the relationship of the two countries. Subsequent to the Yom Kippur War, the civil war in Lebanon and the Syrian occupation have led to new concerns in Israel that the Lebanese border might also become a "confrontation" area in Arab-Israeli relations.[8]

Israeli Relations with Other Arab States

Israeli relations with the "rear area" Arab states have been hostile, particularly with Libya and Iraq, since these countries vigorously maintain the common Arab position that Israel should be expelled from the Middle East or at least should return all conquered Arab lands prior to any other settlement. However, the absence of common frontiers has prevented this hostility from impinging severely upon Israeli security. The rear-area oil states have furnished funds to Syria, Egypt, and the Palestinians with which to purchase arms, have transferred some of their Soviet-acquired weapons directly to the front-line states, and have pressed other countries to adopt pro-Arab policies. While causing difficulties for Tel Aviv, not until the October War did these activities become a serious threat to Israel.

The only concrete issue in Israeli relations with the more distant Arab states concerns Israeli control of Jerusalem. This issue is especially important to Saudi Arabia, since the late King Faisal regarded himself as the protector of the religious heritage of Islam.[9]

Linking Oil with the Arab-Israeli Problem

In May 1973, Prime Minister Sadat announced that a state of "total confrontation" between Egypt and Israel had begun. The pivot of this policy was to be a much closer relationship between Egypt and Saudi Arabia.

This strategy was made possible by the forging of a link between oil and politics. The Egyptians managed to persuade the Saudis, without whose cooperation the political use of oil is impossible, that the time had finally arrived to "mix oil and politics."[10] Several elements in the situation contributed to this outcome. First, it had become apparent that the industrial nations were heavily dependent on Arab oil. Second, the United States, whose oil surplus in the past rendered ineffective the use of the oil weapon, had also become, albeit to a much lesser degree, dependent on Arabian oil. Third, the United States had no oil policy or, for that matter, no Persian Gulf policy and no plan for helping resolve the Arab-Israeli issue. When the United States declined to enter into a so-called special arrangement with Saudi Arabia in the fall of 1972, King Faisal became increasingly critical of American policy.[11] Finally, King Faisal apparently did not view Sadat as a threat to traditional Gulf regimes; Sadat has neither the pan-Arab dreams of Colonel Nasser nor the charismatic qualities that might make those dreams a reality. A significant factor involved in Faisal's change of policy was economic in character. For years, oil has been Saudi Arabia's primary source of revenue, and most of the revenue generated was required to meet the needs of the country. With rising world demand, increased production, and rising prices, oil revenue rose above fiscal requirements, thus giving the Saudi government much more leeway in deciding whether or not to employ the oil weapon.

Having agreed to use the oil weapon, the Saudis increasingly began to warn the United States that unless pressure was put on Israel to return Arab lands, including Jerusalem, oil production would be decreased and possibly an embargo instituted. Apparently Sadat and Faisal had by this time concluded that the oil weapon could be an effective policy instrument.

Cooperation of the oil ministates in the Persian Gulf was facilitated by the presence in their countries of large numbers of Palestinians, who have pressed their host governments to use the oil weapon. This was especially the case in the United Arab Emirates.

By the fall of 1973 all the conditions for an Arab attack on Israel were present. First, the Egyptian government apparently was convinced that without war the Americans and the Soviets would not pressure the Israelis into withdrawal from Arab territories. Second, the Soviet government had resumed arms deliveries to Egypt as well as Syria and may have pledged resupply of arms in the event war occurred. Third, full agreement on cooperation between Egypt and Syria had been achieved. Fourth, the Egyptians and Syrians were confident that their military forces would perform acceptably and that it was possible that the Arabs would secure at least a limited military success. Finally, Sadat's strategy for the use of the oil weapon was to intimidate and coerce other countries, particularly the United States, Europe, and Japan, so that they would lend diplomatic help to the Arabs in their struggle with Israel. The oil weapon was also an insurance policy for Egypt and Syria in that, should they face crushing defeat in the war with Israel, they could expect not only the USSR but the United States, and possibly others, to prevent Israel from reaping political benefits from military victory. Sadat also had assurances of money from the Saudi treasury to finance the war.[12]

Events during and immediately after the war, which began with a coordinated Egyptian-Syrian attack in the early afternoon of 6 October 1973, demonstrated in all essential particulars the wisdom of Prime Minister Sadat's cautious planning and established him as a preeminent practitioner of the political use of warfare. The October War produced a number of diplomatic changes—notably the renewal of United States relations with Egypt and Syria—but in terms of inter-Arab relations the most significant were the reemergence of Egypt as the leading state in the Arab world, the newly recognized importance of Saudi Arabia, and the developing relationship between these two key states.

Egypt is the only Arab state that possesses all the recognized attributes of nationhood, including an ancient political tradition, historically accepted territorial dimensions, linguistic and cultural homogeneity and a centralized, bureaucratic administration somewhat in the Western mold. While Egypt's preeminence had been somewhat obscured prior to the 1973 conflict, it was probably inevitable that sooner or later it would reassert its strong role in the Middle East.

Saudi Arabia's claim to authority in the Arab world is based on oil and on its religious leadership of Islam. Saudi Arabia was the key to the Arab oil embargo; Saudi Arabia alone can determine whether there is an oversupply or shortage of world oil. It was Saudi Arabia's agreement to employ the oil weapon that apparently played a significant role both in Egypt's and Syria's decision to go to war and in denying Israel any benefits from its fourth military victory.[13] In 1976 Saudi Arabia, in improbable coordination with Syria, impressively demonstrated its new power in Arab affairs by successfully demanding an end to the civil conflict in Lebanon.

In addition to Egypt and Saudi Arabia, a third "winner" emerged from the Yom Kippur War—the United States. This seems paradoxical; the United States was embargoed by Saudi Arabia, faced a confrontation with the Soviet Union, was divided diplomatically both from its European and Japanese allies, and was roundly condemned by much of the Third World. Yet it came to be realized, especially by Egypt, that only the United States could play the role of "honest broker" in the Arab-Israeli struggle. This gave Secretary Kissinger the opening he needed to begin his famous shuttle diplomacy, which resulted in the fall of 1975 in the Sinai Agreements. It is important to note that these agreements are very limited in scope and do not settle any basic Arab-Israeli issues. Nevertheless, they granted the world time to seek more fundamental solutions that, regrettably, have not yet been forthcoming.

STRATEGIC AND ECONOMIC IMPLICATIONS OF OIL DEPENDENCE

Decisions taken by the oil-producing countries since the October 1973 Arab-Israeli war have resulted in a multidimensional, worldwide crisis of nearly unparalleled severity. The ultimate consequences of these developments for oil-dependent nations and for global economic and political institutions and practices cannot yet be predicted with confidence, let alone controlled. The essential elements of the situation, however, that made feasible the actions of the oil-producing governments are now well known. Briefly these are as follows:

- The world demand for energy has been growing and is expected to continue to grow for perhaps an indefinite time because of three interrelated factors: (1) the increasing world population; (2) rising per capita consumption throughout the world as living standards improve; and (3) the increasing industrialization of the less-developed world. Oil will have to provide the bulk of this energy demand at least for the next dozen years and perhaps to the twenty-first century and beyond.
- Oil reserves are distributed very unevenly in the world. The Middle East, and especially the Persian Gulf area, is the most fortunate, with two-thirds of the world's proven reserves. Saudi Arabia alone, the oil superpower of the world, possesses about a third of the oil reserves in the entire world. The Middle East currently (1977) produces more than 40 percent of the world's oil and controls 70 percent of the export market, but consumes only 2 percent.

- Petroleum production in other areas of the world is not expanding at a sufficient rate to cope with a continually rising global demand. There is little spare productive capacity in the rest of the world. In the United States, one of the three largest oil-producing countries in the world, output leveled off around 1970 and began a slow decline by 1972, expected to last until at least into 1978.
- Western Europe and Japan are very dependent on Middle Eastern oil, importing about 80 and 90 percent respectively of their requirements from the area.
- The United States, although a very large oil producer, consumes nearly one-third of the world's oil. United States imports of oil rose from 0.9 million b/d (13 percent of consumption) in 1950 to 6.0 million b/d (37 percent of consumption) in 1974. In 1977 the United States was expected to import about 40 percent of its consumption requirements.
- The Soviet Union also possesses large oil reserves and imports only small amounts from the Middle East at present. However, domestic demand is rising rapidly while production is not keeping pace. The Soviet outlook is complicated by the fact that, for political and economic reasons, the USSR finds it desirable to export oil to both its allies and the nations of Western Europe. In 1972, the USSR exported over 28 percent of its total oil production, with about two-thirds going to Eastern Europe, North Vietnam and Cuba, and about one-third going to the countries of Western Europe. Faced with rising domestic demand, the need to obtain hard currency from Western Europe, and the desire to maintain political leverage over its satellites, the Soviet Union may decide to import more oil from the Middle East as the decade progresses.
- The developing nations of the Third World are generally oil-poor and must depend on imports for most of their oil requirements. For example, Brazil and India, two countries at opposite ends of the development spectrum, must import approximately 70 percent of their total requirements from the Middle East.

The factors cited above resulted in a change in the oil situation to one where "shortages of supply have replaced shortages of demand

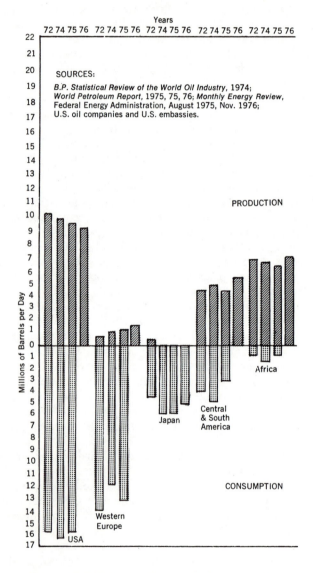

Figure 1: Oil Production and Consumption

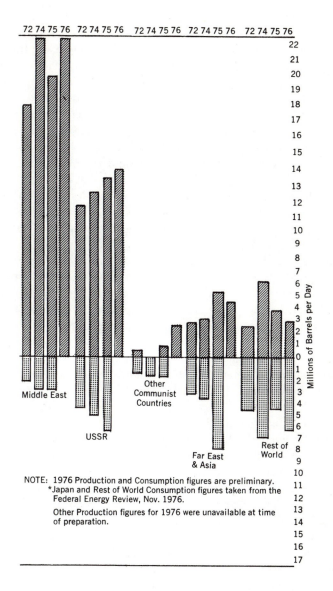

72 74 75 76   72 74 75 76   72 74 75 76   72 74 75 76   72 74 75 76

22
21
20
19
18
17
16
15
14
13
12
11
10
9
8
7
6
5
4
3
2
1
0
1
2
3
4
5
6
7
8
9
10
11
12
13
14
15
16
17

Millions of Barrels per Day

Middle East

Other
Communist
Countries

USSR

Far East
& Asia

Rest of
World

NOTE: 1976 Production and Consumption figures are preliminary.
   *Japan and Rest of World Consumption figures taken from the
   Federal Energy Review, Nov. 1976.

   Other Production figures for 1976 were unavailable at time
   of preparation.

Figure 1 (continued)

as the dominant force in world economics . . . and the power position of suppliers and consumers has thus changed dramatically."[14] Furthermore, the Organization of Petroleum Exporting Countries (OPEC) has been able to engage in oligopolistic pricing, with charges for oil becoming totally unrelated to production costs.[15] Figure 1 summarizes the worldwide oil production and oil consumption situation.

The oil situation would be sufficiently disturbing even if relationships between the Arab countries and the West had been cordial. In fact, however, for some time even prior to the oil embargo in 1973 there had been tension between the OPEC countries and the Western and Western-oriented developed states. These tensions were at one and the same time part of the growing hostility between the less-developed countries (LDCs) and the industrial world (the so-called North-South conflict) and the problems peculiar to relations between the Western nations and the Middle East. The North-South conflict in general turns on the belief among the LDCs that the terms of trade between the manufactured goods produced in the industrial states and the raw materials furnished by the LDCs are grossly inequitable. Put otherwise, the LDCs believe the prices for their products are too low and those of the goods they import from the developed countries too high.

To these economic tensions are added the sociopolitical tensions resulting from a colonial past, and those generated by attacks on Western "racism" emanating from nonwhite LDCs. The United States is singled out for special hostility, both because it is the richest country in the world and because American resistance to the advance of Soviet and Communist influence and power has taken priority over correcting what the LDCs see as social and economic injustice. Three of the world's "pariah regimes"—South Korea, Israel, and Taiwan—are viewed as American "client" states; one pariah regime (Republic of South Africa) is allegedly viewed "with sympathy" by Washington; only one pariah, Rhodesia, is seen as not closely associated with the United States.[16] Such an attitude was demonstrated anew in August 1976, when eighty-five Third World nations meeting in Columbo reacted to the murder of American officers by North Koreans along the DMZ in Korea by criticizing the United States presence in South Korea and deploring "imperialist aggression" on the peninsula.[17] Figure 2 is illustrative of the divergence of views between the United States and the OPEC nations which has developed in recent years.

With regard to the relations between the Middle Eastern states and the West, several elements were added to the usual Third World attitudes. The presence of Israel is seen as a continuation of Western imperialism, reinforced by British and French collaboration with Israel in the 1956 Arab-Israel war and the subsequent assumption by the United States of the role of principal supporter (and weapons supplier) of Israel after Britain and France moved away from Israel and toward a pro-Arab position. Furthermore, OPEC was formed to strengthen the hand of the oil countries vis-à-vis the oil corporations. Since the oil companies were Western-owned (largely American), still another source of conflict arose as the hard bargaining began over oil country participation in the ownership of the companies. Finally, and very importantly, the increasing dependence of the industrial countries on OPEC oil led oil country leaders to perceive that the United States, Western Europe, and Japan were vulnerable to oil exporter economic and political coercion. The catalyst for action was the fourth Arab-Israeli war in October 1973.

The oil producers took three basic actions regarding oil: (1) they decided to reduce production by certain percentages each month until their political demands were met; (2) they imposed a selective embargo, originally aimed at those nations that actively demonstrated their support for Israel (the United States and the Netherlands), and later expanded to include the principal adversaries of black Africa (Portugal, Rhodesia, and South Africa); and (3) they took advantage of the short supply of oil to raise prices drastically. Not all producers participated in all of these actions, but a sufficient number adhered to each action to make all of them at least partially effective.

The initial Arab decisions to reduce production and impose the selective embargo against the United States and the Netherlands led to a number of actions by oil consumers designed to appease the Arabs and avoid further reductions in their oil supplies:

- The countries of Western Europe, by and large, refused to cooperate with the United States and instead competed to see which country would prove itself most pro-Arab. This noncooperation was most immediately evident in their refusal (with the exception of Portugal) to permit the United States to overfly their territories or to use their ports in resupplying Israel (the West Germans did permit covert use

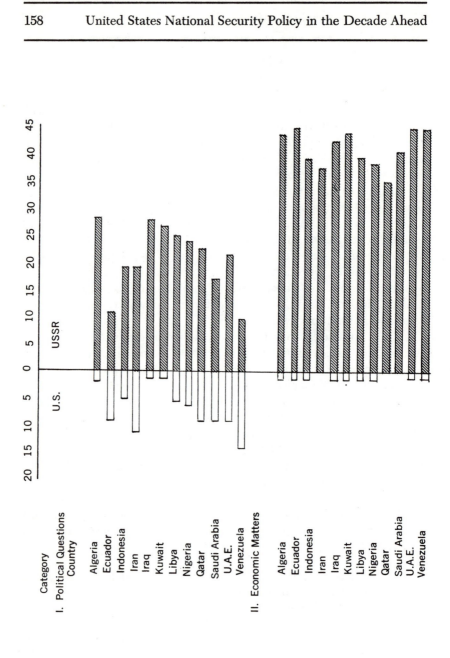

SOURCE: U.S. Department of State Roll Call votes at the 29th Regular
Session of the General Assembly, 17 September 1974–18 December.
Associate member Gabon is not included in this table.

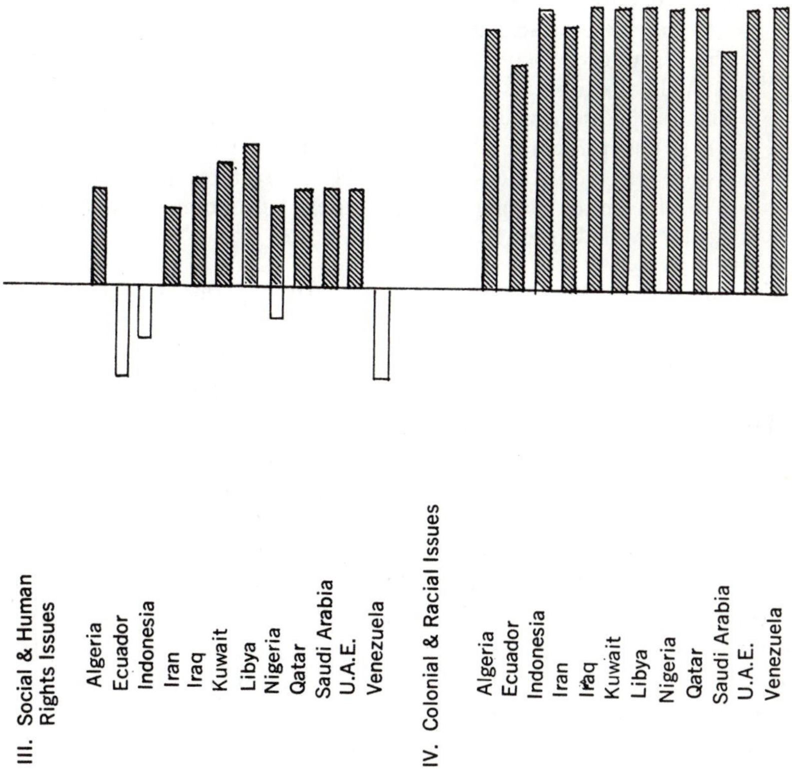

III. Social & Human Rights Issues

Algeria, Ecuador, Indonesia, Iran, Iraq, Kuwait, Libya, Nigeria, Qatar, Saudi Arabia, U.A.E., Venezuela

IV. Colonial & Racial Issues

Algeria, Ecuador, Indonesia, Iran, Iraq, Kuwait, Libya, Nigeria, Qatar, Saudi Arabia, U.A.E., Venezuela

Figure 2: Voting Patterns of OPEC (Organization of Petroleum Exporting Countries Compared to Those of the U.S. & USSR in the 29th UN General Assembly 1974–75 (number of Complete Agreement Votes)

of Bremerhaven, but after this became public knowledge, they notified the United States that they would not permit further usage).

• Holland's fellow members of the EEC were unable to come to its aid by sharing their oil for fear of being embargoed themselves.

• Japan resisted the intense pressure from the Arab oil producers to sever relations with Israel, but it did become decidedly pro-Arab in its diplomatic stance.

• Black African nations (twenty-one in all) broke relations with Israel in order to curry favor with the oil-rich Arabs.

• In November, Saudi Arabia forced Aramco to suspend the supply of products derived from Saudi oil to United States military forces. This created a potentially dangerous situation for the Sixth Fleet.

• Saudi pressure was also applied to the Philippines, resulting in a government order that no Philippine-processed oil or oil products would be sold to the United States military after 15 November. Singapore also ordered oil companies to halt sales to the United States military.

The success of these maneuvers demonstrated the inability and unwillingness of the consuming states to take effective counteraction against the oil producers. Even a hint of collaboration with the United States was scrupulously avoided by the more vulnerable nations.

While the political situation was eased in the aftermath of the October War by increases in oil production and an end to the embargo against the United States, the world economic situation was seriously aggravated by the December decision by the Persian Gulf oil producers to raise the posted price of oil to $11.65 per barrel (which meant that there had been an increase of about 400 percent in the posted price within the space of one year). This action further demonstrated the ability of the oil producers to take steps inimical to the rest of the world with little fear of political, military, or economic countermeasures by other powers.

Although the tensions between OPEC and the oil consumers remain, the dire predictions made earlier have not materialized. As regards the posted price, it was, as of mid-1977, approximately $13.34 (varying by types of crude), better than 10 percent higher than that established in January 1974. Considering world inflation, however, the price in constant dollars has remained about the same or actually eroded somewhat. In terms of the surplus revenue problem, David Rockefeller of Chase Manhattan predicted in 1974 that OPEC reserves would be about $145 billion by the end of 1975; the actual figure turned out to be about $52.7 billion. And as regards the Arab-Israeli conflict, the Sinai Agreements have temporarily reduced tensions, although the full impact of the Likud victory in the 1977 Israeli election has yet to be felt. It is clear that Saudi Arabia—without whose cooperation a boycott is out of the question—would prefer not to utilize the oil weapon directly again. Furthermore, Saudi Arabia is engaged in an extensive development program, heavily reliant upon the West and especially the United States. The enormous military buildup in the Persian Gulf is conditioned on a continued flow of American weapons, training, and other types of assistance. Thus the United States is not without some countervailing power. Hence there is little likelihood that another oil embargo will occur, although a new Arab-Israeli war might force the hand of the Saudis.

With regard to oil prices and the resulting transfer of wealth to the oil producers, this problem remains severe and is exacerbated by the failure of the OECD countries to adopt a unified consumer policy. The only concrete steps in this direction resulted from the Washington Energy Conference in February 1974, which (except for France) agreed to an American set of proposals for common action.[18]

The key source of tension between OPEC and the consuming nations is likely to be the price of oil. When the current surplus is eliminated and oil demand grows, it is likely that prices will rise again. No countervailing pressures are likely to be successful until the United States decides to move firmly against price rises. The United States position is critical: the United States consumes more than 40 percent of the world's energy; North Sea oil will ease the problem in Western Europe in the future, especially for Britain and Norway; China may ease Japan's dependence on the Middle East; only the United States can exercise influence over Israel; and finally, both Iran's and Saudi Arabia's security are heavily dependent on the United States. Future OPEC-oil consumer tensions, accordingly, will depend largely on United States energy and national security policies. Given the lack of a comprehensive United States energy policy and little prospect for a fundamental Arab-Israeli settlement, it is likely that until at least 1985 relations between OPEC and oil consumers will remain strained.[19]

THE FAILURE OF DETENTE

The significance of the Middle East to the Soviet Union predates the Russian Revolution. Traditional Russian interests include protecting its southern borders, exercising influence over countries near or adjacent to itself, and attempting to expand the Russian empire southward.[20] Such policies led to conflicts first with Turkey and Iran, subsequently with Britain, and, since the Truman Doctrine in March 1947, with the United States. It was not until the 1954–55 period, however, that the Soviet Union, through the provision of economic and military aid to selected Middle East nations, became a significant factor in Middle Eastern politics. The principal target of the Soviet offensive was Egypt, the largest and most influential Arab nation, and also one that, under the charismatic leadership of Colonel Nasser, had adopted a revolutionary, anti-Western, pan-Arabic stance.[21]

Moscow's courtship of Egypt in the 1950s initially was defensive in character. Aid to Egypt was to counteract the Western-sponsored Baghdad Pact, which linked Iraq and Turkey and subsequently Iran and Pakistan to complete a link in the containment circle around the USSR, extending from South Korea, around Southeast Asia, through the Middle East and Europe to Norway. The Soviet government appeared anxious to break this link and thus reduce the value of the Middle East as a base for Western operations. Soviet spokesmen have consistently stressed the strategic importance of the Middle East, noting its proximity to important industrial centers of the USSR and arguing that it is imperative that the area not be dominated by its superpower rival.[22]

It would appear that the Soviet government has now largely achieved its goal of eliminating the Middle East as a Western base of operations against the USSR; there has not been for some years a Western monopoly over the Mediterranean side of the region. Given Britain's withdrawal east of Suez and the Russian construction of a "blue water" navy, it may now be said that Western dominance of the Persian Gulf side of the Middle East has also ended. Finally, the Soviet Union is the principal beneficiary, from a military point of view, of the opening of the Suez Canal, since the canal greatly shortens the sea routes from the Black Sea to the Indian Ocean. This enables the Russian fleet to maintain a stronger presence in and around the Persian Gulf and Indian Ocean, should it decide to do so.[23]

In view of the long-standing and often-demonstrated Soviet interest in the Middle East, it is surprising that the American government apparently thought that "detente" would restrain Soviet behavior in the region. In fact, despite the alleged ending of the Cold War, the October 1973 Arab-Israeli conflict ushered in the most serious Soviet-American clash since the predetente Cuban missile crisis eleven years earlier. During this confrontation the Kremlin dispatched messages to the White House that were described as "brutal," partaking of the character of ultimatums, and readied airborne divisions for direct military intervention in the Middle East. Goaded by Soviet threats and pressured by Israel, the United States administration finally responded with a worldwide alert of American strategic forces, thus directly threatening the Soviet Union. These actions by the superpowers made a mockery of the idea of detente.

More significant than the details of superpower relations during the crisis, however, was the fact that the Soviet Union was attempting to alter the balance of power in an area of the world of enormous strategic and economic significance to the West. Moscow's leaders knew full well that Soviet domination of the Middle East, with its strategic location and vital oil resources, would pose literally a life-or-death threat to America's Western European and Japanese allies and thus imperil the entire structure of East-West relations. Less critical but nonetheless significant, orchestrated Soviet-Arab oil actions would seriously damage the American economy and substantially increase worldwide inflationary pressures. Nevertheless, during this crisis period the Soviet government took a number of highly provocative actions:

- Arming to an unprecedented degree Egypt, Syria, and Iraq, all of which were in confrontation with countries allied to or friendly with the United States. Beginning in the spring of

1973, massive new Soviet arms deliveries to the Middle East began. Thus an attack on Israel became a reasonable policy option for Egypt and Syria: without this sharp qualitative and quantitative increase in weapons deliveries in the spring and summer of 1973 there would have been no Yom Kippur War.[24]

- Urging the Arabs to use the oil weapon. For some years the Soviet government had argued that the Arabs should embargo oil to the West unless they ceased supporting Israel. Moscow at various times also urged the Arabs to manipulate their currency holdings in such a way as to damage Western financial institutions. The Soviets have long urged oil-producing states to raise significantly the price of their oil. Finally, the Soviet government for many years has attempted to persuade the oil countries to nationalize the oil companies and to take oil properties without compensation, thus helping to "liquidate imperialism" in the Middle East.
- Failing to inform and consult with the United States, as required by the Nixon-Brezhnev agreements of May 1972 and June 1973, in order to attempt to prevent the impending Arab attack on Israel with its attendant risk of escalating to an American-Soviet confrontation.[25]
- Failing to support United States initiatives for a cease-fire in the Security Council of the UN on 8 October 1973, and appealing to other Arab states, such as Algeria and Morocco, to join in the conflict. The Soviet government supported United States efforts to halt the conflict only after Israeli military sucesses and only in order to prevent an Arab military disaster.[26]
- Resupplying of the Arabs during and after the war, including the provision of SCUDs and advanced MIG fighters. Since the war Syrian armed forces have been especially strengthened. Soviet arms agreements have also been signed with the Libyan government, probably the most violently anti-Western regime in the Middle East.[27]
- Threatening direct Soviet armed intervention during the war.[28]
- Supporting maximum Arab demands on Israel, just short of the extinction of the Israeli state. This position included stronger support of Palestinian claims and anticipated improved relations between the Palestinian organizations and Moscow.[29]

These actions by the Soviet government were in direct contravention of the Soviet-American summit agreements of 1972 and 1973 and could in no way be called consistent with the spirit of detente that President Nixon and Premier Brezhnev had agreed was now governing superpower relations.[30] Yet the United States government did not hold the Soviet leaders even verbally accountable for their aggressive behavior in the Middle East. In fact, Washington, although obviously displeased with Moscow, clearly preferred to downplay the extent to which detente had proved illusory; to acknowledge this would be to admit a failure in national security policy not as dramatic as the collapse of America's Southeast Asia posture, but in the long run much more threatening.

FUTURE POLICY DIRECTIONS

Prior to 1970 the United States had no Middle East policy except a "low profile" one of basically "leaving it to the others." In the Persian Gulf this took the form of allowing most American-Gulf relationships to be handled by the oil corporations. On the Mediterranean side, the Sixth Fleet provided a military presence. The United States also supported Israel and enjoyed good relations with some other Middle Eastern states, especially Iran and Saudi Arabia. Politically, the United States, especially in the Persian Gulf, followed the lead of Britain.

As late as September 1973, the United States was still reluctant to play a leading role in Middle East affairs. Just before the Arab-Israeli war began, Secretary of State Henry Kissinger stated: "In the Middle East, we are prepared to use our influence to urge the parties toward a spirit of compromise—to encourage them in the process of negotiation. But you cannot expect—and no one should ask—us to produce all the formulas and all the will as a substitute for that of the other parties."[31] Ten days later the unexpected war began, and the United States quickly became heavily involved in the crisis, in which it did substantially "produce all the formulas" for the complicated and still ongoing negotiations searching for a stable peace. When the crisis of the war and its aftermath arose, the uniqueness and inevitability of the United States role came from the combination of being able to carry out a dialogue with the Arabs and the possession of political influence with Israel, a role the Soviets could not fill. Thus contrary to the implication in Dr. Kissinger's September statement that the United

States should take only an indirect part in Middle East affairs, that option now seems to be ruled out. The Arab-Israeli problem is the focal point of what has become an enduring United States involvement, but because this problem is linked to many other facets of regional affairs, the implications for United States policy pertain to the whole area. Therefore, realistic policy choices in the Middle East should not be based on whether the United States will take a direct part in the evolution of regional affairs but how the role will be carried out.[32]

The United States can pursue one of three broad approaches to the Middle East. The first would be to continue what has been a general pattern of the past, which was to concentrate on diplomatic relations with major "friendly" states, to have only minimal contacts with lesser countries and almost none with "unfriendly" states, and to adopt a "low profile" stance in the Middle East. To a considerable extent this approach has been overtaken by conscious policy change and by recent events. Even before the crisis of the 1973 war, it was declared that the United States would seek to broaden diplomatic and economic contracts in the Middle East, to strengthen existing relationships, and to restore diplomatic relations where they had been broken.[33] Pursuant to this, diplomatic ties were restored with the Yemen Arab Republic and the Sudan, and a United States "presence" was established in Baghdad. Since the war, ties have been restored with Egypt, Syria, and Algeria, and others may follow. The quality and diversity of United States representation has been raised in such lesser states as Bahrain, Qatar, the United Arab Emirates, and Oman.

Although this trend towards expanding diplomatic and economic ties seems clearly established, a reversion to a somewhat more restricted United States role remains a possible option. Such a United States policy course would not seem likely to be chosen on American initiative, but would be one that could come about as a result of an adverse turn in the climate of international relationships. If, for example, the rapprochment between Washington and Cairo should falter and the Egyptians once again become primarily a client of the USSR, political polarization would once more occur and a new war would become more likely. In that event, United States policy would concentrate mostly on Israel, Iran, and to the extent Saudi leaders could be persuaded not to ally with Egypt, on Saudi Arabia and the other traditional regimes of the Persian Gulf. Trade, transfer of technology, economic asistance, and arms sales would be limited to countries that adopted a cooperative attitude toward the United States.

A second broad approach would call for expansion of United States relationships throughout the Middle East, that is, a policy of strong United States participation in the region. The United States would give priority to the problem of oil-producer investments, to United States–Middle East trade and to arrangements for transfer of United States technology to Middle East countries. Both governmental and private sector activities in the Middle East would be stepped up. Diplomatic, economic, and cultural representation would be expanded, and specific efforts would be made to encourage and coordinate government policy with commercial activities. The states that have been hostile, such as Iraq and (until recently) Syria, are in need of United States technology and management expertise. Iraq, for example, needs help in agricultural development. The United States could exploit this and probably other such opportunities for openings to Iraq and Syria. The possibility of United States purchase of Iraqi oil should not be ruled out. A broader base of United States oil sources would be a natural part of this approach. In short, the United States would involve itself heavily in the entire Middle East and become the preeminent external power.

A third option would be an activist, involved policy as in the case of the second approach, but one much more selective in application. The three "great powers" (in addition to Israel) of the region—Egypt, Iran, and Saudi Arabia—would be cultivated. Ongoing programs of trade, technology exchange, and economic and social development would be expanded. Such a policy would recognize that Egypt, as the most powerful and populous Arab state, is the key to stability on the Mediterranean side of the Middle East. Saudi Arabia, in contrast, owes its preferred position primarily to oil and secondarily to its recognized religious leadership of the Islamic world. Iran, currently the strongest military power in the Middle East, except possibly for Israel, is clearly the regional power to be reckoned with in the future. A United States policy that deliberately recognized the overriding importance of these three states, and that included a strategy for cultivating close ties with them, would not be hostile to the other countries of the region; it would simply be a case of United States recognition that certain powers will determine the course of the Middle East for the foreseeable future.

While it is analytically convenient to delineate three separate United States policy approaches to the Middle East, in the "real" world foreign policy choices are severely constrained by past events and domestic and international factors. This means that ordinarily diplomatic moves are incremental in nature; while sweeping policy reversals for a great nation are not unknown, they occur only infrequently and usually in times of crisis. Sometimes constraints are such that only one option or varying emphases on one choice may be feasible. Also, policies are rarely "pure," with each component element harmonizing with all others. Rather, realistic choices frequently will reflect an eclectic mixture of the desirable and feasible. Finally, the United States has had— and will have—only limited influence over events in the Middle East and policy approaches must reflect this limitation. These caveats should be borne in mind when considering the future of the Arab-Israeli conflict, the oil problem, and Soviet-American relations in the Middle East.

Arab-Israeli Policies

Policy choices with regard to the Arab-Israeli conflict must begin with the fundamental premise that the United States of necessity will have important relationships with both Israelis and Arabs for the foreseeable future. Polarization of the political forces in the Middle East, which would be a likely consequence of a United States decision to abandon "evenhandedness" and strongly favor one or the other side, would jeopardize important American interests. Accordingly, courses of action such as reversing alliances and "abandoning" Israel on the one hand or deliberately seeking confrontation with the Arab world through total and unquestioning support of Tel Aviv on the other, are essentially "throwaway options." Realistic choices must be constructed within much narrower policy parameters.

It is also important to note that the United States, as a superpower and leader of the Western security system, cannot adopt a "hands off" attitude toward the Arab-Israeli conflict; it carries so much potential for affecting the world's security and economic well-being that Washington must play an active rather than a passive role. At the same time, neither the United States nor any other outside forces can dictate a solution. Rather, the parties to the conflict must in the final analysis themselves resolve it. The task for the United States is to work in the broad environment affecting both sides, facilitating a rational settlement by the parties themselves.

Finally, while there are certain aspects of the Arab-Israeli dispute that lend themselves to the formulation of alternative options, there are other aspects which have come to be imperatives in United States policy, as folows:

- The existence of Israel is not negotiable. Most Arabs have now come to accept this, and the United States must not adopt a policy position which leaves any room for doubt on this question. To do otherwise, aside from the moral implications, would do irretrievable damage to United States credibility and lead an isolated and desperate Israel to adopt a declaratory nuclear retaliation policy with attendant consequences for nuclear proliferation in the region.
- While the United States is comitted to defend Israel's right to exist, it is not committed to particular boundaries. The United States supports UN Resolution 242, which calls for Israeli withdrawal from teritories occupied in the 1967 War. That resolution envisions such withdrawal in the context of Arab recognition of Israel's right to live in peace within secure and recognized borders, not mere armistice lines.
- The United States supports "normalization" of relations in the region. This means direct negotiations of issues by the immediate participants, with external powers assisting but not dictating outcomes. It also means the acceptance of negotiations as a bargaining process in which each side makes certain concessions in order to arrive at a solution not wholly satisfactory but at least minimally acceptable to all concerned.
- Pending resolution of the dispute, the United States must attempt to maintain a balance of military power between the two parties. This does not necessarily mean matching in all particulars Soviet (and other) arms transfers to the Arab

countries. A serious imbalance of forces must be avoided, however, as either an Arab attack or Israeli preemption may result. Arab military preponderance may also result in an Israeli decision to inform the world that it has adopted a nuclear stance and will respond to an Arab attack with nuclear weapons.

- It is not sufficient to maintain a military balance between Israel and the Arab opponents. While it is possible that a no-war, no-peace situation could persist a long time, the inherent instabilities make it essential to move beyond this condition to some form of settlement, and United States policy should be geared to this goal.

While these "ground rules" should govern United States policy considerations, there is a need to develop alternatives, both in terms of a broad approach to the conflict and with respect to specific substantive issues. With regard to broad policy alternatives, there are two logical choices. The first is to attempt a "grand settlement," linking all aspects of the conflict together. Such an approach would go much beyond associating the Israeli border question with Israeli security; it would require the settlement of all aspects of the conflict in one stroke. Borders and security would not be negotiated, in such an approach, without settlement of such questions as the Palestine refugee problem, Israel's transit rights in the Suez, sovereignty or jurisdiction over Jerusalem, and so on. Israel, in such an approach, would have peace with all Arabs or with none; all issues would be resolved or none would be. Alternatively, Israel and the United States could concentrate heavily on bringing about a settlement of all issues between Egypt and Israel. Bluntly put, since the geography of the area favors an Israeli-Egyptian accord, unlike the situation between Israel and the rest of its Arab neighbors, Egypt might possibly be the "weak link" in Arab insistence to date on an all-or-nothing settlement. Recognition of this led Secretary Kissinger in 1975 to concentrate most strongly on Egyptian-Israeli relations.

When the Sinai Agreements were achieved, this was hailed as a great step toward peace. In fact, of course, Dr. Kissinger had merely selected by far the easiest Arab target for an agreement. The softness of the Egyptian position was verified by the Sinai Agreements. They required Israeli withdrawal only from the Sinai mountain passes of Gidi and Mitla, leaving Tel Aviv in possession of approximately 87 percent of the Sinai Peninsula, that which had been seized from Egypt during the 1967 war.[34] This is not to disparage the accomplishment; as has been pointed out, the accords, for the first time, represented not only a departure from previous Israeli and Egyptian attitudes, but required both Israeli and Egyptian leaders to justify the agreements to domestic critics by alleging good faith on the part of their opposite numbers.[35]

There has been no further progress toward an Arab-Israeli settlement since the agreements of 1975. Critics, accordingly, are now arguing that the Sinai accords were a mistake:

> Viewed in retrospect, the Sinai agreement clearly bears the Kissinger imprimatur. Like the Paris accords that ended the Vietnam War, it . . . was primarily intended to buy time—a "decent interval" in the case of Vietnam and, with luck, three or more years in the Middle East. Like those accords, the Sinai agreement, by avoiding the tough issues, has created a situation of inherent instability. . . . It is the work of a tactician when the times call for a strategist.[36]

This view is surely correct. On the other hand, the technique of "divide and conquer" is an ancient one; there is nothing inherently wrong with it if it works. Put otherwise, the problem with the Sinai Agreement is not that it was aimed at detaching Egypt from the Arab cause generally but that Dr. Kissinger failed in this effort and settled for a temporary respite instead. But an approach that deliberately concentrates on Egypt, as distinct from a "grand settlement" with all Arab protagonists, is not necessarily an incorrect approach, given the failure of numerous statesmen during the last thirty years to achieve a comprehensive Arab-Israeli peace settlement. So long as the United States insists that ultimately Israel return to the 1967 borders it should not feel morally constrained from attempting a complete settlement first with Egypt.

While Israel would undoubtedly favor an "Egypt first" policy, constraints on Egyptian freedom to negotiate may defeat this approach. Sadat's position in the Arab world is not as strong as his successful political use of warfare would lead one to think. He has proved to the Soviets that he is an unreliable ally and undoubtedly

Moscow would like him replaced. Additionally, Egypt has become very dependent on income from Saudi Arabia and other conservative regimes. Coupled with closer relationships with the capitalist West and especially the United States, this means that, in essence, Sadat has abandoned Nasser's revolutionary pan-Arabic goals. This coincides with the views of many Egyptians who never were at ease with the grandiose ambitions of Nasser. The military successes of Egypt in the war, however, have been greatly exaggerated by Cairo and ironically by Tel Aviv as well. Such a situation rekindled in Egypt, if not Nasser-like revolutionary fervor, a feeling that the Arabs are winning the struggle against Israel. Thus it is essential for Sadat to wring further concessions from Tel Aviv.

In addition to the principals, two countries are central to Egyptian and Israeli negotiations: Saudi Arabia and the United States. Egypt must continue to have Saudi support, both financial and diplomatic. Yet since the Yom Kippur War the Saudis have moved from a passive to an active role as guardian of the heritage of Islam. Specifically, this means that Saudi Arabia is adamant in insisting that the status of Jerusalem, captured by Israel in 1967, be negotiated before any Arab-Israeli peace agreement is reached. It would be helpful if this very sensitive issue could be worked on subsequent to and not coincident with an Israeli-Egyptian accord.[37]

The United States is also very significant to an Egyptian-Israeli settlement. As mentioned earlier, only Washington can be an "honest broker" in their negotiations. Only the United States, too, can replace the Soviet Union as a great power supporter of Egypt. Unless the United States is more forthcoming in both economic and military assistance to Egypt, Cairo will inevitably, as it has several times previously, turn to the Soviet Union. The pattern of Israeli-Egyptian hostility, both backed by and abundantly supplied with advanced weapons by the rival superpowers, will reassert itself.

It is not clear whether a pan-Arab or an "Egypt-first" approach would be more likely to lead to a settlement of the Arab-Israeli conflict. What is clear is that former Secretary Kissinger's Sinai Agreement is not only not a solution, it is hardly even an approach to one. It is, rather, a postponement of the hard questions and tough policy choices. As of this writing the outlines of the Carter administration's preferred approach have not clearly emerged (ritualistic calls for a reconvening of the Geneva Conference hardly constitute a policy), but hard choices cannot be indefinitely postponed.

Oil, Arms, and the Persian Gulf

Choices with regard to oil policy have to be formulated that will cope with the many and varied facets of the problem. The most basic policy requirement, however difficult to implement, is simple and obvious: the United States can and must bring energy production and energy consumption into a much closer balance than presently exists. The situation will worsen in the future unless present trends—an annual increase in consumption and level or declining domestic energy production—are reversed.

It is convenient to consider oil policies in terms of immediate, mid-term (1980–85) and long-term (1985–2000) solutions. Each of these time-oriented options must, in turn, be related to the various aspects of the energy problem: security and adequacy of oil supplies; the tremendous rise in oil prices and the many effects high oil costs have on nations throughout the world; balance of payments and liquidity problems; adequacy of international economic institutions to handle massive monetary flows; and the economic and national security implications of an enormous transfer of both current liquidity and capital resources from the industrial to the oil-exporting countries.

Measures to curtail demand can be effective much more quickly than those intended to increase energy supply. Accordingly, the most crucial immediate step that could (indeed must) be taken by the United States is to put into effect a series of steps that would add up to a massive conservation program intended to reduce American oil consumption—a target goal might be a reduction of about 10 percent in the present consumption rate. Beyond conservation, other immediate actions could include: greatly increasing oil stockpiling; imposing (as France has done) a dollar ceiling on the amount the United States will pay for imported oil; adopting a standby rationing and control system; undertaking steps to strengthen international banks; improving coordination with other consuming countries; considering rules to guide foreign investments in the United States; developing a comprehensive raw materials import and export policy, which would recognize the foreign policy implications of shortages not only of oil but food and other commodities as well; and encouraging American trade with the oil-exporting countries. Additionally, existing legislation regulating energy should be reviewed to eliminate any artificial barriers to increasing oil and gas supplies found to be unnecessary. Data disclosure legislation should be enacted so that all aspects of the energy situation are known by the government and the public. Finally, a well-financed and politically supported research and development program should be an essential element in energy policy.

Mid-term solutions involve a continuation and expansion of conservation measures plus determined efforts, led and where necessary financed, by the federal government, to exploit fully existing energy resources. Incentives should be provided also for efforts to find new oil and gas fields, and where necessary, environmental legislation impeding these efforts should be relaxed on a temporary basis. Cooperation with non–Middle Eastern countries which in the future might be large oil producers, such as China and Indonesia, should be explored. Construction of independent tanker fleets to prevent the distribution . system from coming completely under Middle Eastern control should be undertaken. Superport facilities should be built. Increased use of oil shale, coal gasification, and solar energy should be considered. Bearing in mind environmental risks and the problem of both accidents and nuclear sabotage or terrorism, the nuclear reactor program, under strict safeguards and security, should be expanded.

Long-term solutions involve phasing out oil as a source of energy and its replacement by energy sources not now at the stage of technological, economic, and industrial feasibility. It should be one goal of the research and development program to accomplish this replacement of oil as fuel at the earliest practical date.

The general principles of an energy policy, as described here, are well known. Basically, they add up to a recognition that energy policy is national security policy and that the government, accordingly, cannot leave this to the oil companies and the oil producers. Unfortunately, while a beginning has been made on some of the measures suggested here, the requisite determination to deal effectively with the energy problem has not yet been forthcoming, despite the publication in November 1974 of the Project Independence Blueprint (PIB) by the Federal Energy Administration. Absence of an energy policy undoubtedly reflects the strength and unwillingness to compromise of powerful contending forces in the United States. These (overlapping) groups are the energy expansionists versus energy conservationists; environmentalists versus corporations; energy corporations versus consumers; energy corporations versus advocates of divestiture; and OPEC conciliators versus confrontationists. In addition, there is little agreement as to which alternatives to oil hold the most promise.

Given this situation, it is clear that the United States needs to cooperate with Saudi Arabia. Saudi Arabia is the key to the oil problem. Indeed, not only is an embargo impossible without Saudi cooperation, the Saudis, with substantial spare capacity, have the power virtually to dictate the price of oil through substantially increasing their oil production. Between October 1973 and December 1976, the Saudis agreed to regular OPEC price increases, although presumably counseling price moderation. At the OPEC meeting on 17 December 1976, however, the Saudis (and also the United Arab Emirates) refused to agree to a 10 percent increase in posted prices decided upon by the other eleven members of OPEC. Instead, Saudi Arabia and the UAE raised prices by 5 percent. This signaled the first open break in the oil cartel. Other OPEC members, such as Iran, were particularly incensed at Riyadh's decision to increase oil production, which should have the effect not only of diverting some of their customers to cheaper Saudi oil but also will lead to a further accumulation of oil surpluses and at least some price reductions.[38] For the United States, unless prices are reduced, or consumption cut, the oil import bill is expected to total about $40 billion in 1977, with approximately 40 percent of United States needs supplied by imports.

The Saudi Oil Minister, Sheik Zaki Yamani, made it clear that he expects the United States to be grateful to Saudi Arabia for its "restraint" in oil pricing; this "gratitude" should take the form of additional progress on the Arab-Israeli situation and on the North-South dialogue in Paris with regard to the "new international economic order."[39] Subsequently, Yamani stated that the Saudis held down the price increase because they were worried about the economic situation in Europe, especially in Britain, France, and Italy.

Regardless of Saudi motives, it is indisputedly true that the United States needs to cultivate the closest possible relations with Saudi Arabia. In practical terms, in addition to the Arab-Israeli and North-South questions, this means continued access for Saudi Arabia to United States technology, expertise, and management assistance, as well as providing an outlet for the investment of surplus Saudi revenues. These are not really diverse issues; what is more likely to cause problems is the resistance by some in the United States, including influential members of Congress, to large-scale Saudi purchase of American weapons. President Carter has also criticized the amount of sales to Saudi Arabia, both during the 1976 election campaign, and since assuming the presidency, on the grounds that the weapons might be used against Israel and also due to his moral objections to the United States's having become "the world's leading arms salesman."

It is certainly true that United States arms sales to the Persian Gulf have risen dramatically in the past four years. In fiscal year 1972, the combined arms sales totals for Saudi Arabia and Iran were $854 million; three years later, in fiscal year 1975, the dollar value of United States arms sales worldwide totaled $9.5 billion with $4.8 billion accounted for by Israel, Iran, and Saudi Arabia. In fiscal year 1976, worldwide United States sales of arms were $8.4 billion, of which just under $1 billion went to Israel, $1.3 billion went to Iran, and $2.5 billion to Saudi Arabia. Estimates for new sales during fiscal year 1977 are $1 billion for Israel, $1.2 billion for Iran, and $1.5 billion for Saudi Arabia.[40]

Enormous arms transfers to the Persian Gulf reflect changes both in the United States and in the Persian Gulf. In the United States, as long as arms transfers were via grants, there existed a built-in adversary system, with both Congress and competing recipient nations dividing relatively scarce resources. With sales, an arms advocacy system assumed dominance as nonmilitary reasons, such as redressing the balance of payments, came to dominate arms transfer decisions. With regard to Persian Gulf states, they feel a new sense of threat, both because of their affluence in a poor world, and for other reasons associated with the retreat of Western power in the region. And subsequent to the Yom Kippur War and the attendant quadrupling of oil prices, they are now in a position to upgrade substantially their military forces.

It would be hard to imagine Saudi Arabia posing a threat to its neighbors, despite the recent large expenditures for new weapons systems. It is necessary, however, for the United States to continue to monitor the Saudi program to ensure that Saudi weapons are not transferred to Israeli "confrontation" states.

Iran, with a population five or six times larger than that of Saudi Arabia, a developing economy, an emerging middle class, and all the major ingredients to become a modern state, is in a very different situation from Saudi Arabia. Large-scale arms for Iran are clearly more justified than for Saudi Arabia. Further, since Iran is not an Arab nation, there is no need to be concerned that American weapons will be used against Israel. Iran's commitment to maintaining stability in the oil-rich Gulf is also vital. Finally, Iran has for many years maintained a staunchly anti-Soviet posture, thus making Tehran a valuable ally in containing possible Soviet penetration of the Gulf area.

At the same time, Americans naturally question whether the United States should continue the military buildup of a nation that has been in the forefront of the drive for higher oil prices. If the Iranians were in a position to significantly influence oil prices, then it would be valid to argue that the United States should demand Iranian oil price moderation as a quid pro quo for United States arms sales. But the reality is that Iranian oil price rhetoric should be ignored; Iran has little power to affect oil prices. And the United States has a decided interest in a strong and viable Iran, especially in an era when it is not regarded as permissible for the United States to maintain significant military forces of its own in the Persian Gulf area.

It is not suggested here that the unprecedented amounts of weapons now being acquired by Iran and Saudi Arabia should not be a cause for concern. What is needed is not a policy of arms denial, however. Rather, the Carter administration needs to develop arms sales guidelines, tailored specifically for Iran and Saudi Arabia, which reduce the risk of inappropriate use without incurring tensions with these two countries. A successful American policy in the Middle East will be on firm grounds if it is rooted in good relations with four key countries: Israel, Egypt, Saudi Arabia, and Iran.

The Superpowers: The Conflict of Interests
Earlier in this essay it was argued that Soviet actions in the Middle East just prior to, during, and immediately after the 1973 Arab-Israeli war were wholly inconsistent with either the spirit or letter of the detente agreements of 1972 and 1973. More critical is the fact, however,

that even if their conceptions of detente were identical, the interests of the two superpowers in the Middle East are sufficiently divergent as to make continued tension and possibly a renewal of outright conflict in the area likely.

Important examples of asymmetries in goals and divergences of interests are the following:

- The United States, and even much more so its European and Japanese allies, need the oil of the Middle East and do not want to disrupt the flow of oil supplies. The Soviet government, while it finds the oil useful, can view with equanimity disruptions in the supply of oil, at least in the near future.
- The Soviet Union (and before it czarist Russia) has long regarded the Middle East and the Indian Ocean as areas of critical importance to its security. The United States, on the other hand, has not had a clear and consistent policy regarding the Middle East, and only since the crisis of the 1973 war has it taken an active and leading role in Middle East affairs.
- The United States has been more closely associated in a diplomatic and military sense with the non-Arab regimes in the Middle East, Israel and Iran. The USSR has been a supporter of the Arabs, anti-Israeli and, to a lesser extent, anti-Iranian. Currently the United States is attempting to be "evenhanded," whereas the Soviet Union is not.
- The Soviets have associated themselves with the "radical" Arabs of the Persian Gulf, in opposition to conservative regimes such as that in Saudi Arabia. The United States supports the existing governments and opposes their replacement by radical regimes.
- The Soviet Union regards the Persian Gulf–Indian Ocean area as an arena essential to the general Soviet policy of containing China; the United States does not.
- The United States would benefit from a "just" and peaceful resolution of the Arab-Israeli conflict, while the Soviets wish to exploit its continuation.
- Disruption in the Middle East and conflicts in the area, such as the one between Greece and Turkey over Cyprus, weaken the southern flank of NATO and hence adversely affect the United States alliance system. This problem does not exist for the USSR.

American and Russian interests are in sharp conflict in the Middle

East; to expect these differences to be eliminated through Soviet-American detente is wholly unrealistic. Superpower rivalry will continue in the Middle East, Persian Gulf, and Indian Ocean areas, restrained primarily by the mutual interest both sides have in preventing this conflict of interest from escalating into a nuclear confrontation. This situation acts to inhibit direct military intervention by either the USSR or the United States in the Middle East. Given the intraregional problems, however, it will remain very difficult for the superpowers to realize even the negative goal of not allowing events in the Middle East to get completely out of control. Furthermore, given the tremendous transfer of sophisticated weapons into these areas, events could develop so rapidly that effective superpower intervention to prevent the development of a major conflict would not be feasible.

After the October 1973 war, the United States gained an important diplomatic victory in that the Arabs realized that only the United States could mediate the conflict with Israel. It would be a mistake, however, to believe that this American advantage is more than temporary. Also, the favorable position achieved by the United States is more than offset by the demonstrated inability of the Western Alliance members to act in concert on Middle East policy, and by their vulnerability to the oil weapon.

The conflict of strategies between the superpowers means that long and arduous negotiations lie ahead. The threat of oil force will cast an ominous and omnipresent shadow over these negotiations; the outcome will affect not only the Middle East but the entire global balance of power and the future of the Western alliance system.

Over four years have passed since the Yom Kippur War. Once more American policy has become complacent with the status quo, lulled into a false sense of security by a temporary easing of Arab-Israeli tension, by remarkably friendly attitudes by the Saudi Arabian oil superpower, and by the continuing belief in the chimera of detente. A new administration in Washington should put these illusions to rest and accord the highest priority to an equitable Middle Eastern settlement.

POSTSCRIPT

One of the principal themes of this article is the possibility of separate Israeli-Egyptian negotiations that optimally would lead to an all-inclusive Israeli-Arab settlement but short of that to an agreement between Israel and Egypt alone. It was pointed out that both terrain and circumstance favor such a course of action, not possible to date because of the Egyptians' reluctance to separate themselves from the general Arab cause, for both external and internal reasons. It was also pointed out that Egypt is one of four key countries for United States policy in the Middle East and that closer United States relations with Cairo would be useful. The dramatic visit of Prime Minister Anwar Sadat to Israel and the subsequent negotiations further emphasize these conclusions. It will be difficult, however, to sustain the momentum of the negotiations unless the United States pursues a more vigorous and bolder policy of pushing both Egypt and Israel into a settlement. For Israel, this means making territorial concessions; for Egypt, it means a (separate if necessary) peace treaty with Isreal. For the United States, it means a formal treaty guarantee of Israeli security, including possibly the semipermanent stationing of American troops in Israel to compensate for the diminution of Israeli security that territorial concessions will entail. It also means, despite Israeli objections, that the United States become the source of Egyptian arms so that there will be no need, as has occured in the past, for Egypt to become dependent on the Soviet Union for its security.

NOTES

1. For discussion of this dimension of the conflict see Robert Freedman, "The Partition of Palestine: Conflicting Nationalism and Great Power Rivalry," in *The Problem of Partition: Peril to World Peace,* ed. Thomas Hackey (Chicago: Rand McNally, 1972).
2. Embassy of Israel, "Current Prospects for an Israel-Arab Settlement," mimeographed (Washington, D.C.: 12 February 1975), p. 4.
3. While the Israelis refer to the October 1973 conflict as the Yom Kippur War, the Arabs refer to it as the War of Ramadan. The Israeli term is used here since it is the one familiar to American readers. The 1973 war also frequently is referred to as the October War and the fourth Arab-Israeli war.
4. By "secure borders," the Israelis apparently mean frontiers lying somewhere between the 1949 armistice lines and the cease-fire lines of June 1967. See, for example, Prime Minister Golda Meir's speech to the Knesset, as reported in the *New York Times* (5 May 1969).

5. There is, of course, a close relationship between Israeli control of Arab territory and the military necessity to launch a preemptive air strike in a period of crisis. See, for example, General Dayan's statement on this point, as quoted in Steven Rosen and Martin Indyk, "The Temptation to Preempt in a Fifth Arab-Israeli War," *Orbis* (Summer 1976), p. 273.

6. At Rabat, Arab representatives agreed that the PLO was to be the "sole legitimate representative of the people of Palestine." See *Middle East Monitor* (1 October 1974), p. 4.

7. For a discussion of the position of Palestinian "moderates," see the (admittedly biased) analysis of Mordechai Nissan, "PLO 'Moderates'," *The Jerusalem Quarterly* (Fall 1976), pp. 70–82.

8. Prime Minister Rabin, in a speech to the Knesset in June 1976, warned of the "dangers to Israeli security interests" should Lebanon be dominated by either the PLO or Syria. Quoted in the *New York Times* (16 June 1976).

9. See Malcolm Peck, "Saudi Arabia's Wealth: A Two-Edged Sword," *New Middle East* (January 1972), p. 6.

10. Numerous visits were exchanged between Egyptian and Saudi officials to discuss the use of the oil weapon, from about April 1973 to October 1973. See, for example, articles in the *Washington Post* (20 April 1973), *New York Times* (17 August 1973), and *The Economist* (22 September 1973).

11. See the *New York Times* (2 December 1972) and *The Oil and Gas Journal* (30 April 1973).

12. Saudi Arabia initially agreed to provide funds to Egypt "until the traces of the Israeli aggression are removed" at the Arab summit conference in Khartoum in August 1967. *The Arab World* (3 May 1973). Subsequently, Saudi Arabia annually provided subsidies to Egypt and renewed these pledges in 1973.

13. For a detailed examination of the effectiveness and limitations of the oil weapon, see Hanns Maull, *Oil and Influence: The Oil Weapon Examined, Adelphi Paper No. 119* (London: International Institute for Strategic Studies, 1975).

14. F. Bergsten, "The Threat Is Real," *Foreign Policy* (Spring 1974), p. 85.

15. The posted price, for example, of Saudi Arabian light crude oil as of 1 October 1974 was $11.65 per barrel, while production costs were approximately ten cents a barrel. See "OPEC Freezes Fourth-Quarter Oil Prices," *The Oil and Gas Journal* (23 September 1974).

16. Use of the word *pariah* is not intended to be descriptive of an active state of affairs but rather is a shorthand expression to connote attitudes toward these countries.

17. One reason why the "nonaligned" nations take such anti-American positions is that the group includes the Communist regimes of Cuba, North Korea, Cambodia, Vietnam, and Yugoslavia.

18. The text of the United States proposals may be found in the *Department of State Bulletin* (4 March 1974).

19. Saudi Arabian policy will be the critical factor in determining OPEC-consumer relations. Without Saudi cooperation an oil embargo is impossible. Furthermore, maintaining even the present level of oil prices depends upon Saudi Arabia's continued willingness to produce oil far below capacity. In December 1976, Saudi Arabia announced it would increase its production significantly in 1977.

20. See Bernard Lewis, "Great Powers and the Middle East," *Foreign Affairs* (July 1969), p. 652.

21. The initial Soviet-Egyptian arms agreement was announced in September 1955, providing for Soviet weapons and training, with Czechoslovakia acting as agent for the USSR. See Wynfred Joshua and Stephen P. Gibert, *Arms for the Third World: Soviet Military Aid Diplomacy* (Baltimore: Johns Hopkins Press, 1969), chap. 2. Between 1955 and the third Arab-Israeli war (June 1967), Egypt received more Soviet military aid (about $1.5 billion) than did any other Third World country. Ibid., p. 102. Subsequent to the arms deal, in October 1958, the USSR agreed to undertake the mammoth Aswan Dam project. See Marshall Goldman, *Soviet Foreign Aid* (New York: Praeger, 1967), pp. 61-70, for a discussion of this undertaking.

22. For relevant comment, see Ye. M. Primakov, the deputy director of the Institute for World Economics and International Relations of the USSR Academy of Sciences, writing in *Mezhdunarodnye Konflicti*, ed. V.V. Zhurkin and Ye. Primakov (Moscow: 1972), translated in *JPRS, International Conflict*, no. 58443 (12 March 1973), p. 103.

23. For a speculative discussion of these points, written, however, before the Suez Canal was opened, see T.B. Millar, "Soviet Policies South and East of Suez," *Foreign Affairs* (October 1970), p. 72. There is no evidence to date, however, of a significantly expanded Soviet naval build-up in the Indian Ocean, although total Soviet ship days have increased.

24. A. Mirskiy, "New Factors in the Near East," *New Times*, no. 48 (30 November 1973): 18. A recent *Pravda* editorial provided unexpected—and remarkably detailed—confirmation of the extent of Soviet military aid to Egypt between 1967 and late 1973. The USSR, *Pravda* stated, had rapidly reequipped the Egyptian armed forces after the 1967 defeat and at one point even "assumed the defense of Egyptian airspace." During the 1973 war, the Soviet Union "took urgent measures" to deliver "additional large quantities" of arms by air and sea, and provided vigorous political support of the Arab countries in the UN and

elsewhere. See Christopher Wren, "Pravda Charges that Sadat Lies on Soviet Role," *New York Times* (20 February 1977).

25. In the Basic Principles of Relations Between the USA and the USSR, signed in Moscow on May 29, 1972, the two powers agreed "to do everything in their power so that conflicts or situations will not arise which would serve to increase international tensions." *Weekly Compilation of Presidential Documents* 8, no. 23 (5 June 1972): 943. In the Agreement on Prevention of Nuclear War, signed in Washington on 22 June 1973, the United States and the USSR agreed that anytime there appeared to be a risk of nuclear conflict the two countries "shall immediately enter into urgent consultations with each other and make every effort to avert this risk." *Department of State Bulletin,* 23 July 1976, pp. 160–61.

26. Robert O. Freedman, "Soviet Policy Toward the Middle East from the Exodus of 1972 to the Yom Kippur War," in *The Middle East, 1974: New Hopes, New Challenges,* hearings before the Subcommittee on The Near East and South Asia of the Committee on Foreign Affairs, U.S. House of Representatives (Washington, D.C.: Government Printing Office, 1974), p. 190.

27. See the *Military Balance 1974–75* (London: The International Institute for Strategic Studies, 1974), pp. 89–90.

28. See Secretary of State Henry Kissinger, Press Conference, U.S. Department of State *News Release* (6 December 1973), p. 7.

29. See *Pravda* (17 April 1974).

30. The present writer, at a symposium held by Stanford Research Institute for Soviet and American academicians in May 1975, called attention to Soviet behavior in the Middle East to Ye. Primakov and V.V. Zhurkin, deputy directors respectively of the Institute for World Economy and International Relations and the Institute for the United States and Canada. Their rejoinder was to the effect that detente required the USSR and the United States not to threaten each other. The Soviet government during the Yom Kippur War threatened Israel; it did not threaten the United States. Conversely, the American strategic alert threatened the USSR. Hence the United States violated detente, not the USSR. Since detente did not preclude superpower threats against third countries, Soviet threats against Israel were not a violation of detente.

31. News conference at the United Nations, 26 September 1974, *Department of State Bulletin* (15 October 1974), p. 480.

32. The Cyprus crisis of the summer of 1974 seems to have borne out the thesis that the United States cannot escape responsibility in a Middle East crisis. The United States, perhaps partly because of the crisis in

the presidency, acted late and impulsively, alienating all parties in the dispute, and probably worsening the crisis in its overall effect.

33. *U.S. Foreign Policy for the 1970s* (Washington, D.C.: Government Printing Office, 1973), p. 142.

34. For details of the 4 September 1975 accords, signed at Geneva, see *Department of State Bulletin* (29 September 1975), pp. 466–70.

35. Nadav Safran, "Engagement in the Middle East," *Foreign Affairs* (October 1974), pp. 48–49.

36. George Ball, "Kissinger's Paper Peace," *The Atlantic* (February 1976).

37. The Saudi position on Jerusalem may have softened somewhat since King Faisal's death.

38. As previously noted, posted prices later rose to more than $13.00 per barrel, but there is no doubt that the Saudis have been a restraining force.

39. Interview on NBC-TV, 19 December 1976.

40. U.S. Congress, Committee on International Relations, *International Security Assistance and Arms Export Control Act of 1976* (Washington, D.C.: Government Printing Office, 1976), pp. 91–92. Figures quoted are for arms orders, not deliveries.

Chapter Nine

United States China Policy: Basic Assumptions

Franz Michael

No other political drama has provided the spectator-analyst with so many surprises as has the Chinese scene of recent years. Nowhere have predictions been more hazardous and misdirected. Thanks largely to Chairman Mao, the Chinese scene has been vexed with more upheavals and turmoil than was expected or could be handled by the current analytical concepts in use in the academic profession in the last decades. And yet, when one attempts to assess the Chinese political potential in order to determine how United States policy should be directed, one must clarify the basic elements of the Chinese equation with which we deal. Before we decide on United States policy, we must understand what China we are dealing with.

The argument among the contending factions within the People's Republic of China since the Cultural Revolution was based on ideological justifications of what, in essence, has been a political power struggle. When one faction, the so-called Maoists, attacked the opposition as "capitalist-roaders" and removed them from power, as happened to Teng Hsiao-p'ing at the beginning of 1976, and when a few months later, the new man in power attacks those same Maoists also as "capitalist-roaders," the ideological argument is led *ad absurdum*. The only valid part of the argument is the factional struggle itself. In order to relate United States policy to this situation, one must interpret and analyze the factions and their policy goals; hence terminology is important. Western specialists, agreeing with the tenet set forth by Chairman Mao, of the "battle between the two lines," have usually labeled these opposing factions "radicals" or "Maoists" on one side and "moderates" or "pragmatists" on the other. It is this latter classification of "moderates" or "pragmatists" with which one must take issue. The use of terminology would not matter if the definitions were understood by all. However, the problem with the terms "moderates" and "pragmatists" is that they lead to the assumption that we deal with people whose thinking and aims are similar to our own and that we can therefore come to terms with them on policies leading toward goals that are shared by these Chinese leaders with the West. This assumption is often combined with the notion that "ideology is dead," meaning other people's ideology, not our own, and in particular, that the Communist ideology of world revolution is dead. The words and actions of the Chinese leaders fly in the face of this assumption. Chinese Communists of all colors quote Mao's sayings:

> The current international situation is one of great disorder under heaven and one in which the winds sweeping through the tower herald a rising storm in the mountains. . . . Countries want independence, nations want liberation and the people want revolution.

This belief that the international "situation is excellent" for the cause of world revolution is the leitmotiv for the fluctuating policies of Peking. It would appear therefore better not to use the terms "moderate" or "pragmatist" for the entrenched bureaucracy in the People's Republic. These terms are as misleading as was once the term "agrarian reformers" applied by so many commentators to the Chinese Communists at the end of World War II. Instead, this faction might better be called orthodox Communists—not in Moscow's usage, where "orthodox" means dogmatic, but rather in the sense of traditional Communists —those who follow the model of staged economic development provided by the Soviet Union, rather than of perpetual revolution and instant communism espoused by Chairman Mao.

The history of the People's Republic of China since the Great Proletarian Cultural Revolution has been one of confrontation between these two lines, with Mao always reasserting himself, his concept of perpetual revolution, and his leadership against the challenge of the Chinese Communist party bureaucracy. This challenge first surfaced in 1956 when the de-Stalinization policy in the Soviet Union, never accepted by Mao, caused the introduction of "collective leadership" in China. In opposing the line of Moscow's new leaders, whom he labeled "revisionists" and "capitalist roaders," Mao became more and more extreme, combining his Marxism with a vulgarized form of Darwinism that led him to propagate eternal struggle—indeed, struggle as a law of nature and goal in itself. As long as he lived, Mao's authority and political skill was extraordinary enough to continually renew the revolutionary fervor of his followers and to prevent any stabilization and institutionalization of the Communist system in China. Once Mao left the scene, the Maoist epigones could not perpetuate a policy that had no goal except revolution itself. Sooner or later, the Maoist faction would be defeated; that their fall occurred so soon demonstrated the disgust of the public and the strength of the opposition.

Actually, the new men who came to power in Peking were not—with the exception of the again-restored Teng Hsiao-p'ing—the leaders of the bureaucratic faction of traditional communist policies. Hua Kuo-feng, Wang Tung-hsing, and Ch'en Hsi-lien represented essentially the primary power of the police and the army. Hua, the head of the security system, controlled the most decisive factor, the secret police. Wang Tung-hsing, the head of the palace guard, Mao's former bodyguard and loyal palladin, surprised not only foreign observers but presumably Madame Mao and her friends, by turning against them and participating in their arrest. Ch'en Hsi-lien, the commander of Peking Military Region and the Peking garrison, provided the military backing. Behind them stood such military leaders as the old man, Yeh Chien-ying, the dean of the People's Liberation Army (PLA) commanders. The basic justification for the coup by these men was, however, their determination to do away with utopian Maoism. With the Maoists out of power and accused as "capitalist-roaders," the new leaders will clearly return to the traditional Communist policy line of staged economic growth, particularly since they were joined by Teng Hsiao-p'ing. The remaining question is whether the new triumvirate of Hua Kuo-feng, Yeh Chien-ying, and Teng Hsiao-p'ing will be able to continue its collective leadership or whether the power struggle will go on. Whatever the outcome of this new relationship, as of now the Maoists seem to have lost.

Whatever documentation we have from the last months of Mao's life indicates that he wanted his faction to retain control after his death; Mao's displaced trust in Hua Kuo-feng aborted his plan. The coup, in effect, demonstrated Hua's flexibility and his astuteness in sensing the realities of power. In joining the opposition, Hua could count on the PLA and on substantial support from the party regulars and large dissatisfied sections of the population, as demonstrated by the massive anti-Mao demonstrations in April of 1976 in Peking and other cities. Hua's price was the chairmanship of the party. To embalm Mao's body for preservation in a crystal coffin was an artful maneuver enabling Chairman Hua to claim Mao's blessing for his rather different political course. In his crystal coffin, the silent Mao will not be able to remonstrate against the betrayal of his vision by new leaders claiming political legitimacy, while reinterpreting Mao's broad, vague, and often contradictory directives, to serve their new policy line.

The new course seems thus to indicate at least for the time being the end of the Maoist utopian dream of perpetual revolution, and of instant communism, which could indeed not be expected to survive the prophet.

Yet, there is still uncertainty and instability. In a continuing shift of authority within the triumvirate, Teng Hsiao-p'ing has steadily enlarged his influence. Teng's men have assumed the posts of minister of security, head of the party's Organization Department, head of the Party School, commander of the Peking garrison, Peking garrison political commissar, and other leading positions. Teng, who holds the real administrative power, is the true head of the regular Communist bureaucratic faction. United States policy will have to consider this Chinese change of line toward regular communism.

There are of course other possible political developments in China. If the power struggle is not over, it may erupt into open conflict. Such conflict may invite Soviet intervention. This eventuality should not be construed to mean war between the two countries, which would only unify the Chinese leaders, but would more likely take the form of Soviet political action supporting one faction against the other, if feasible with military force along the Chinese border combined with their considerable leverage in offering as temptation economic and technical aid—the carrot on the stick. There is also the possibility, however remote, yet never to be excluded, of a new revolution in China, caused by the alienation and impatience of an intelligent people, tired of all the shifts in policy and doctrine, cynical when black today becomes white tomorrow, bitter about so much suffering and suppression caused by Mao's doctrinal fantasies. The outcome of either course of events is unpredictable, yet whatever course ensues will necessarily affect United States security and global peace, and must be taken into consideration in any discussion of United States foreign policy toward China.

If, however, the triumvirate retains power, or is replaced by Teng's authority, and one stipulates a return to Communist normalcy—orthodox planned economic development by stages, "revisionism," if you like—a Soviet type of communism will be back in China. It will affect not only domestic policies, with a new emphasis on production based on incentives and systematic planning, but foreign relations as well.

In the field of economic policy we have already learned something of the shift in gears. The slogans turn back to rapid economic advancement, to the fulfillment of the plan proclaimed by Premier Chou En-lai at the National People's Congress in January 1975, when Chou spoke of two stages in the development of the national economy of the People's Republic:

> The first stage to build an independent and relatively comprehensive industrial and economic system in 15 years, that is before 1980; the second stage to accomplish the comprehensive modernization of agriculture, industry, national defense and science and technology before the end of the century, so that our national economy will be advancing in the front ranks of the world.

To accomplish such economic growth there will have to be a new emphasis on productivity; wages will have to be raised to counter workers' dissatisfaction; education will have to be reorganized to reintroduce standards—in recent years sacrificed for the sake of revolutionary activism; and foreign technology will have to be introduced to accelerate industrial development. There will be need for far more capital than is available today. Much has been made of the potential oil resources on the mainland and on the continental shelf under the China Sea; these, too, however, can only be developed with foreign technology and capital. Chou, quoting Mao, proposed a careful balance:

Chairman Mao points out, "Rely mainly on our own efforts while making external assistance subsidiary, break down blind faith, go in for industry, agriculture and technical and cultural revolutions independently, do away with slavishness, bury dogmatism, learn from the good experience of other countries conscientiously and be sure to study their bad experience too, so as to draw lessons from it. This is our line."

This economic program, then, cannot be approached in isolation. How much and whose foreign support will Peking seek? For the United States the crucial question is the possibility of a realignment of relations between Moscow and Peking.

There are strong arguments on both sides of the speculation about the possibility of a Sino-Soviet rapprochement. Those who hold that the gap is unbridgeable and that at the very most some civility in diplomatic relations between the two Communist powers may return, argue in terms of historical incompatibility, of national interests and pride, and of historical claims and problems along the Sino-Soviet border. The question is, how valid are most of these arguments in the world of twentieth-century communism?

On the other side of the ledger is the history of Sino-Soviet relations since the founding of the Chinese Communist party. Moscow was the midwife and the nursemaid to the fledgling Chinese Communist party, giving decisive aid toward the seizure of power in 1949 and providing massive support for economic development during the First Five-Year Plan. This changed only when Khrushchev decided to apply his de-Stalinization and Moscow's general policy line to China, threatening Mao's position within his own party. Khrushchev's highhandedness also threatened the autonomy of Chinese communism within the framework of a socialist order that was rapidly moving in a centrifugal direction. When Chairman Mao's defiance of Khrushchev's policy and authority widened into a challenge to Soviet leadership in the socialist camp and led to the splitting of the Communist world movement, the question remained, how much this test of strength between Khrushchev and Mao was limited to the dramatis personae. When Khrushchev fell, there was a short flurry of feelers between Moscow and Peking, but the conflict continued and hardened. Now the other leading actor has gone, and thus the personal obstacle to reconciliation has disappeared. But in the meantime conflicting policies have created hurdles and entrenched positions on both sides that may be hard to abandon.

It must not be forgotten, however, that throughout the conflict all opposition leaders in China were, falsely or correctly, accused by Mao of favoring reconciliation or even secretly dealing with the Moscow "revisionists." Leaving aside the earlier history of Chinese communism, the three major purges during the period of the Sino-Soviet conflict—the attack against Mao by P'eng Teh-huai, following the disaster of the Great Leap Forward; the acceptance of cooperation on Vietnam in 1965 by the party leaders, and their subsequent purge in the Cultural Revolution; and the purge of Lin Piao in 1971—all had their acknowledged or suspected Soviet connection.

Even after Lin Piao's purge the question of realignment with Moscow remained an issue in the Chinese factional struggle. Chou En-lai's last speech in January 1975, which referred to the Sino-Soviet conflict as "a debate" and included an invitation to unconditional negotiations, hinted at a move in that direction. Teng Hsiao-ping's gesture in December 1975, releasing the Soviet helicopter pilots who had been prisoners in China for eighteen months, was clearly a signal comparable to the Ping-Pong policy vis-à-vis the United States. Indeed, it seems plausible that it was this gesture that may have aroused the Chairman's ire and sealed Teng's fall a short time later.

Then, after Mao's death, there were many signs of a new Soviet political offensive with the goal of reestablishing Sino-Soviet cooperation. Chinese media attacks against Moscow continued, but the Soviets abruptly ceased their anti-Peking propaganda. Soviet congratulations to the Chinese party leadership at Hua Kuo-feng's ascension to power, though not accepted, must be seen as an opening move. And, at the Soviet revolutionary anniversary, the Chinese message was more cordial than it had been for a long time. For the first time in many years Chinese representatives not only appeared at official celebrations, but listened to the end to Soviet speeches. In Washington and in Tokyo, the heads of the Chinese Mission had what appeared to be cordial discussions with the Soviet ambassadors. In the People's Republic of China, Soviet films of the Bolshevik Revolution were shown in Peking and other cities, presumably to improve the climate in Moscow-Peking relations. These were only first steps, and they were succeeded from the early months of 1977 by more discordant notes, but it is significant that they occurred rather quickly after the changeover in Peking. In assessing the situation in the People's Republic, it ought also to be noted that among the rehabilitated and reappointed cadres in the provinces, and especially among the military men, were several who had been Soviet trained and spent considerable time in the Soviet Union. All this raises at least the possibility of a reconciliation that would go well beyond the limited improvement of state-to-state relations that is now regarded as possible among United States officials and specialists.

There have been the visits to Peking of President Tito and the Vietnamese Communist leaders. Tito, who had been to Moscow, was most cordially received, and his visit led to a realignment of the Chinese Communist party, cleansed of its Maoists, with the "archrevisionist" Yugoslav Communist party. At the visit of the Vietnamese Communist leader, his speech and that of Chairman Hua stated by side the respective Soviet and Chinese interpretations of the world situation without any protest from either side.

If one seriously considers the possibility of a Sino-Soviet realignment, the question has to be answered, On what basis could the conflict be overcome? On the positive side of Moscow-Peking relations there remains a common doctrinal basis and commitment to Communist strategy. Both sides assert their belief in, and support of, world revolution, revolutionary wars, and wars of national liberation. Though true to the imperatives of their conflict, Moscow and Peking accused each other of betraying these common revolutionary goals, such accusations could be easily discontinued; there is no disagreement on the basic final goal of a Communist world order. The conflict may have started largely as a move by Chairman Mao to counter the Soviet de-Stalinization policy, moving on from there to challenge the Soviet leadership of the socialist camp to follow his vision of perpetual revolution; with the death of Mao, these policies could be quietly abandoned. Indeed, some change can already be discerned. But there are by now other obstacles in the way of Sino-Soviet reconciliation resulting from competitive policies that have hardened and have created entrenched positions on both sides, hurdles that might be more difficult to remove.

The often-mentioned border conflict between the Soviet Union and the Chinese People's Republic presents in this assessment no such major obstacle. The territory taken by czarist Russia in the treaties of 1858 and 1860, the large area north and east of the Amur and Ussuri Rivers ceded by the Manchu dynasty, poses no real problem. There is no Chinese population, no Chinese irredenta, and no Chinese demand for repossessing this whole area. Peking's references to the imperialism of the Soviet Union's czarist predecessors have been rather in the category of propaganda ploys in the Sino-Soviet negotiations. The only real border issues are local quarrels over islands and small areas along the Amur and Ussuri rivers, which could be settled readily given the will to do so.

There is of course the possibility of renewed large-scale Soviet economic and technical support, as given in the past and certainly both needed and welcome today. No major problem should arise in negotiating such aid between Moscow and Peking, in connection with and as part of a political settlement.

A more crucial issue standing in the way of cooperation, however, remains the Sino-Soviet competition for leadership of the revolutionary forces in the so-called Third World. In this rivalry, especially in Southeast Asia, in the Middle East, and in Africa, the Soviets have the advantage. Whether they are willing to make concessions and to accept a true partnership with Peking in supporting Communist revolutionary expansion remains to be seen. There was once a Soviet willingness to assign the Chinese People's Republic a special role in this so-called Third World strategy, as indicated in the Moscow Declaration of 1957 and the Moscow Statement of 1960. The Chinese Communists were then encouraged to assume a major part of the training of Communist functionaries to implement the bloc's revolutionary strategy. Whether today the Soviets are willing to afford Peking a role in their Third World strategy or whether they will be unwilling to forego their existing advantage is difficult to predict. The Soviets have rarely shown themselves willing to share power and influence within the Communist world, but it would not be wise to rely on past Soviet shortsightedness in weighing the dangers to our national security that would result from a viable compromise between Moscow and Peking on a new common global strategy.

There is still another possible area of renewed Sino-Soviet cooperation of direct concern to the United States. One of the issues that hardened the Sino-Soviet conflict was, as Soviet sources indicate, Khrushchev's unwillingness to back Mao Tse-tung's adventurous plan of attacking Taiwan in September 1958. When Khrushchev refused to risk a nuclear confrontation with the United States, committed to the defense of Taiwan, Mao is said to have viewed this Soviet refusal as a decisive turning point in Sino-Soviet cooperation; indeed many Western specialists are agreed that this incident was the point of no return in the growing Sino-Soviet conflict. What of today? Would the new leaders in Peking again ask for Soviet support in such a venture at a time when the military balance between the Soviet Union and the United States has, to say the least, altered considerably and when United States willingness to stand by its commitment to the Nationalist government may, in Sino-Soviet eyes, be worth testing again? Worse still, if one assumes a United States withdrawal from its commitments to the Nationalist government on Taiwan, such Soviet support of a renewed Peking offensive could be offered with less risk and might well be decisive. If the United States has "de-recognized" the Nationalist government on Taiwan and invalidated the security treaty, a Taiwan venture by Peking with Moscow backing could become the starting point in a new phase in Sino-Soviet cooperation. It is in this light that the United States government should weigh its decision on the conditions for normalization of United States relations with Peking.

These then are the realities of the situation that the United States must face in devising its China policy. What is to be done? On the negative side, if Moscow and Peking decide on a rapprochement there is very little the United States can do to keep the two apart. Those who speak of the concept of balance of power normally conceive of a three- or four-power system in northeast Asia, and count on the "national interests" of the two Communist countries to make such a system function. In the view of this author, this is nineteenth-century thinking. The balance of power concept is related to the politics of a past world, the Western international system, essentially limited to state-to-state relations. The Thirty Years War that initiated this new system ended with a detente, a detente that included an "ideological" detente. The famous principle of *eius regio, cuius religio* meant non-interference in each other's internal ideological affairs; and this was the basis of international law and international agreements, including the well-known agreements of the Congress of Vienna. Balance of power systems, therefore, can work even if the participating states have conflicting interests if they accept the basic international order and its rules.

This is no longer the case. Since the advent of international communism with its international movements and its propagation of revolutionary wars and wars of national liberation in disregard of international rules and without ideological detente, the concept of the balance of power has become largely obsolete. Ideological warfare, political warfare, psychological warfare, and international movements have become major aspects of global politics in the twentieth century. Ideological detente has been expressly excluded by the USSR from the ongoing negotiations between the Soviet Union and the United States. To deal with the Moscow-Peking relationship in purely military terms or as a matter of relations between states concerned with their assumed "national interests" misjudges the underlying factors in relations within the Communist world and in particular misunderstands the issues that have caused the Sino-Soviet conflict and affect the possibility of a reconciliation. It was to our benefit, particularly in the Vietnam situation, to attempt to take advantage of the Sino-Soviet conflict. But the suggestion, for instance, that the United States attempt to influence Peking's basic policy vis-à-vis the Soviet Union by political accommodations or military support is predicated on the belief that traditional state interests completely transcend ideological interests in the foreign policies of Communist states. It ignores the need to remember that intra-Communist relations are based on common ideological goals, and the need to understand the Sino-Soviet dispute as a new type of fraternal rivalry within the Communist order.

It is the traditional interpretation of international relations that has led to the argument that the United States could exert influence on Peking by a variey of political and territorial concessions and by the establishment of full diplomatic relations. The slogan for this policy is that the "normalization of relations" between Washington and Peking, initiated in the Shanghai Communique following former President Nixon's visit to Peking in 1971, must be completed. It has never been made clear what "complete normalization" was supposed to mean and what obligation, if any, the administration of former President Nixon assumed. On the face of it, all that was said in the Shanghai Communique was that the United States took note of the view held by both Peking and Taipei that there was only one China, of which Taiwan was a part. There was no promise—at least no open promise—by the United States to recognize only the People's Republic of China and to abandon the Republic of China in order to complete normalization. In fact, the continued United States obligation to the government of the Republic of China was reasserted at the time in Dr. Kissinger's press conference in Shanghai and in former President Nixon's promise that the United States would "not abandon old friends." Even if the former president or Dr. Kissinger should have secretly promised a move towards "derecognition" of the Nationalist government on Taiwan, no later administration in the United States is bound by any such personal promise. On the other hand, since the Shanghai Communique there has been an exchange of missions between Washington and Peking, establishing full diplomatic relations in everything except in name. There is no obstacle to "normalizing" this relationship by raising Peking's mission to formal embassy status while continuing to deal with both the People's Republic of China and the Republic of China. The precedent is the establishment of such diplomatic relations with both East and West Germany. It is not "normalization" that is an issue, but Peking's demand that the United States should break relations with the Republic of China as a condition for formal diplomatic relations. There is no obligation to do so. All diplomatic and military wisdom weighs against such an appeasement, which would compromise disastrously the United States position in northeast Asia.

Such a move would also run counter to United States public opinion that in the final analysis is the foundation of United States foreign policy. Repeated opinion polls have indicated that a large majority of the American people, while willing to accept full recognition of the People's Republic, is opposed to sacrificing Taiwan. The argument has therefore been made that United States acceptance of Peking's demand for derecognition would not mean abandoning Taiwan, if it could be linked with a "tacit" promise by the People's Republic of China not to use force in the process of "liberating" Taiwan. What guarantee such a "tacit" promise would provide is difficult to imagine. To help support this precarious argument it has sometimes been claimed that Peking is militarily in no position to use force against Taiwan. This is at best wishful thinking; once the United States has given up recognition of the Republic of China and the defense treaty, there is no obstacle to Peking's military action, the use of tactical nuclear weapons not ex-cluded—although to be sure the defensive capabilities of Taiwan should not be underestimated. Should military action against determined na-tional resistance on Taiwan prove difficult, an economic blockade of Taiwan, with which the United States would have some difficulty cop-ing, could be disastrous for Taiwan. Indeed the legal and political consequences of a United States abrogation of its treaties with the Republic of China appear not to have been thought through, let alone taken into serious consideration.

Equally fallacious is the assumption that such action would endear the United States to Peking or enable the United States to influence Peking's policy decisions on relations with the Soviet Union. On the contrary, the weaker the United States proves to be, the less restraint she will be able to exercise over Peking's actions. Once the United States position on Taiwan has been abandoned, Peking can reunite with Moscow in a new political marriage, and a part of the marriage contract might even be Moscow's support of Peking's "liberation" of Taiwan. In that case a United States retreat from our Taiwan obligation would be our dowry to the reunited couple. If the United States has any leverage at all that would cause Peking some hesitation in moving toward a re-alignment with the fraternal Communist power, it would come from a strong United States military position within reach of the Chinese shores, and not from a retreat and weakening of the United States position in northeast Asia, nor from a "friendly" gesture that would have little im-pact on the power-conscious Peking realists. If the United States yields to Peking's pressure and surrenders its alliance with the Republic of China, it more than likely would have the opposite effect from that pro-claimed by the advocates of "full normalization."

United States security as well as the stability of northeast Asia has in the eyes of past and present administrations depended on the alli-ance with Japan, as "the anchor" of our regional position. If so, the security of Japan, in turn, depends on the security of South Korea and of Taiwan. A loss of either of these countries to communism would constitute, in the Japanese view, a most serious threat to her security.

Alarmed by the uncertainty of the United States position on South Korea and Taiwan, Japanese spokesmen have openly expressed their anxiety over weakening United States resolve to maintain its commitments in northeast Asia. Former Foreign Minister Miazawa Kiichi stated to Senator Mansfield his concern about a possible United States recognition of Peking at the expense of Taiwan, remarking that the so-called Japanese model of shifting recognition from the Republic of China to the People's Republic of China could not be regarded as precedent for the United States, because Japan provided no guarantee for the security of Taiwan. This statement still stands. For Japan, the United States guarantee means not only the so-called nuclear umbrella —our willingness to risk our own cities in defense of Japan—but also the United States protection of the security of the sea lanes on which Japan's essential energy resources, her trade, and her whole economic survival depend. A glance at the map will show the danger that would be posed to Japan's lifeline if Taiwan were in Communist hands. The Japanese tankers that pass along the western coast of Taiwan sail in a continuous procession almost in sight of each other. Taiwan's location at the edge of the continental shelf would make her an ideal blind for hostile submarines assuming a threatening position against Japanese sea lines of communication.

From the point of view of United States security and that of the allies on whom United States security depends, United States policy ought to make certain that as we reach out into the hazardous world of negotiations with potential Communist adversaries we will not abandon our traditional commitments to friends and allies. The United States role as power broker has not increased the confidence of friends and allies. The United States has lost considerable credibility and trust in the wake of the weakness and retreat characteristic of United States Asian policy over the last decade. We have to assert most emphatically that we are loyal to our commitments and alliances, and that behind these commitments and alliances are principles for which we stand and which are more lasting and permanent than the doctrinal assertions of the Marxist-Leninist world. United States relations with both Peking and Taiwan will be a test case both of our Asian policy and of United States credibility and willingness to stand by its commitments.

Chapter Ten

The United States in Asia: A Forward Strategy in the Pacific Basin

Alan Ned Sabrosky

THE AMERICAN RECORD: POWER AND PURPOSE IN ASIA

Few Americans can contemplate with equanimity the future role of the United States in the Pacific Basin. In some respects, of course, the American attitude toward Asia always has been ambivalent, reflecting a complex blend of self-confidence and insecurity. Even the unprecedented degree of United States military and political involvement in Asia following World War II did not represent the pursuit of a clearly defined set of goals in that region.[1] Instead, it occurred in conjunction with the general expansion of American influence in the postwar world,[2] and specifically with the globalization of the Cold War prompted by the Communist invasion of South Korea in 1950.

The importance of the fact that the American presence in Asia over the past three decades has been largely a function of global geopolitical considerations cannot be overestimated. Perhaps the most significant implication of this circumstance is that the United States has tended to define its interests in Asia in global rather than regional-specific terms. Thus, the primary American interest there has been to prevent any single state or coalition from gaining control of the resources of Asia,[3] and thereby upsetting the global balance of power. All other American interests in the Pacific Basin have been of only secondary importance.[4] Yet this has presented the United States with a fundamental problem. Those areas in which conflict was most likely to occur all too often could be linked only indirectly, and therefore unper-

199

suasively, to the maintenance of the global balance of power. It therefore became necessary for this country to apply to Asia a doctrine that would legitimize a major American involvement in areas, and over issues, whose intrinsic value to the United States might be very slight indeed.

Since 1950, the United States has adopted three principal approaches in its effort to explain—and justify—its involvement in Asia. For nearly two decades after the onset of the Korean War, the doctrine of containment provided the basic theoretical rationale for American participation in Asian affairs.[5] The central characteristic of this doctrine was the belief that the stability of the regional and global balances of power required the United States to oppose any Communist state that pursued an expansionist policy. According to a derivative of this doctrine, the so-called domino theory, security was indivisible. A threat to one state was a threat to all, and the loss of a single additional state to communism would set off a chain reaction that ultimately would topple other states as well.[6] Seen in this light, the Vietnam War was not a "dangerous deviation" from a more modest Asian policy to which this country could, and should, return, as some observers have asserted.[7] Far from being an aberration, the costly and frustrating American intervention in Indochina was a logical consequence of a foreign policy predicated on the global containment of communism.

By 1968, the impasse in Vietnam had become all too apparent. The following year, with a new administration in power, the United States began searching for another doctrine to replace the then discredited doctrine of containment. The new American strategy was embodied first in the Nixon (or Nixon-*Kissinger*) Doctrine, entailing "detente among the great powers ... combined with ... supremacy over most of the rest."[8] Essentially, the Nixon Doctrine was an attempt to bring American objectives more into line with American capabilities, thereby gaining for the United States an added measure of diplomatic maneuverability while we disengaged from Vietnam.[9] Washington would assist its allies in Asia to defend themselves. Direct American military intervention on their behalf, however, was likely only under the most extreme circumstances—and, as the South Vietnamese and Cambodians learned in 1975, perhaps not even then.

Less than a year after the inadequacies of the Nixon Doctrine were highlighted with stark clarity in Indochina, President Ford announced the so-called Pacific Doctrine. Even more than its predecessor, this doctrine was Kissinger's work; not surprisingly, it renounced none of the key tenets of the Nixon Doctrine. Yet it did convey an impression of a somewhat more active and determined American security role in Asia than was envisioned under the Nixon Doctrine itself, despite the withdrawal of American combat forces from Southeast Asia.[10]

Whatever their deficiencies (and they were many), the two post-containment strategies did at least provide some theoretical foundations on which a more realistic United States policy for Asia might have been built. Unfortunately, what once was seen as an area of opportunity has come to be viewed in some circles as a highly competitive and largely unfriendly arena, in which success is increasingly elusive. This has made many Americans reluctant to support an assertive foreign policy in Asia, despite the continuing importance of that region to the United States.[11]

Three principal developments have contributed to this shift in the American perspective on Asia. First, and of greatest significance, was the collapse of three decades of American policy in the wreckage of Indochina in the spring of 1975. However legitimate it might have been, the unsuccessful American intervention in Southeast Asia was widely seen to have marked the high point of the *Pax Americana*, with consequences whose full measure is still to be taken.[12] Second, there was the incontestable growth of Soviet and, further back, Chinese power, due in no small part to the dissipation of American resources and political will during the Indochina misadventure. This development has called into question the stability of both global and Asian balances of power based essentially on United States strategic superiority.[13] Finally, the appearance of a number of political and economic problems within the United States and other Western nations cast doubt on the long-term cohesion and capabilities of the American-led coalition. The fact that a number of this country's allies in Asia and elsewhere also are ruled by authoritarian regimes has decreased their legitimacy in the eyes of many Americans, thereby inhibiting effective cooperation between those countries and the United States.[14]

The net effect of these developments has been to underscore the passing of American paramountcy, throw the Asian balance of power into a state of flux, and add a substantial degree of uncertainty to regional affairs as each nation there reassesses its options in light of the changing circumstances.[15] Most Asian states clearly appear to place far less reliance on American commitments to them than once was the case, despite Washington's reassurances.[16] In addition, many questions have been asked, and too few persuasive answers provided, with respect to the definition of legitimate and defensible American interests and objectives in the Pacific Basin. But of far greater significance is the fact that the increasing stature of regional powers such as China and Japan, plus the expanding global reach of the Soviet Union, limits the ability of a trans-Pacific power such as the United States to pursue successfully an independent foreign policy in Asia.[17] At the very least, what is decided in Moscow, Peking, and Tokyo will in the future have far more impact on the course of Asian international politics than would have been possible if the United States had won in Vietnam.

THE SOVIET UNION AND THE PEOPLE'S REPUBLIC OF CHINA: RIVALS IN COMPETITION WITH THE U.S.

The USSR: In Quest of Paramountcy

In some respects, the Soviet Union and the United States have similar concerns in Asia. Both states are global powers, with global interests to safeguard. Thus, what each does in Asia must be seen in a global context, and the relative success or failure of a given policy must be assessed in considerable measure in terms of its impact on each state's position in the world at large.[18] Unlike the United States, however, the Soviet Union is geographically part of Asia. Thus, its goal in that region is not merely a matter of preserving or extending a sphere of influence. It is also a question of maintaining the territorial integrity of its Asiatic provinces. This is a mixed blessing for Moscow. The possession of bases and lines of communication adjacent to the principal areas of contention does give the Soviet Union an added measure of tactical flexibility, political leverage, and staying power in a protracted conflict in the region. But that same proximity also means that the USSR is more vulnerable, and has less strategic flexibility, than the United States. In a worst-case analysis, for example, the United States —faced with the collapse of its entire Asian policy—at least has the option of withdrawing to a less exposed line of defense, or even going home (whatever the long-term consequences of that step might be). Under similar circumstances, the Soviet Union has no such option. It cannot disengage easily from a major confrontation without increasing the risk to its own territory, something it is most unlikely to do.

What sets the Soviet Union apart from the United States the most, however, is the fact that the USSR, unlike the United States, is an expanding power. This is reflected in a number of ways, not least of which are the Soviet views on detente and the Soviet assessment of the proper role of military force in world politics. Unless one is willing to discount the entire body of Soviet writing on the subject, the Soviet leadership is convinced that the global and regional "correlation of forces" has shifted in favor of the USSR.[19] Needless to say, this does not augur well for the future of American relations with Moscow, at least from the perspective of the United States.

For the USSR, the principal regional objective is the creation and maintenance of a new balance of power in Asia that enhances the role of the USSR, alters and restricts American and Chinese influence, and disengages Japan from its alliance with the United States.[20] In many respects, of course, to speak of Soviet policy in Asia is to speak of Soviet policy toward China. The USSR's greatest long-term concern is that a de facto Sino-Japanese-American axis directed against the Soviet Union might, as one observer already has suggested, take shape.[21] For the present, the USSR must at least minimize Peking's hostility to itself, or—failing that—work for the political isolation and military containment of China.

To date, Moscow's record in Asia is far from an unblemished string of successes. On balance, however, it must be conceded that the Soviet Union has been able to establish and maintain a respectable presence there.[22] By assuming a relatively low profile in the area and adopting a cautious Asian policy, the Soviet Union has gained more in Asia than it has lost, if only because its principal competitor for global influence—the United States—has had the opposite experience. The USSR continues to pursue a policy of minimum direct involvement while hawking its still unpopular concept of an Asian collective security system.[23] Such an approach does not suggest that striking successes are in the offing, but it does ensure that whatever gains are realized in Asia by the USSR will be achieved at relatively low cost and with little risk to its own vital interests. All things considered, it is an approach that the United States itself might once have been well advised to have adopted.

China: The Principal Regional Adversary

As the chapter on China[24] indicates all too clearly, the "Middle Kingdom" of Asia is both an enigma and a problem. China's basic strategic requirement is to pursue a foreign policy that capitalizes on the gains it has made to date, while minimizing the danger of incurring significant setbacks in its more vulnerable areas.[25] China clearly sees itself as the model for the new world order it believes to be emerging, with the PRC acting as the de facto leader of a composite Third World center of power.[26] In a sense, Peking believes that it must simply bide its time until its full power is realized, while its adversaries are weakened through internecine war or as a consequence of their internal contradictions.[27]

Given this perspective, it is not surprising that China has pursued a relatively conservative foreign policy. A state whose leadership is convinced of its country's ultimate success has little reason to risk everything for short-term gains. If Chinese foreign policy has a single operational principle, it is to prevent the formation of a major-power coalition against it. So long as the Soviet-American Cold War continued, that possibility did not exist, even though China might have only poor relations with both superpowers. If one's enemies are also enemies, a coalition cannot form easily.

With the apparent waning of Soviet-American hostility, however, a different policy was required to stave off what China saw as a deliberate (if uncoordinated) attempt to encircle it.[28] First, China modified its earlier Manichaean view of the world to accommodate a "Second Intermediate Zone" composed of all industrial states other than the Soviet Union and the United States, arguing that such states had more in common with China and the Third World than they did with the superpowers.[29] Second, using the standard Communist practice of aligning oneself with secondary adversaries in order to ward off or destroy a more immediate threat, China moved to improve its relations with the United States, even to the point of supporting a continuation of the American military presence in Asia.[30] Finally, China continued its earlier practice of improving governmental relations with other countries, especially in Southeast Asia, while simultaneously encouraging and supporting insurgent movements in most of them.[31]

This situation has produced a paradox in Asian affairs. On the one hand, China does seem genuinely concerned about being encircled. In a sense, this is not surprising. Given the Chinese Communist world view and long-term objectives, the Chinese leadership must find it difficult to believe that rational governments in other countries would *not* combine against it. For their part, most Asian nations of any political complexion are clearly apprehensive about the consequences of a continued growth in Chinese power for their own security and well-being.[32] Unfortunately for them, there is no certainty that any Asian state, or even one of the superpowers, could preclude further Chinese growth without resorting to nuclear war—and, perhaps, not even then. China's nuclear capability cannot be dismissed out of hand; its conventional forces, although unimpressive by NATO and Warsaw Pact standards, are suited sufficiently well for the type of defense China would be conducting that their strength should not be underestimated; and China's economic potential as a major oil producer of the 1980s gives it a degree of economic leverage that may alter radically the entire range of Asian international politics.[33]

It is, of course, far from certain that China will realize its ambitions. The difficulties inherent in the long-term resolution of the Chinese political succession are substantial, with significant implications for international affairs.[34] Whether the present government represents a viable successor to Mao-Tse-tung, or simply an interregnum of aging leaders acting as caretakers pending the accession of a more stable regime, cannot be ascertained with precision. It does seem that the more radical faction that had advocated recurrent upheavals such as the Great Proletarian Cultural Revolution of the 1960s is unlikely again to become dominant. Yet the likelihood that the ensuing Chinese regime may not be of the radical Maoist faction does not necessarily augur well for the United States and its Asian allies. China might acquire a relatively moderate, pragmatic government that would play a balancing role among the major powers. But it may also produce a PLA-heavy regime more inclined toward detente with the Soviet Union than toward accommodation with the United States,[35] even if there is no resurgent radical-heavy regime likely to forego detente with both superpowers. Needless to say, neither of these outcomes would be in the American interest.

Second, China's growing nuclear capability remains something of a double-edged sword, at least for the near future. On the one hand, China's possession of even a nominal nuclear capability may well have given the USSR reason to pause during those periods when influential circles in the Kremlin were arguing for a surgical nuclear strike against China.[36] That capability may even have provided China with a measure of prestige as a power with which to be reckoned. But that same capability also has created apprehension in many parts of Asia concerning Chinese intentions. Peking's claims to the contrary notwithstanding, most nations find it difficult to imagine a state acquiring a major nuclear capability and then declining to translate that capability into political influence. The Chinese nuclear program also has forced the Soviet leadership to acknowledge that the continued growth of Chinese nuclear capabilties will work to the disadvantage of the USSR under virtually any forseeable circumstances. The Soviet Union simply cannot look with equanimity on the continued rise of Chinese power, regardless of which faction rules in Peking. The rise of any powerful new competitors inevitably must detract from Soviet freedom of action in Asia. It would be unrealistic for China to assume that the USSR would acquiesce willingly in such a development.

The Sino-Soviet Dispute and the United States
Finally, there is the pervasive question of the outcome of the Sino-Soviet dispute itself. The present Asian Cold War is being waged by the two major Communist powers, with the United States observing but not participating.[37] As a consequence, neither Communist power appears to desire a reincarnation of the earlier confrontation with the United States, at least at this time. Both the Soviet Union and China are too concerned with one another now to wish to be so distracted. The Sino-Soviet confrontation clearly is the most war prone of the disputes among the major powers. The impressive Soviet military presence along the Sino-Soviet border, its still active alliances in Asia, the rise of Soviet influence in the newly unified Communist Vietnam, and the continuing Soviet effort to create an implicitly anti-Chinese "collective se-

curity" arrangement in Asia all attest to Moscow's efforts to contain the
growth of Chinese influence. The possibility that China's support of the
Vietnamese Communists may turn out to have been a colossal blunder,
should the USSR gain access to the excellent American-built bases in
Vietnam while still hostile to China, must haunt Peking.

In general, prospects for a Sino-Soviet reconciliation are not favorable for the immediate future. Long-term prospects for a detente between them may be somewhat better, although even then the Sino-
Soviet alliance is unlikely to be restored.[38] The peculiar intractability of
ideological disputes in particular cannot be a comfort to the leadership
of either state. Under the People's Republic of China, the East may
well become Red, but it is unlikely to be of a shade that will bring
relief to the Kremlin. There may even be a sense of grim irony in
both Peking and Moscow over their seemingly irreconcilable dispute.
We in the West sometimes assume that a general war between China
and the USSR would work against our interests.[39] Yet it may be that
the territorial, political, and ideological differences that divide the two
Communist powers will deny both of them the ultimate hegemony each
believes to be its due, thereby giving the victory to the "capitalist-
imperialist" West by default.

JAPAN: PRESENT ALLY, FUTURE RIVAL?
In some respects, Japan is more of an enigma than any other state in
Asia. Few would deny the importance of that country to the stability
of the Asian balance of power. Most recognize that the alliance between
the United States and Japan has been both the cornerstone of the
American position in the Pacific Basin and the principal determinant
of Japanese foreign policy since the end of World War II.[40] Yet at the
same time, Americans and Japanese alike have become increasingly
uncertain about the role that Japan can, or should, play in the future.
Some observers, remarking on the impressive size of the Japanese
economy and the likelihood that such economic power will eventually
be translated into political influence, have suggested that Japan will
become one of the superstates of the future.[41] Others, noting the military weakness of Japan, as well as its economic dependence on foreign
markets and raw materials, have described that country as a "fragile
blossom."[42] Ironically, both views may be correct. That is, Japan may

be at present a "fragile blossom" that, if it expands its power and influence more rapidly than pressures on its vulnerable areas increase, may well join the United States and the Soviet Union in the first rank of global powers in the future.

For the present, however, one thing is certain. Japanese foreign policy is now in a period of reassessment.[43] The alliance with the United States is itself being scrutinized, in part because American overtures to China and the Soviet Union have raised questions in Japan about the reliability of the American commitment to that country, in part because of the developments in world affairs indicated earlier, and in part because the need for American protection has declined along with its credibility.[44] What decisions Japan will eventually make on this point will depend in large measure on the degree to which Japan remains willing to rely on a foreign power for its own security, relative to its desire to play a greater part in the fundamental political and military aspects of world politics.[45]

The difficulties encountered by Japan in its search for a new, or at least more defensible, role are likely to be compounded by a number of external and internal constraints. Perhaps the most fundamental external constraint is that Japan is an economic power in a world of military powers, less able to defend its own interests than even the European community, and all too conscious of its very real vulnerability to coercion if left to its own devices.[46] Japan is also the possessor of a set of attributes that inhibit its ability to pursue independently a more assertive policy. First of all, Japan is a large, politically dissatisfied nation that, like France, has never quite adjusted to a more vulnerable position in world politics than it occupied before World War II. Its desire to reassume at least some measure of its former stature has never been discounted entirely, either in Japan or in the rest of Asia. Second, like other resource-poor and industry-rich nations such as Great Britain, Japan is vulnerable to the external interdiction of its vital lines of communication to a degree greater than that of continental nations. This requires it to have either an independent capability to ensure access to necessary resources, or an ally that can fulfill that function reliably. Finally, there is the recognition that any increase in Japanese power or status, much less the adoption of a more activist foreign policy, would raise *very* great concerns throughout Asia that might run counter to Japan's best interests. Like the Germans in Europe, the Japanese are disliked, mistrusted, and envied throughout much of Asia. This is due in part to the events attending World War II, in part because of Japan's own variant of an economic miracle in a region where such miracles are all too rare, and in part because of what some Asians perceive as Japanese cultural arrogance.

Internally, Japan is a psychologically fragmented society that suffered a major cultural shock with its defeat in 1945, yet seems not to have altered its entire set of traditional values. At some point in the future, Japan may experience a partial return to its prewar values, with an assertive nationalism taking the place of an acquiescent internationalism in key circles. Psychological determinants of foreign policy are always important, of course, and psychological moods are essentially unstable phenomena.[47] Yet in the case of Japan, these factors are extremely important and unusually volatile, despite the fact that they are all too often underestimated or misunderstood in analyses of Japanese foreign relations.[48]

Perhaps the most important question, given the above considerations, is what Japan might do if it chose to modify its present role in world affairs. No consensus on what, if anything, Japan *should* do has yet been reached. A number of different courses of action are open to that country if it chooses to follow a different course in international politics.[49] Lacking a reliable American ally, however, only two basic options seem feasible, barring an unlikely decision to accept indefinite dependence on the goodwill of other states. That is, Japan could: (1) seek another ally, or (2) pursue an independent course of action.

The only other states in Asia able to give Japan some added measure of security as an ally are the Soviet Union and China. Some change in Japan's relationship with both of those countries might well obtain, particularly if there is a continuation of some form of detente between the United States and its principal Communist rivals, and at least no further deterioration in the state of Sino-Soviet relations.[50] It has been suggested, in fact, that it might be to the advantage of Japan as well as the other major powers if Sino-Japanese relations in particular improved, even to the point of joint nuclear cooperation between the two countries.[51] Such a development, however, seems unlikely to occur, and highly destabilizing if it were to take place. It would be more to

Japan's advantage to maintain equally good relations with both Peking and Moscow, perhaps acting as a balancer between them, than to align itself with one of them and thereby incur the overt hostility of the other.[52] This would hold even if Japan continued to adhere to its alliance with the United States. For a Japan following a more independent course, however, such prudence would be essential.

Precisely what such an independent course would entail is the crux of the matter. It has been suggested that "[an] independent Japan could become a stronger ally for the United States."[53] Yet this would be true only if such a Japan were still militarily dependent on the United States, and thus still subject to an American veto if its policies diverged too far from what Washington considered to be desirable. To adopt such a policy would require Japan to recognize that it would continue to deal with both allies and adversaries from a position of weakness in any situation where important interests of the contending powers were at stake.[54] Such a halfway house would be unacceptable to any state that had determined not to allow its foreign policy to be subordinated, in whole or in part, to the wishes of a foreign power.

What must therefore be recognized is that the shift in public and elite attitudes that would be required for Japan to decide to pursue a significantly more independent role in world affairs almost certainly also would entail an equivalent rearmament of Japan, *including the acquisition of nuclear weapons.* Anything less would not achieve the guarantee of autonomy that a truly independent Japan would seek. Few subjects are likely to be as controversial within Japan, or as significant outside that country, as a decision to acquire nuclear weapons. There is little doubt that the Japanese have the capability to deploy an impressive nuclear capability within a relatively short time, once the decision was made to do so.[55] It is too often overlooked that, as one writer has noted, Japan's determination to forego acquiring an independent nuclear capability is not irrevocable.[56] Once that determination was set aside, many of the existing preconceptions about Japan likewise would have to be discarded.

On balance, it seems that Japan is likely to be reentering world affairs in the near future on a considerably more active scale than at any time since the end of World War II. It would be most unwise to think of the Japanese as a pacified people who will acquiesce indefinitely in a subordinate role. A more assertive Japan could be either a stabilizing or a destabilizing factor in Asian affairs, at least in theory. In practice, however, the attitudinal change that would prompt the adoption of a more assertive role by a rearmed Japan, with or without its acquisition of nuclear weapons, suggests that an activist Japan would be more interested in securing national objectives than in perpetuating what would have come to be seen in Tokyo as a constricting regional balance of power.[57] Unfortunately, there is no sound reason to assume that a militarily strong and independent Japan would be either inherently neutral or an American ally. On the contrary: perhaps Washington's only consolation, should Japan adopt such a course of action, is the certainty that a better-armed and more assertive Japan would be a greater concern to China and the Soviet Union than the United States.

WHAT IS TO BE DONE?

Faced with the need to organize effectively to overcome major obstacles to success, Lenin asked: "What is to be done?" Unlike many who pose such a question to themselves and others, Lenin provided an answer. Having described the situation in which the United States finds itself, and having delineated weaknesses in past policies that must be avoided in the future, we must ask the same question. All too often, however, otherwise sophisticated analyses end with the recommendation that the United States do more of the same, or asume a lower profile to present less of a target to its opponents. And in fact, few expect any significant change in American policy in Asia from the present administration.[58]

This, in my opinion, is utterly unacceptable. From the preceding discussion, it is all too apparent that the situation now emerging in the Pacific Basin is both complex and challenging. It must be conceded that the American ability to influence events in Asia has been diminished by both global and regional developments of the past decade. American assets are still substantial, but so are American liabilities. Our capabilities have decreased, both absolutely and in relation to our adversaries and our allies. Our principal rivals are more confident of themselves, our principal allies are more assertive, and our smaller allies and clients are much less certain of the constancy of

Washington, should war occur, than once was the case. The all too apparent absence of any clear sense of direction and priorities in the American government inhibits corrective action, while the uncertainties attending the current state of affairs in Asia preclude a clear and easy solution to the American dilemma.

One thing, however, is clear: a continuation of existing trends cannot be tolerated. Otherwise, the dominant characteristic of the next decades could well be the terminal contraction of American influence in Asia, and possibly elsewhere as well. Interests are not maintained, influence is not exerted, and security is not guaranteed by a policy of phased withdrawal, no matter how adroitly the recessional is managed.

In Search of a Policy

There is, admittedly, no dearth of proposals in the literature on how the United States should deal with its Asian challenge. A broad range of policy alternatives has been suggested, reflecting different degrees of reliance on military power, formal alliances, interactions with other regional states, and direct United States involvement in Asian affairs.[59] Some assert that this country should rely in large measure on a quadrilateral Sino-Soviet Japanese-American balance of power to provide a needed measure of stability in Asia.[60] Others argue that the United States should concentrate on creating a trilateral "united front" of the United States, Western Europe, and Japan that would place the resources of a global coalition at the service of any of its threatened regional members.[61] Some recommend reducing the traditional reliance on military power and formal security alliances, concentrating instead on promoting the establishment of regional collective defense pacts that specifically exclude the major powers in any capacity.[62] With few exceptions, it is also recognized that unless the United States is willing to become irrelevant in Asia, outright withdrawal is not feasible.

Underlying most of the different approaches is a clear, if often implicit, recognition of a fundamental dilemma confronting the United States. The more this country disengages militarily from its commitments to the non-Communist states of Asia, the more freedom of action it will acquire vis-à-vis the Communist states, and the less likely it will be to become involved in another potentially frustrating land war in that region. Yet that same disengagement may facilitate the further rise of power centers potentially hostile to the United States, or contribute to the outbreak of a war in some part of Asia that might have been averted had the onshore American deterrent still been in place.

In many respects, the principal distinction among the different policy alternatives is not so much *what* ought to be done—it is with which states America should combine, and in what fashion, to maximize its prospects for success. Each of the possible alternatives has at least some theoretical merit, yet most are substantively flawed. The ineffectiveness of regional defense pacts that lack a major power guarantor is too great for them to serve as surrogates for an active American foreign policy in the region.[63] It is also both inaccurate and misleading to describe the emerging order in Asia as a balance of power system. To do so presupposes the existence of a basic community of interests among the four principal regional powers, plus a common willingness to promote a peaceful regional order, that is simply not in evidence.[64] Nor is the trilateralist approach more promising, as one scholar recently pointed out with forceful clarity.[65] Despite the existence of some common interests (largely economic) among the three core members of such a grouping, the likelihood that they would be willing to conduct joint action on one another's behalf on political-military issues of immediate concern to only one of them is extremely low. All things considered, the United States is unlikely to be able, in Canningesque fashion, to call into being either a global trilateral concert or an Asian quadrilateral balance of power in order to compensate for this country's decline as the principal guarantor of regional stability.

"Lessons" of the Past

Despite the all-too-clear deficiencies in American policy in Asia in the past, there is no need for any future American policy to overlook what lessons can be learned from that experience. That is, before one can prescribe what the United States can, or at least should, do in Asia, we must come to terms with what we neither can nor should attempt to undertake.

Perhaps the first point that must be understood is that long-term accommodation between the United States and either China or the Soviet Union is unlikely either to occur or to be of much benefit to the United States in Asia. China in particular pursues a form of detente with the United States only because of its fear of the Soviet Union. Thus, the ending of the Sino-Soviet rift likely would end Sino-American (and possibly Soviet-American) detente, with serious consequences for the American position in the Pacific Basin. Assertions that the United States ought to institutionalize its relationship with China in order to counter Soviet policy in Asia[66] are therefore fundamentally misguided, whatever their theoretical appeal. China, like the USSR, is fundamentally hostile to the United States and its non-Communist allies, and analyses that choose to overlook this point simply do not come to terms with political reality.[67] Even without an accommodation between Moscow and Peking, however, there is little to be gained from sacrificing American allies or interests to either Communist power in hopes of earning a nonexistent goodwill from them. Such gratuitous gestures are all too likely to be self-defeating in the long term. They create an impression of weakness and uncertainty, give up something that we have while receiving nothing in return, and risk upsetting what may be a stable, if wearisome, situation. There may be little objective point to retaining an alliance with Taiwan, for example, but there is even less reason to abandon that pact. Recognizing the PRC would gain us little that we do not now have. Cutting loose yet another American client in Asia would not enhance the reliability of American guarantees abroad. Similarly, any withdrawal of American ground forces from South Korea would only increase the danger of war in that area, reduce American leverage over the South Korean government and American credibility with our other Asian allies, and perhaps give additional impetus to Japanese rearmament. None of these developments would be desirable from the American perspective, and no policy that might lead to any of them ought to be adopted.

Second, we must recognize that we are most unlikely to be able to pursue simultaneously detente with the Soviet Union and China on the one hand, and policies intended to promote the cohesion of our alliances on the other. To be sure, it has often been argued that some type of accommodation with China and the Soviet Union is not only essential, but also compatible with a strong system of alliances.[68] Yet there is little doubt that the very success of negotiations between Western nations and the Communist states undermines the basic sense of purpose of a Western alliance system predicated on the existence of a Communist threat to the well-being of its members.[69] Accordingly, a realistic future American policy will have to choose between: (1) a precarious detente with China, the Soviet Union, or both powers at the expense of a weakened network of United States–centered alliances; and (2) a stronger Western alliance system in Asia (and elsewhere) at the risk of some deterioration in American relations with one or both major Communist states.

Third, the American experience in Vietnam underscored the lesson that *some* people had learned from the earlier Korean conflict: the United States cannot wage a limited protracted war on the Asian mainland with any significant hope of success. This is not because military power is no longer useful as an instrument of policy (at least for the United States) in regional conflicts, as some have suggested.[70] On the contrary, it can be argued persuasively that whatever stability is likely to obtain in Asia will do so largely as a function of the continued presence there of American military capabilities.[71] Nor is it that such an intervention is politically unthinkable, at least in terms of mustering the initial electoral support for such a war. After the Korean conflict, for example, it was frequently said that the United States would never again wage a limited war in Asia.[72] But memories are short, and a decade later the United States did precisely that in an even more remote part of Asia called Vietnam. Thus, it is possible that in a decade or so, memories of the Vietnam experience would have faded sufficiently to support the initiation of another such venture. Yet any support of that kind would be deceptive. For it is all too clear that popular support for a limited war in Asia cannot be maintained in an open society such as ours for the length of time necessary to win it. Accordingly, any policy that relies on the American ability to wage limited war on the Asian mainland is not viable.

Finally, we must recognize that strengthening the military power of the PRC (much less that of the USSR!) via the transfer of military or computer technology is inherently counterproductive. So long as the Sino-Soviet rift continues, a stronger China might well constrain Soviet influence in Asia, as a number of the proponents of such transfers have suggested.[73] But a China that was better able to defend itself against the Soviet Union also would be a China better able to exert itself in Asian affairs against pro-Western or neutral states, if not against the United States directly. Moreover, the ending of the Sino-Soviet rift—a possibility that proponents of American defense aid to the PRC conveniently seem to overlook—would place the United States and whatever allies still remained aligned with it in a difficult and embarrassing situation. For they would face not only a Soviet Union no longer distracted by China, but also a China made stronger by the very nation against which it would now be directing its augmented power. No realistic person can look at the character of the Chinese regime, regardless of which faction rules in Peking, much less the foreign policy goals accepted by most Chinese of any political faction, and still believe that it is in our long-term interest to contribute to the strengthening of a state whose future status is predicated on America's departure as a power of any consequence in Asia.

Toward a Forward Strategy

Given these considerations, what *is* to be done? All of the "grand designs" of America's Asian policy, from the doctrine of containment to the search for a quadrilateral balance of power, have a single common flaw. *Each conceded the strategic initiative to our principal geopolitical and ideological opponents.* Such forbearance may be admirable in terms of abstract ethics. But in the realm of practical international politics, it is tantamount to conceding eventual strategic success to those opponents, since it is left to them to determine the time and place at which challenges to the existing order will be made. When the United States had a clear margin of nuclear superiority over the USSR, that flaw nonetheless contributed to a weakening of the Western coalition over time. Now that the nuclear balance has shifted, such a flaw could prove fatal in Asia as well as in other parts of the world.

What is obviously needed is a replacement for the earlier doctrines that provides a more flexible, yet equally coherent, framework for United States policy, reassuring American allies while permitting a reassertion of United States influence in the Pacific Basin. Under the present circumstances, an approach once described as a "forward strategy"[74] seems particularly appropriate. Essentially, this entails rejecting a passive, defensive posture for an activist, offensive strategy. Only in this way can confidence be restored in the ability of the United States not only to defend its interests, but also to undermine those of its opponents, and thereby regain the essential strategic initiative. A forward strategy demands an acknowledgment, however grudging, of the overriding importance of the creative use of military power *and the outcome it produces* in world politics.[75] Finally, this doctrine requires a clear determination to apply the leverage our considerable assets still allow us to exercise in our dealings with adversaries and allies alike. Reciprocity would be the hallmark of policy in both instances. No favors would be given, no concessions would be made to our adversaries without matching concessions from them in concrete and clearly deliverable terms. No guarantees of continued support would be given to our allies without a clear and binding understanding that assistance from the United States entails an obligation on the part of the recipient to support the United States elsewhere, when *this* country deems such support to be necessary. This need not be the preferred strategy under all circumstances, of course. It is simply that, given the present trends in the Pacific Basin, anything *except* a forward strategy can do no more than stabilize temporarily our currently weakened position.

CONCLUSION

On balance, it is difficult to be optimistic about the long-term prospects of the United States in the Pacific Basin. The problems with which this country must deal are great, and the assets available to us to deal with those problems are finite and declining, though still substantial. We cannot improve relations with our principal adversaries and reinvigorate our alliances simultaneously. A choice must be made between the two sets of powers; and we should give precedence to our allies, even if it means the end of detente with the Soviet Union and a cessation of any further improvements in relations with China. A forward strategy, although a high-risk approach, offers the best prospects of at least stabilizing, and perhaps reversing, what is an increasingly unfavorable situation for the United States.[76] Even then, with the rejection of the defensive mentality implied in most earlier doctrines, many of the specific policies that can be attempted are intended to minimize losses, rather than maximize gains. Yet the alternatives to such an approach seem to augur far worse for the United States and the stability of the Pacific Basin.

Finally, despite the fact that some erosion of American influence has occurred, the United States certainly has not become a "spectator" in the Asian power game, as one writer has concluded.[77] This country can neither recoil from involvement in Asia, nor allow its interests in that region to be defined or guaranteed by other states. It would be grossly unrealistic for the United States to assume that other nations would do for it anything that it was demonstrably unwilling to do for itself. America *is* "in Asia," geopolitically speaking, and how it defends its interests and deals with both allies and adversaries there will determine in large part the future of the United States as a world power. In a very real sense, American prospects in the Pacific Basin correspond with the dual meaning of the Chinese character for crisis: a combination of danger and opportunity.

NOTES

1. See Wayne A. Wilcox, *Asia and United States Policy* (Englewood Cliffs, N.J.: Prentice-Hall, 1967), p. 11, and Akira Iriye, "The United States as an Asian-Pacific Power," *Sino-American Detente and Its Policy Implications,* ed. Gene T. Hsiao (New York: Praeger, 1974), pp. 3–4 for discussions of the sense of ambiguity in the American approach to Asian affairs.
2. Graham T. Allison, "American Foreign Policy and Japan," *Discord in the Pacific: Challenges to the Japanese-American Alliance,* ed. Henry Rosovsky (Washington, D.C.: Columbia Books, 1972), p. 7.
3. Russell H. Fifield, "America in East Asia: The Dimensions of Change," *Pacific Community* 6, no. 2 (January 1975): 201–202, 204; William V. Kennedy, "The United States in Northeast Asia," in *New Dynamics in National Strategy: The Paradox of Power* (New York: Thomas Crowell, 1975), p. 245; Foreign Policy Research Institute, "United States–South Asian Relations: A Conference Report," *Orbis* 17, no. 4 (Winter 1974): 1394.
4. Bernard K. Gordon, *Toward Disengagement in Asia? A Strategy for American Foreign Policy* (Englewood Cliffs, N.J.: Prentice-Hall, 1967), pp. 9–17; Robert A. Scalapino, *Asia and the Road Ahead: Issues for the Major Powers* (Berkeley: University of California Press, 1975), p. 281; Coral Bell, "The Asian Balance of Power: A Comparison With European Precedents," *Adelphi Paper No. 44* (London: Institute for Strategic Studies, February 1968), pp. 4–5.
5. Ralph N. Clough, *East Asia and U.S. Security* (Washington, D.C.: Brookings Institution, 1975), pp. 5–17; Wilcox, *Asia and United States Policy,* p. 84.

6. Alan Ned Sabrosky, "An Imperial Recessional: The 'Domino Theory' Revisited," *Intercollegiate Review* 11, no. 2 (Winter-Spring 1976): 83, 85–86; Saul B. Cohen, *Geography and Politics in a World Divided*, 2d ed. (New York: Oxford University Press, 1973), pp. 59–63.

7. Edwin O. Reischauer, "Back to Normalcy," *Foreign Policy* 20 (Fall 1975): 199.

8. J.L.S. Girling, " 'Kissingerism': The Enduring Problem," *International Affairs* (London, July 1975), p. 324.

9. James E. Dornan, Jr., "The Nixon Doctrine and the Primacy of Detente," *Intercollegiate Review* 9, no. 2 (Spring 1974): 77–98; Fifield, "America in East Asia," p. 199.

10. O. Edmund Clubb, "China and the West Pacific Powers," *Current History*, September 1976, p. 52; William R. Van Cleve and S.T. Cohen, "Nuclear Aspects of Future U.S. Security Policy in Asia," *Orbis* 19, no. 2 (Fall 1975): 1156; Sol W. Sanders, "Doctor Kissinger's Asia: Balance or Vertigo?" *Asian Affairs* 1, no. 1 (September-October 1973), p. 15; Russell Spurr, "The new balance of terror," *Far Eastern Economic Review*, 7 May 1976, p. 27.

11. See, for example, Zbigniew Brzezinski, "The Global Triangle: The Changing Power Balance in Asia and Its Consequences for the Foreign Policy of the Atlantic Nations," in *The New Atlantic Challenge*, ed. Richard Mayne (New York: Wiley, 1975), p. 315; and Stephen Barber, "The new balance of power," *Far Eastern Economic Review*, 2 July 1976, especially p. 36.

12. See, for example, Sabrosky, "An Imperial Recessional." Concurring arguments anticipating this development appear in Henry Brandon, *The Retreat of American Power* (Garden City, N.Y.: Doubleday, 1973) and J. William Fulbright, *The Crippled Giant* (New York: Random House, 1972). For a dissenting view, see Reischauer, "Back to Normalcy," pp. 199–208.

13. John R. Swanson, "The Superpowers and Multipolarity: From Pax Americana to Pax Sovietica?" *Orbis* 15, no. 4 (Winter 1972): 1050.

14. See Marshall D. Shulman, "On Learning to Live With Authoritarian Regimes," *Foreign Affairs* 55, no. 2 (January 1977): especially 334ff.

15. Clubb, "China and the West Pacific Powers," p. 50; Gaston Sigur, "U.S. Interests and an Emerging Asian Balance," *Orbis* 19, no. 2 (Fall 1975): 1141 et passim; Allison, "American Foreign Policy and Japan," p. 8; Bhabani Sen Gupta, "Soviet Perceptions of Japan in the Seventies," *Pacific Community* 7, no. 2 (June 1976): 179; Sabrosky, "An Imperial Recessional," pp. 91–92; Y. Melnikov, "U.S. Foreign Policy: Traditions and Present Trends," *International Affairs* (Moscow) 10 (1976): 92–93.

16. Denzil Peiris, "Carter and the pragmatists," *Far Eastern Economic Review*, 12 November 1976, p. 19; Ralph N. Clough, *Deterrence and Defense in Korea: The Role of U.S. Forces* (Washington, D.C.: Brookings Institution, 1976), p. 50; Sigur, "U.S. Interests," pp. 1142–1143. But Kazushige Hirasawa, "Japan's Emerging Foreign Policy," *Foreign Affairs* 54, no. 1 (October 1975): 165–166, disagrees, arguing that confidence in the United States remains high in Asia.

17. Fifield, "America in East Asia," p. 201.

18. See, for example, E. Stuart Kirby, "Russia in East Asia: Perspectives of a Major Presence," *South-East Asian SPECTRUM* 4, no. 1 (October 1975): 25–34. See also the chapter on the USSR in this anthology.

19. See, for example, Georgy Arbatov, "A New Stage in Soviet-American Relations," *Social Sciences* (Moscow), 1974, p. 12; N. Kapchenko, "Socialist Foreign Policy and the Restructuring of International Relations," *International Affairs* (Moscow), April 1975, pp. 3–13; S. Sanakoyev, "The World Today: Problems of the Correlation of Forces," *International Affairs* (Moscow), November 1974, pp. 40–50. Melnikov, "U.S. Foreign Policy," observes explicitly that the American "policy of negotiations and cooperation with the Soviet Union" is due to United States acknowledgment of Soviet (and other Communist) successes and increasing power (pp. 92–93).

20. Jane P. Shapiro, "Soviet Policy Towards North Korea and Korean Unification," *Pacific Affairs* 48, no. 3 (Fall 1975): 351; Gupta, "Soviet Perceptions of Japan," pp. 196–98; Malcolm Macintosh, "Soviet Interests and Policies in the Asian-Pacific Region," *Orbis* 19, no. 3 (Fall 1975): 773–74.

21. Spurr, "New Balance of Terror," p. 27.

22. Bhabani Sen Gupta, "The Insecurity of Asia: The View from Moscow," *Pacific Community* 6, no. 2 (January 1975): 259.

23. Ian Clark, "Soviet Conceptions of Asian Security: From Balances 'Between' to Balance 'Within'," *Pacific Community* 7, no. 2 (January 1976): 162–78; A. Sergeyev, "Problems of Collective Security in Asia," *International Affairs* (Moscow) 8 (1975): 48–56.

24. See Franz Michael's Chapter Nine in the present volume.

25. For discussions of the factors influencing China's foreign policy, see Robert A. Scalapino, "China and the Balance of Power," *Foreign Affairs* 52, no. 2 (January 1974); A. Doak Barnett, *Uncertain Passage: China's Transition to the Post-Mao Era* (Washington, D.C.: Brookings Institution, 1974), pp. 279–86; Clough, *East Asia and U.S. Security*, pp. 117–19; Peter Van Ness, "Dilemmas in Chinese Foreign Policy," *Contemporary History*, September 1976, pp. 60–63, 83; Harry Gelber, "Nuclear Weapons and Chinese Policy," *Adelphi Paper No. 99* (London: International Institute for Strategic Studies, 1973), pp. 1–2.

26. W.A.C. Adie, "China and the Detente: Theory and Practice," *Lugano Review* (1975); M. Cranmyr-Byng, "The Chinese View of Their Place in the World," *China Quarterly* 93 (January/March 1973): 67–79.

27. Peter G. Mueller and Douglas A. Ross, *China and Japan: Emerging Global Powers* (New York: Praeger, 1975), pp. 59–60, 68–71; Shao-chuan Leng, "China's Strategy Toward the Asian and Pacific," *Orbis* 19, no. 3 (Fall 1975): 775–92.

28. Francis J. Romance, "Peking's Counter-Encirclement Strategy: The Maritime Element," *Orbis* 20, no. 2 (Summer 1976): 445; Clough, *Deterrence and Defense in Korea*, p. 43.

29. Yung H. Park, "The 'Anti-Hegemony' Controversy in Sino-Japanese Relations," *Pacific Affairs* 49, no. 3 (Fall 1976): 476ff.; and see the Soviet critique of the Chinese position in B. Koloskov, "Foreign Policy Concepts of Maoism," *International Affairs* (Moscow) 2 (1976): 58.

30. Stephen Barber, "Checking China's shopping list," *Far Eastern Economic Review*, 7 May 1976, p. 20; Clubb, "China and the West Pacific Powers," pp. 49–50; Leng, "China's Strategy," p. 792.

31. Jerry Mark Silverman, "The Domino Theory: Alternatives to a Self-Fulfilling Prophecy," *Asian Survey* 15, no. 11 (November 1975): 935.

32. Donald C. Hellmann, *Japan and East Asia: The New International Order* (New York: Praeger, 1972), p. 31; Bell, "Asian Balance of Power," pp. 2–3.

33. Russell Spurr, "China's Defense: Man Against Machines," *Far Eastern Economic Review*, 28 January 1977, pp. 24–30; Selig S. Harrison, "Time Bomb in East Asia," *Foreign Policy* 20 (Fall 1975): 3–27.

34. Thomas W. Robinson, "Political Succession in China," *World Politics* 27, no. 1 (October 1974); Maxwell D. Taylor, *Precarious Security* (New York: W.W. Norton and Company, 1976), p. 8; Alan Ned Sabrosky, "Foreign Policy Implications of the Chinese Political Succession," *Asian Affairs* 2, no. 1 (September/October 1974).

35. Ross Terrill, "China and the World: Self-Reliance or Interdependence," *Foreign Affairs* 55, no. 2 (January 1977): 304.

36. H. Adomeit, "Soviet Risk-Taking and Crisis Behavior: From Confrontation to Coexistence?" *Adelphi Paper No. 101* (London: International Institute of Strategic Studies, 1973), p. 37; William Welch, "Containment: American and Soviet Versions," *Studies in Comparative Communism*, Autumn 1973, pp. 236–37.

37. Marie-Luise Näth, "Soviet and Chinese Policies Toward South-East Asia in the Early '70s," *South-East Asian SPECTRUM* 3, no. 1 (October 1974): 20. See also Harold C. Hinton, *The Sino-Soviet Confrontation: Implications for the Future* (New York: Crane, Russak, 1976) for a careful and extensive discussion of the intricacies of the Sino-Soviet dispute.

38. Obaid ul Haq, "The Changing Balance of Power in the Pacific and Its Implications for Southeast Asia: A Possible Scenario," *Pacific Community* 6, no. 3 (April 1975): 386; Terrill, "China and the World," p. 303.

39. Uri Ra'anan, "The Washington-Moscow-Peking Triangle: A Re-Examination of Chinese and Soviet Concepts," *Orbis* 19, no. 3 (Fall 1975): 837.

40. See, for example, Evelyn Colbert, "National Security Perspectives: Japan and Asia," in *The Modern Japanese Military System*, ed. James H. Buck (Beverly Hills, CA: Sage, 1975), pp. 199, 216; and William H. Overholt, "Japan's Emerging World Role," *Orbis* 19, no. 2 (Summer 1975): 433.

41. Herman Kahn, *The Emerging Japanese Superstate* (Englewood Cliffs, N.J.: Prentice-Hall, 1970); Overholt, "Japan's Emerging World Role," pp. 412, 418–21.

42. Zbigniew Brzezinski, *The Fragile Blossom: Crisis and Change in Japan* (New York: Harper, 1972).

43. John K. Emerson, "After Thirty Years: Japan and America," *Pacific Community* 6, no. 4 (July 1975): 476–86; Brzezinski, "Global Triangle," pp. 323–24; Susumu Awanohara, "Japan changes direction," *Far Eastern Economic Review*, 1 October 1976, pp. 10, 13.

44. Harrison M. Holland, "The U.S.-Japanese Alliance: A Post-Vietnam Assessment," *Pacific Community* 7, no. 2 (January 1976): 199–215; James H. Buck, "Japanese Defense Policy," *Asian Affairs* 1, no. 3 (January/February 1974): 141; Allison, "American Foreign Policy and Japan," p. 9; Hellmann, *Japan and East Asia*, pp. 114, 191; Overholt, "Japan's Emerging World Role," pp. 421 et passim.

45. Buck, "Japanese Defense Policy," p. 150; Hellmann, *Japan and East Asia*, p. 45.

46. John Roderick, "Japan-China Relations: Some Questions," *Pacific Community* 6, no. 2 (January 1975): 230ff.; Hirasawa, "Japan's Emerging Foreign Policy," p. 155; Overholt, "Japan's Emerging World Role," p. 415.

47. Gabriel A. Almond, *The American People and Foreign Policy* (New York: Praeger, 1960 ed. of 1950 text), p. 54. See also Joseph de Rivera, *The Psychological Dimension of Foreign Policy* (Columbus, Ohio: Charles Merrill, 1968).

48. Brzezinski, *Fragile Blossom*, pp. 14–16; Hellmann, *Japan and East Asia*, p. 60.

49. Masatake Kosaka, "Options for Japan's Foreign Policy," *Adelphi Paper No. 97* (London: International Institute for Strategic Studies, 1973); Robert A. Scalapino, *Asia and the Major Powers* (Washington, D.C.: American Enterprise Institute-Hoover Policy Study 3, November 1972), pp. 10–20; Brzezinski, *Fragile Blossom*, pp. 61–92.

50. C.G. Jacobson, "Japanese Security in a Changing World: The Crucible of the Washington-Moscow-Peking 'Triangle'?" *Pacific Community* 6, no. 3 (April 1975): 365; Hirasawa, "Japan's Emerging Foreign Policy," p. 162; Elizabeth Pond, "Japan and Russia: The View from Tokyo," *Foreign Affairs* 52, no. 1 (October 1973): 141–52.

51. Gene T. Hsiao, "Prospects for a New Sino-Japanese Relationship," *China Quarterly* 60 (December 1974): esp. pp. 740–41; Hirasawa, "Japan's Emerging Foreign Policy," p. 162.

52. Park, "Anti-Hegemony Controversy," p. 490; William J. Barnds, "Japan and Its Mainland Neighbors: An End to Equidistance?" *International Affairs* (London) 52, no. 1 (January 1976): 38; Hong N. Kim, "Sino-Japanese Relations Since the Rapprochement," *Asian Survey* 15, no. 7 (July 1975): 573; Brzezinski, *Fragile Blossom*, p. 92.

53. Franz Michael and Gaston Sigur, *The Asian Alliance: Japan and United States Policy* (New York: National Strategy Information Center, 1972), pp. 74, 82.

54. Scalapino, *Asia and the Major Powers*, p. 16; Kennedy, "The United States in Northeast Asia," p. 249.

55. Jay B. Sorenson, "Nuclear Deterrence and Japan's Defense," *Asian Affairs* 2, no. 2 (November/December 1974): 55–69; Brzezinski, *Fragile Blossom*, pp. 108–110; Buck, "Japanese Defense Policy," p. 146; George Quester, *The Politics of Nuclear Proliferation* (Baltimore: Johns Hopkins University Press, 1973), pp. 103–121.

56. Jay B. Sorenson, "Japan: The Dilemmas of Security," *Asian Affairs* 2, no. 6 (July/August 1975): 370.

57. Clough, *East Asia and U.S. Security*, p. 235; Obaid ul Haq, "Changing Balance of Power in the Pacific," esp. pp. 383, 388.

58. See, for example, Stephen Barber, "Asia waits for the word from Carter," *Far Eastern Economic Review*, 12 November 1976, pp. 10–11.

59. See, for example, Amos Yoder, "Options for a New Policy in East Asia," *Asian Survey* 16, no. 5 (May 1976): 478–91; Robert A. Scalapino, "U.S. Policy Alternatives in Asia," *Parameters* 5, no. 1 (Fall 1976): 14–24; Scalapino, *Asia and the Road Ahead*, pp. 277–81; Fifield, "America in East Asia," p. 202; Yuan-li Wu, *U.S. Policy and Strategic Interests in the Western Pacific* (New York: Crane, Russak, 1975), pp. 191–93; Jack H. Harris, "Northeast Asia: The Problem of Balancing Power," in *Foreign Policy and U.S. National Security*, ed. William Whitson (New York: Praeger, 1976), pp. 139–53; Maynard Parker, "One of Four," *Foreign Policy* 20 (Fall 1975): 209–224; and Gaston Sigur, "Northeast Asia: Area of Confrontation or Accommodation?" *Orbis* 21, no. 1 (Spring 1977): 45–60.

60. Clough, *East Asia and U.S. Security*, pp. 44–54, 235–39; Hellmann, *Japan and East Asia*, p. x; Harold C. Hinton, *Three and a Half Powers:*

The New Balance in Asia (Bloomington, Indiana: Indiana University Press, 1975), p. 295. Silverman, "The Domino Theory," p. 938 describes the system as multilateral rather than quadrilateral, according a substantial role to the smaller regional states.

61. Robert L. Pfaltzgraff, Jr., "The American-European-Japanese Relationship: Prospect for the Late 1970's," *Orbis* 19, no. 3 (Fall 1975): 809–826; Brzezinski, "The Global Triangle," pp. 324–28.

62. Sheldon W. Simon, *Asian Neutralism and U.S. Policy* (Washington, D.C.: American Enterprise Institute, 1975).

63. Wilcox, *Asia and United States Policy*, p. 95.

64. Scalapino, *Asia and the Major Powers*, p. 115; Obaid ul Haq "The Changing Balance of Power in the Pacific," p. 385; Iriye, "The United States as an Asian-Pacific Power," p. 19; Melvin Gurtov, "A New Asian Balance of Power," in *Southeast Asia Under the New Balance of Power,* eds. Sudershan Chawla et al. (New York: Praeger, 1974), p. 2.

65. Richard H. Ullmann, "Trilateralism: 'Partnership' for What?" *Foreign Affairs* 55, no. 1 (October 1976): 1–19.

66. Barnds, "Japan and Its Mainland Neighbors," p. 38; Parker, "One of Four," p. 223.

67. Harvey Sicherman and Alan Ned Sabrosky, "The Efficacy of Technique: 'Protracted Conflict' Revisited," *Orbis* 20, no. 4 (Winter 1977): 51–64. See also L. N. Moskvichov, *The End of Ideology Theory: Illusions and Reality* (Moscow: Progress Publishers, 1974), and Robert Strausz-Hupé, William R. Kintner, and Stefan T. Possony, *A Forward Strategy for America* (New York: Harper & Row, 1961), p. 35.

68. Stanley Hoffmann, "Choices," *Foreign Policy* 12 (Fall 1973): 12–18, 42.

69. See Fred Greene, *Stresses in U.S.-Japanese Security Relations* (Washington, D.C.: Brookings Institution, 1975), pp. 12–13 for a discussion of this point.

70. Clough, *East Asia and U.S. Security*, p. 45; Dwight H. Perkins, "The United States and Japan in Asia," in *Discord in the Pacific*, ed. Henry Rosovsky (Washington, D.C.: Columbia Books, 1972), p. 48.

71. Kennedy, "The United States in Northeast Asia," p. 257.

72. Herbert S. Dinerstein, *Intervention Against Communism* (Baltimore: Johns Hopkins University Press, 1967), pp. 18–19, 23.

73. Michael Pillsbury, "U.S.-Chinese Military Ties?" *Foreign Policy* 20 (Fall 1975): 51–64.

74. Strausz-Hupé et al., *A Forward Strategy for America*. A more recent rendition appears in Wu, *U.S. Policy and Strategic Interests*, pp. 196–203.

75. Colin Gray, "Foreign Policy—There Is No Choice," *Foreign Policy* 24 (Fall 1976): 114-27; Klaus Knorr, "On the International Uses of Military Force in the Contemporary World," *Orbis* 21, no. 1 (Spring 1977): 5-28; Chawla et al., *Southeast Asia Under the New Balance of Power,* p. 106; Strausz-Hupé et al., *A Forward Strategy for America,* p. 1ff.

76. The implications of this strategy with respect to United States policy toward specific states and areas of contention are being explored by the author in a study now in progress.

77. Näth, "Soviet and Chinese Policies Toward South-East Asia," p. 20.

Chapter Eleven

United States Policy in Latin America

John J. Tierney, Jr.

INTRODUCTION

For over three decades Latin America has been a tertiary area of American political and military interest. The issues that dominated early Cold War policies—Berlin, Turkey and Greece, and so forth— were in part an outgrowth of the "Europe first" military demands of World War II, and after the war, reflected the continuing priorities of Washington in the face of the massive Soviet military presence in Europe. The Communist victory in China, the need to manage the post-war administration of Japan and, in June of 1950, the attack on South Korea by the Communist North pushed American interests into the "rimlands" of Asia. United States involvement in Southeast Asia officially began with the SEATO Pact of 1954, although we had been supporting the French effort in the first Indochina War for some time. During the remainder of the 1950s, United States policy focused on Western Europe and the Asian periphery that, together with Israel, became the central concerns of American foreign policy. It was not until the late 1950s that the United States began to take serious notice of Latin America. The rude reception given Vice-President Nixon in Venezuela in 1958 and, one year later, the takeover of Cuba by an avowed Marxist-Leninist movement were the principle catalysts. Nevertheless, the Western Hemisphere was still believed to be a relatively secure area for the United States. While the introduction of missiles into Cuba by the USSR shook American complacency, the crisis did not result in a fundamental reordering of priorities. The 1962 missile crisis removed the imminent threat of attack from the Soviet's Cuban base, while for the remainder of that decade, diplomatic support from the OAS plus effective counterinsurgency activities in the Caribbean area stopped the spread of Castro-style Communist revolutions.

The neglect of Latin America since the end of World War II, therefore, is explained both by the near-absolute strategic control that the United States had come to exercise over the area,[1] and, in turn, by the extensive United States involvement in other areas of the globe after World War II. The continued low profile toward the region assumed by the Nixon administration, however, revealed the extent to which the United States had come to believe that its control over the hemisphere would persist forever. This belief was entrenched so deeply within United States history that it approximated an article of faith. As such, it has tended to undercut efforts to develop a relevant long-term policy toward the region, especially necessary due to ongoing social and political modernization in Latin America. Neither the much-heralded Alliance for Progress nor the continuing desire to "contain communism" in Latin America has succeeded in inspiring a careful examination of current United States interests there.

As a result, the United States may one day discover that its control of hemispheric politics has irreparably slipped from its grasp. Beneath a tranquil surface have emerged a number of developments since the early 1960s which have already shifted, glacierlike, the pattern of relationships throughout the entire area.[2] Not only must the Carter administration acknowledge these changes (both of substance and style), but it must confront them directly in the policy initiatives that it undertakes. Supreme American authority—once unquestioned—is already a nostalgic remembrance of a bygone era. The task ahead for the United States is to devise imaginative policies that match the changing national interests of the area states with those of the United States while, at the same time, retaining the paramountcy of American strategic power during what will be a period of profound political transition.

UNITED STATES POLICY AND
THE DECLINE OF HEGEMONY

The authority that Washington exercised in Latin America during this century will not be completely eliminated in the near term. A transition period of uncertain duration is more likely, especially if the United States is able to deal constructively with the emerging realities that, perforce, will dominate hemispheric politics for the remainder of this century. Many of these trends have been underway since the early 1960s. The continuing existence of the Castro regime, as a bastion of communism ninety miles from United States shores, stands as a reminder that American desires alone no longer determine Latin American politics. As long ago as 1961, a new Democratic administration discovered at the Bay of Pigs that the Castro government was not to be toppled without a serious use of force and that, unlike the nations against which our past military interventions in the Caribbean had been directed, a hostile Cuba armed and aided by an outside power was a formidable rival. For the first time in over seventy years a foreign navy has been able to penetrate the Caribbean Sea, bringing to an end the era in which that body of water was the American *mare nostrum*. Ironically, the same Johnson administration that dispatched more than half a million men thousands of miles away to Vietnam was unwilling to use force to eliminate communism in what had been the traditional and unquestioned United States sphere of influence. The stubborn existence of Soviet influence and Cuban communism inside the region testifies not only to an important shift in the hemispheric balance of power, but it underscores the much more decided change in world politics from strict bipolarity to a condition of bi-multipolarity and, in certain respects, true multipolarity. Behind this global pluralism other states of the region have also found room to maneuver away from traditional American hegemony. Their capacity to wrest free from United States influence has been manifested in a variety of ways, and such shifts should continue to characterize regional politics indefinitely into the future.[3]

For the first two decades after World War II almost all of Latin America was dependent on the United States market as a source of military weapons. By way of contrast, from 1968 to 1972 nearly 90 percent of Latin American arms purchases came from countries other than the United States. All six countries in the area with jet aircraft fly the French Mirage. Peru's military relationship with the Soviet Union includes the first ongoing training program operated by an outside power in the region since World War II. In November 1976 the Peruvian government announced the purchase of thirty-six sophisticated Soviet jet fighter-bombers (the SU-22), the first such purchase by a Latin American country other than Cuba.

On important foreign policy issues many countries have in recent years adopted stands remarkably independent of the United States. In the United Nations and in other international organizations some Latin American states have been only too willing to defy the United States position. Under former President Echeverria, Mexico assumed a leadership position in a loose coalition of Third World nations that voted consistently against United States economic and political positions. Brazil's refusal to sign the Non-Proliferation Treaty and its subsequent nuclear accord with Germany are early indications of the growing independence of that country. The almost universal assertion by South American states of a 200-mile fishing zone has led to continual conflicts with the United States. Mexico's initiative in drafting the Charter of Economic Rights and Duties of States had a blatant anti-American tone. Panama has been able to marshal regional and even worldwide support for its effort to end perpetual United States control of the Panama Canal. Colombia ended its bilateral aid pact with Washington with a public rebuke against United States military interventions in the world. Communist Chile nearly succeeded in opening up a second Soviet "front" in the hemisphere, and the subsequent downfall of the Allende regime produced an outpouring of anti-American abuse throughout the area over alleged United States involvement. The dispatch of Cuban soldiers to Africa has brought Angola, at least temporarily, into the Soviet sphere of influence and has created a series of problems for Western policy in southern Africa that will continue for years. The Cuban move, in retrospect, was one of the boldest assertions of independence from the United States in the history of the Western Hemisphere and underlines dramatically the declining capacity of the United States to determine the foreign policies of regional states.

In their economic policies hemispheric nations have been even more assertive. Ever since the Consensus of Vina del Mar in 1969 various Latin American states have been attempting to put pressure on the United States on several issues. Many opposed the 1971 import surcharge and the anti-OPEC provisions of the 1974 Trade Act. Until Cuba's military intervention in Africa there were clear signs that the OAS economic embargo against Castro's regime, which had been sponsored for over a decade by the United States, was about to be repealed. Many countries throughout Latin America have formed regional economic pacts in an effort to enhance their bargaining strength with

Washington. The first of these was the Latin American Free Trade Association (LAFTA) formed in 1960. In the same year came the Central American Common Market (CACM), followed by the Caribbean Free Trade Association (CARIFTA) in 1968 and, one year later, the Andean Group. (The latter was originally formed by the five Andean nations of South America; Venezuela became a sixth member in 1973.) Although none of these regional arrangements have resulted in true economic integration, their very existence—despite discouraging setbacks—indicates an evolving sense of economic independence from the United States.

This independence has also been manifested in other ways. Latin American exports to the United States have fallen from 50 percent of the total to 32 percent in the past twenty-five years. United States exports to Latin America have likewise declined in the same period by 20 percent. Japan and the countries of Europe have sharply increased both trade and investment in the region. In 1973, for example, Japanese investment in Brazil exceeded American investment for the first time. The Arab states have also begun to invest in Brazil as well as in other Latin American states. In an increasingly multipolar economic world, some Latin American states have resorted to nationalization of United States industries. In addition to the obvious cases of Cuba and Chile, Peru and Venezuela have nationalized foreign industries on a wholesale basis. The entire Venezuelan petroleum industry is now in the hands of local authorities. That nation's participation in OPEC is a continuing example of a traditional United States supporter assuming the role of an economic adversary, or at the very least, powerful competitor armed with an economic weapon (oil) that could equalize its relationship with the United States.

Politically, regimes that once could be counted upon as perennial friends of the United States have gradually shifted ground. The continued aloofness of Argentina is no surprise; that country has a long tradition of envy and fear of the United States. But in other areas of Latin America growing anti-Americanism will pose problems for the United States even if Washington exhibits more interest than has been customary in hemispheric problems. Many of the new elites of both Left and Right, even including the traditional pro–United States military elite, now reject American dominance. New rulers and their bureaucracies, as in Peru, are fiercely nationalistic and not only sought their own identity in part by asserting their independence of the United States, but on occasion as well they have perceived Washington as the immediate threat to their aspirations.

Although anti-Americanism has been a recurrent phenomenon in the area throughout this century, the new drive to cut loose from United States influence is much more real, and undoubtedly will be more sustained, than before. In part, this is due to the nature of the modern Latin American state. In comparison with the weak and dependent governments that habitually looked to Washington for leadership, the new regimes of Latin America have gained enormously in internal cohesion and in the effectiveness—and ambition—of their leadership. They are, in varying degrees, socialistic and militaristic in their ideological orientation and, in general, appear far more confident in their external dealings. To be sure, this is more true of such South American states as Brazil, Argentina, Chile, and Peru than it is of most of the small and still weak governments of Central America. But even in Central America, especially in Panama, a new nationalism has permeated the region. The Caribbean area, likewise, will continue to be governed by weak regimes, but there also things are changing. The reelection of Michael Manley in Jamaica, for example, has moved that country decidedly into a socialistic, pro-Cuban position. Guyana has also moved toward the Left, and socialist parties are contesting for power in several other Caribbean nations. The certainty that a number of other colonies of both Britain and Holland will gain independence in the near future can only have the effect of further diluting traditional United States hegemony.

In its security policies in the area, the United States must thus take into account an evolving diversity of the perceived national interests between the northern and southern halves of the hemisphere. No longer can the assumption be safely made that all the states of the region share the habitual American fear of the spread of communism. The nationalism of Canada and Latin America more frequently targets the United States as the principal enemy. In particular, American economic hegemony is characteristically viewed as the chief obstacle to national autonomy. While the United States may stress an anti-Communist foreign policy, the states of South America, for example, are stressing development economics, including technological transfers from the United States, fair prices for their commodities, trade preferences and so forth. Some of them share the UNCTAD ideology that calls for a "new international economic order," and because of this, they have stressed the North-South economic gap rather than the East-West conflict in their international policies.[4]

Even within the context of anticommunism, the environment of the future will be significantly different than the recent past. During the 1960s, the internal security threat was paramount. In Bolivia, Colombia, Peru, Guatemala, and Venezuela there existed Castro-style insurgencies that threatened the stability of the governing regime. By 1970, however, these rural guerrilla bands had been either defeated or largely contained. The problem of urban terrorism, which existed principally in Argentina, Brazil, and Uruguay, has also largely dissipated, and for the near future, urban terrorism appears to have no greater likelihood of success than rural insurrection. The success of Salvador Allende in Chile, albeit short-lived, has generally symbolized the victory of the Soviet "way" of peaceful struggle, with the concomitant decline of both Chinese and Cuban support for armed struggle.

In South America especially, *external* relations, rather than *internal* security problems, have dramatically captured the attention of leaders in the more advanced countries. The changing regional and international environment of the 1970s has seen a reemergence of traditional balance of power politics as the defining characteristic in relations between several key pairs of states. This trend has been reinforced by the dominance of the military in such countries as Argentina, Brazil, Chile, Bolivia, and Peru. As the priorities of national development claim greater attention in these states, so too will the traditional need to focus on their neighbors as rivals for leadership and economic-military power in the region. This tendency has already gained considerable momentum in the resurgence of a "frontier mentality" over the 200-mile maritime limit and has been stimulated as well by the border problems between Argentina and Chile, Brazil and Argentina, Colombia and Venezuela, and Bolivia and Chile. Indeed, many Latin American leaders are now exhibiting the same geopolitical outlook evident in Europe and the United States during the nineteenth and early twentieth centuries. Brazil and Argentina, for example, have conflicting interests in the economic development of the Rio de la Plata area, while the oil-rich Amazon and Andean territories constitute potential flash points for the states that border them.[5]

For the foreseeable future, therefore, United States foreign policy must seek a way to preserve a Western Hemisphere free from outside intervention, and at the same time, it must oversee the transition in political authority from an almost exclusively United States–dominated region to one that is increasingly pluralistic. At a minimum, American global strategy cannot afford to permit the Soviet Union to gain any more of a foothold in the area than it already possesses. This must continue to remain the fundamental desideratum of American policy. Latin America has always constituted a kind of strategic "reserve" for the United States, and a further decline of United States influence in the region would be little short of disastrous in the continuing global conflict with the Soviet Union. The United States throughout this century has been permitted the luxury of pursuing security policies without real fear that its military predominance in Latin America could be jeopardized. If the Soviets were permitted to extend their strategic influence in the area, the result might very well forecast a final decline in the United States global position. The hovering presence of United States power, therefore, must continue to be a common denominator of hemispheric political life for the foreseeable future.

The *nature* of this power, however, and the manner in which it is exercised, must take into account the new political realities in the area. As such, certain assumptions and attitudes tied to the past should be reexamined. Specifically, traditional United States paternalism toward the region must learn to accommodate resurgent nationalism and the desire of other states to assert a national identity apart from Washington. In this respect, Brazil bids fair to become the "Colossus of the South," with a military and an economic potential that promises to outstrip any Latin American rival. The United States must be increasingly alert to Brazil's ambitions, and in general, it should seek ways to integrate the international outlook of the hemisphere's emerging giant with its own interests and with those of Brazil's neighbors.[6]

At the same time, the United States must become more reticent than theretofore—and certainly more reticent than the Carter administration apparently intends—in asserting the preeminence of its own domestic values and institutions over those preferred by the states of the hemisphere. The moralistic and utopian strains in past American policy must, in the future, give way as necessary to the needs of military and political strategy. At any rate, it is extremely doubtful, as the experience of Alliance for Progress has shown, that United States attitudes and postures can have more than a marginal impact on the internal policies of Latin American governments. In general, therefore, a greater realism in United States foreign policy throughout the region is required: realistic with respect to the degree of economic association with the United States that other states can be expected to accept, and realistic with respect to the capacity of American influence alone to direct the internal and external political affairs of the other states of the region.

These new attitudes must be accompanied by an enduring awareness of the need for the United States to maintain an active vigilance against strategic intrusions from outside Latin America. During the next decade, no other power in the region will have the capability to replace the United States as the primary guardian of hemispheric security. Conversely, only the USSR in the near term will have either the intent or the ability to challenge this American role.

Although few, if any, Latin American states have developed the capacity for sustained conventional war, the shift in the overall security environment in the region has a number of important implications for the future direction of United States foreign policy. In this connection, several of the most important issues facing the Carter administration are the new treaties on the Panama Canal, the nature and scope of United States security assistance to Latin American nations, and the issue of human rights. In the context of an emergent multipolar political environment in Latin America, what specific measures should the United States adopt to preserve stability throughout the region without a heavyhanded attempt to reassert traditional American hegemony?

CRITICAL ISSUES IN LATIN AMERICA
1. The Panama Canal
The 1964 riots in Panama against the American presence in the Canal Zone provided the immediate stimulus for the negotiations which took thirteen years, off and on, to produce an agreement acceptable to both

sides. The submission of the Canal treaties in September 1977 has triggered a debate in the United States, both in Congress and throughout the country, the likes of which has not been seen since the heyday of the Vietnam War. Although emotionalism has been a recurrent phenomenon in United States foreign policy debates with regard to Latin America, the Canal issue tops them all. Strategic and economic considerations aside, the Panama Canal still symbolizes past American technological achievements in history and recalls, as well, traditional policies and policy attitudes toward the Caribbean and Central America. The difficulty that the treaties have had so far (as of March 1978) in the Congress reflects an overwhelming fixation on the part of the American people against any tampering with the status quo in Panama. This attitude is almost generic to American political culture and has surfaced time and again whenever the issue arose.[7]

In 1967 three revised treaty drafts were prepared, but their premature disclosure caused such a public outcry in the United States that any hope for an early agreement was foreclosed. The use of the Canal issue by Governor Reagan in the 1976 Republican primaries caused another commotion over the issue, and probably cost ex-President Ford the Texas primary. Even before that, policy statements and the like had been signed by 38 U.S. Senators and 246 Representatives indicating that they would refuse to ratify any treaty that would dilute, relinquish, or surrender either United States "sovereignty" or "rights" in the Canal Zone. In Latin America, the issue also has great political symbolism, with all states in the region on record as opposed to the indefinite continuation of the status quo. For many of them, the Panama Canal embodies "Yankee imperialism," and recalls the more onerous aspects of past United States diplomacy. OAS Secretary-General Orfila did not exaggerate when he called the Canal "the most explosive issue in Latin America."

The stakes involved in the Canal issue are profound, regardless of whether or not the Senate ratifies two treaties. Apart from the future of the Canal proper, the issue at large will affect America's image and policy throughout Latin America and the world. As the debate grows, the issue becomes more of a bellwether for the nature and direction of American foreign and security policies. In short, the Canal has assumed a symbolic significance far beyond its intrinsic value, a symbolism that typifies America's past ingenuity and creativity, and symbolic, likewise, for what it implies for the nation's future.

Both the basic treaty provisions and the main arguments, pro and con, are by now commonplace to most Americans. More relevant for the future of United States Latin American policies, as discussed above in this chapter, is how the Canal issue, once resolved, will affect United States policy in the context of a changing Latin American international posture.

At bottom, there is a demonstrable need for *some* change in the political status quo. The 1964 riots killed four Americans and eighteen Panamanians and cost $200 million in property damage. The years in between, especially the past several years, have focused worldwide attention on Panama, and a global consensus has developed in favor of revision. The changes in the political environment of Latin America, outlined earlier, indicate that a new United States relationship with Panama would be a *sine qua non* for a more constructive partnership between Washington and the rest of the hemisphere. Although the United States, according to the 1903 treaty, had exercised "sovereign" rights over the Canal Zone "in perpetuity," both of these considerations remain formal legalisms compared to the delicate political situation that currently exists in Latin America. As a mature and responsible superpower, the United States can afford to step down a bit from its mantle, especially in Latin America, to deal with a small and allied country in a reasonable manner.

Nevertheless, the newly negotiated treaty requires the United States to pay a high price in order to secure the continued goodwill of Latin America, especially under the threat of terrorist warfare and sabotage that has come from the Torrijos government. The problems with that regime, as the domestic debate has shown, are deep. The implications of the possibility that a pro-Castro government might be in charge of the Canal in the future are shocking to many Americans who otherwise would be willing to concede political ownership to Panama. The very fact that the treaty has been secured under duress from a country of less than two million people (who owe their very independence to the United States) remains galling to the antitreaty faction. There have been, in addition, several "retreats" of American power from positions of strength throughout the world. In this perspective, the withdrawal of a physical presence in the Canal Zone might represent (or be perceived as representing) another backward step in the erosion of America as a global power in the struggle against communism. The economic agreement initiated between Panama and the Soviet Union in 1977 will hardly allay United States security fears on this score.

Despite the symbolism attached to the Canal issue, and its importance as an indicator of policy, the real heart of the issue remains the waterway itself. Protreaty sentiment will stress its *declining* importance; antitreaty spokesmen emphasize its *remaining* importance. Both marshal facts to support their case. At the same time, both sides continue to accuse each other of undermining the future of navigation through the Canal. The Carter administration maintains that only the present treaties can guarantee passage, and without them there will be violence and disruption of traffic. Those opposed to the treaty claim that Torrijos will raise tolls so astronomically that, in effect, transit will be disrupted or altered drastically. Worse, they claim, he might bring in an outside power (the USSR?) to help supervise navigation, or he might resort to outright nationalization. In addition, it remains a real fear that the instability of Panamanian politics is such that no predictions are even possible. In short, *anything* is possible once the guiding hand of United States administration departs.[8]

At bottom, the dispute is political and is based upon the scenario of political and terrorist warfare in Latin America and Panama if the treaty is rejected. Practically nobody quarrels with the equity and administration of the Canal by the United States. For over sixty-four years, Washington has efficiently and economically operated the Canal, which today still remains a vital artery of world shipping. An average of about 70 percent of all cargo sent through the Canal originates in or is bound for the United States. Japan sends about one-third of its oceanic trade through the Canal. Great Britain is usually the second or third largest user, with over 60 percent of British shipping using the Canal.

For Latin American countries, the trade through the Canal is quite significant. The trade in particular between the countries of South America's West Coast and the Gulf and East Coast states of the United States relies heavily upon the use of the Panama Canal. For example, Nicaragua, El Salvador, Peru, and Ecuador send respectively 77 percent, 68.1 percent, 41 percent and 50 percent of their oceanic trade through the Canal. Countries such as Australia and New Zealand rely on the Canal to reach vital European markets. All have a keen interest in the smooth and nondiscriminatory operation of the Canal.

Today, the Panama Canal Company runs a low-cost operation under a toll structure designed to recover costs of operation and maintenance alone. The current budget for the Canal and Canal Zone (minus defense costs) is about $260 million, out of which $166 million is derived from tolls. Of Panama's annual annuity of $2.3 million, only $700,000 comes from tolls.

The new arrangement, however, in addition to $350 million in assistance, would require that the United States pay Panama an annuity of at least 40 million annually; a figure that at $.30 a ton from toll collection, might easily reach $70 million annually. In addition, there will be a fixed, nondeductible payment to Panama of $10 million, plus still another $10 million if Canal revenues permit. Release of these figures has harmed the treaty's chance for ratification, as they have been widely interpreted as being both psychologically and economically too high a price to pay for Washington to transfer ownership to Panama.

Despite the provisions for the retention of United States security rights, the phasing out of American troops and base facilities gives little confidence that the United States will continue to be in the best position to defend the Canal if it should become threatened. Without a considerable American presence, furthermore, the separate neutrality pact will have little meaning. The Carter-Torrijos communiqué of October 1977, meant to clarify ambiguities regarding future United States military rights, also has little meaning unless it becomes incorporated into the final and ratified document, one way or the other. The closing of the Suez Canal because of the Arab-Israeli conflict offers dramatic testimony to the dangers involved when vacuum areas are created by the withdrawal of a great power presence without compensating legal and strategic rights.

At best, therefore, the treaties are a compromise. They are by no means completely ruinous to American and hemispheric stability, but, in fact, they risk those interests, fundamentally, to avoid the predictions of terrorist violence against the Canal. The basic question remains: will the price of the treaties be worth the risks involved? There is obviously no absolute answer to this question; in the final analysis it depends upon the most logical scenario about the threat against the Panama Canal from inside Panama itself. (With the retention of United States ownership and exclusive rights, there is very little concern about a conventional military attack.)

How real is the threat of General Torrijos that 50,000 Panamanians would die in a war of liberation to get the Canal? Or, put the other way, are the administration's arguments that the Canal is "indefensible" sufficient grounds to cede it over to Torrijos? The threat of sabotage or guerrilla warfare still lies behind most of the arguments advanced by protreaty spokespersons. Yet, the possibility of either, although not to be dismissed, remains unlikely. In Panama, the potential for a national insurgency, à la Vietnam, simply does not exist. Torrijos has neither the training facilities, equipment, terrain, logistical support nor even the chance of outside assistance to sustain a full insurrection. The potential does exist, however, for small, urban terrorism against the Canal, especially from Panama's large and radical student population. Yet it remains to nobody's advantage, least of all the Panamanian's, to sabotage Canal operations. Since the United States would have to rebuild it, sabotage would make Panama as dependent as before on Washington. The Torrijos government, moreover, remains heavily dependent on foreign investment and banks and, from a survival standpoint, would have an interest in eliminating—rather than encouraging—violence and unrest. The potential to outlast United States public opinion via a campaign of sporadic terror is real. But this will always remain no more than an even chance from Panama's viewpoint and, in any event, will continue to be an option for local left-wing radicals until the year 2000, when Panama is supposed to take over completely. It should be remembered, in this context, that the much publicized vulnerability of the Canal to disruption has *always* been the case throughout all the turmoil of the past and, by definition, will be the same regardless of future ownership. Under United States control, the Canal has not been closed for even one minute by sabotage (the only closing that ever occurred, in 1914, was caused by a landslide).

In sum, while the Panama Canal treaties are by no means a national or international disaster, and admitting legitimate pros and cons, the United States should not feel compelled to endanger its strategic leadership in the area by a hasty ratification of the current treaties. The national and congressional debate over ratification, while it has contained overly emotional and extreme dimensions at both ends, has been healthy and appropriate. A Senate rejection of the treaties would not necessarily plunge Panama into protracted bloodshed, nor, on the other side, would ratification automatically invite the Soviet Union into the Western Hemisphere. But the Carter administration, in an obvious effort to win its first major foreign policy test with Congress, may have oversold its product. The protreaty enthusiasts have ignored the fact that private support for General Torrijos in Latin American capitals varies considerably.[9] Insufficient attention, moreover, has been given to the economic benefits that Panama has derived from the Canal—a technological achievement to which Panama owes its very existence. Finally, the basic fact of geopolitical life in Latin America must be confronted directly: under no circumstances can, or should, tiny Panama be exclusively responsible for the long-term strategic defense of the Canal. The amendments to the Canal treaties proposed in the United States Senate, in particular those that protect American defense rights and accessibility to the Canal, are absolutely essential for strategic stability in the Western hemisphere. Whether or not the present treaties provide for an adequate, long-term American presence and responsibility therein must remain a matter of individual judgment.

2. Security Assistance

As the power of the central governments in Latin America has expanded with a resurgence of militarist regimes, internal security considerations have given way to a major preoccupation with external military balances and frontier problems. In the more advanced South American countries especially, security and national development have become central concerns. During the era of American predominance, these considerations remained in the background, overshadowed by United States hegemony. As a result, Latin America has been during this century one of the most harmonious regions of the world.[10] The loosening of United States ties within the region, however, including reductions in military assistance, and the change in the structure of international relations from bipolarity to bi-multipolarity and multipolarity, have begun to affect regional politics. The lessening of the

American presence should result in the strong reemergence of local rivalries, including a marked possibility of border clashes and, less likely, open warfare.

In this context, there will be no direct military threat to United States interests emanating from any state in the area, nor will one likely develop in the foreseeable future. Instead, the United States will find itself dealing with Latin American regimes that are arming in order to balance one another and who increasingly will find it both feasible and profitable to turn to other sources for military aid. As in the case of Peru, this could include the Soviet Union. While the United States will not want to contribute to a spiraling Latin American arms race, United States interests would also not be served if, through default, the Soviet Union were permitted to expand its influence in the area via arms assistance. How should the United States resolve this dilemma?

In reevaluating its recent restrictions on arms transfers to countries in the area, the United States should be guided by several assumptions. First, there is a growing need to develop a security relationship with other states in the hemisphere based upon the partnership concept of interdependence in an increasingly pluralistic world. A total, or near-total, ban on arms transfers amounts to a needless self-denying ordinance and could result in possible destabilizing intrusions by Communist powers. Second, while it is not necessary to develop intimate relations with military dictatorships, both Latin America and the United States should welcome a moderate, restrained military partnership. Washington should also not be deceived by the notion that assistance to military regimes undermines Latin American democracy. In the past, United States efforts to determine the nature of regimes by negative or adversary policies have generally proved ineffective or counterproductive. There is correspondingly (as suggested above in another context), a need for more realism in United States relations with the new military regimes. In the future, United States policy should give priority to the external and strategic needs of hemispheric stability in a diffuse and changing world.

With the military in ascendence throughout Latin America, it is in the American national interest to end paternalistic restrictions against military aid. The request by Mexico for F-5 jets, furthermore, indicates that the desire for American-made equipment is by no means confined to military regimes. The United States should provide moderate levels of military asistance to those countries who will continue to play a vital role in the Western Hemisphere. At the same time, the United States should terminate those legislative restrictions on military assistance (against aid to "dictatorships," against assistance to regimes that have seized United States fishing vessels, and so forth) that have been aimed primarily against Latin America. By providing some form of constructive military assistance, including commercial sales, the United States can end the frustration generated by past restrictions while, at the same time, it can help prevent the sort of balkanization of the region that might come about if Washington remains aloof. The guiding hand of American military cooperation is an indispensable element if a new partnership with the hemisphere is to have any long-term meaning.

3. Human Rights

Even before the Carter administration assumed office, the area of human rights in Latin America was a major concern of United States foreign policy. In Congress, the Harkin amendment to the foreign aid bill (September 1975) prohibited dispensing funds to countries that consistently infringed upon the human rights of their citizens. Both Chile and Uruguay had already been denied access to most forms of United States assistance before Mr. Carter's election. Under the new administration, however, the human rights issue has singularly dominated our Latin American policy. The president's eagerness to push this issue in Latin America has already led to the unilateral rejection of United States military assistance by six countries. Secretary of State Vance's June 1977 speech to the OAS in which he linked United States aid and trade with the condition of human rights in a given country, was the most forceful and uncompromising administration statement to date on this question. Clearly, the United States is on a collision course with some of the most important countries in Latin America. Brazil, for example, has called the United States human rights statements "inquisitorial." Unless United States human rights policies are tempered with a sense of strategic realism, the United States may find itself soon relegated to the status of a political sermonizer throughout most of Latin America. While it will remain important for the United

States to attempt to insure that human suffering under authoritarian governments is reduced to a minimum, it has already been demonstrated that Washington's capacity to influence the internal affairs of Latin American governments is marginal at best.[11] Aside from the smoldering resentment of the country in question, there have been very few concrete results of American "denial" policies. Chile, for example, has proceeded on its own internal course despite widespread official and unofficial American censorship of the Pinochet government.[12] The initial reaction to the Carter initiatives on human rights in Latin America suggests that those countries targeted by Washington for alleged "violations" will turn inward in a reaction against the United States, without having set in motion any of the reforms that the administration demands as the price for American friendship. At best, such reforms will be cosmetic, tailored only to the short-term goodwill of the administration in Washington.

How can the United States do its part to help safeguard human rights without needlessly antagonizing the important states in Latin America? This question will be even more appropriate in the future if the trend toward independent-minded, nationalistic, and military governments continues. The isolation of the particular regime from the United States, and its public embarrassment, may satisfy the administration's ideological needs, but it will not necessarily produce long-term, meaningful results. Consequently, there is need for a careful assessment of the effect that these policies have had on authoritarian governments. Rather than embarking upon unilateral and public moral condemnations the United States might better serve the cause of human rights if a way were found to channel legitimate complaints through hemisphere-wide institutions. As presently constituted, the Inter-American Commission on Human Rights is inadequate for this task.[13] A new agency, composed of nongovernmental civil servants operating under new legislation and under OAS auspices, would be in a better position to protect individuals against the excesses of their own governments. A professional and institutionalized watchdog committee would have the advantage of being more effective against violations of human rights without the concomitant problems that are involved whenever the United States arrogates to itself the responsibility to direct internal changes in allied governments.[14] This does not mean that the United States must surrender its ideals in diplomatic associations with military governments. Rather, these ideals would best be served by a positive and constructive American presence, as opposed to an embarrassingly negative and "harassment" role.

4. Cuba and Soviet Power
Historically, the Soviet Union has been fairly cautious in its attempts to influence events in the Western Hemisphere.[15] Aside from their relationship with Cuba, the Soviets have not expended either large amounts of money or substantial diplomatic effort inside the region. Until very recently, they adhered to the concept of "geographic fatalism," an idea that conceded Latin America and Canada to paramount American influence. The diffusion of United States political and economic power, however, has created a number of opportunities for the Soviets. The military relationship with Peru is the most significant among a series of diplomatic and economic initiatives which they have undertaken over the past several years. If regional multipolarity is accompanied by a further decline in American willingness to remain the *primus inter pares* in the hemisphere, opportunities for the Soviet Union should increase further. Nor should the United States rely upon Latin American nationalism to check Communist ambitions. The combined Soviet-Cuban intervention in Angola provides sufficient evidence of the stubborn capability of Communist powers to overcome geographic or regional obstacles. The continued presence of the Soviet Navy in the area, with port facilities in Cuba, should also remind Americans of the proximity of a hostile military power. Events such as Angola and the 1962 Cuban missile crisis demonstrate the ability of the Soviets and their allies to surprise the West with their daring adventurism.

Continuing attention to the danger of Communist penetration of Latin America must be a major feature of American foreign policy. The new political realities in the area, however, militate against a sterile and negative anticommunism. Positive programs of balanced economic and military assistance will be much more productive in the long run. The United States, for example, could be more supportive of the attempts to achieve regional economic integration in Latin America and the Caribbean. Tariff preferences for Latin American products, increased capital flows (with appropriate insurance against nationalization), and increased technology transfers are further examples of possible United States economic policies.[16] Arrangements for stable and fair commodity prices and general United States support for a more important Latin American role in the OAS would also be forward steps. Such policies have been top priority in Latin America for several years. In moving toward at least a number of them the United States would greatly strengthen the partnership concept in the hemisphere of the 1980s.

In its relations with Communist Cuba, the United States should be guided by dictates of national and hemispheric security. By its actions, the Castro regime has indicated no strong inclination for a rapprochement with Washington. Quite the opposite, in its behavior Cuba has continually flaunted its close ties with the Soviet Union and its contempt for the other states in Latin America that retain good relations with the United States. Until both of those policies undergo a reasonable change, Washington should be in no hurry to mend fences with Havana. As a quid pro quo for a rapprochement, therefore, the United States must insist that Cuba end its close military and political ties with Moscow and demonstrate a sincere intent to collaborate with other states in the region. Not until then should Cuba be allowed the political and economic benefits attendant on American recognition.

In the meantime, the United States should continue to guard against a possible expansion of Soviet power via the Cuban satellite. For the time being it appears that the Soviets are not willing to risk overt military moves of the Angolan type in the area. Such an adventure in Latin America would be foolish from their perspective since it might constitute an American *casus belli* against Cuba. The Soviets appear willing to wait for opportunities to increase their political and economic leverage, and continue to stress "constitutional" paths to socialism, such as occurred in Chile in 1970. They will also attempt to exploit whatever opportunities are offered them as a result of the decline of American influence in the hemisphere.[17] An active and supportive United States involvement in the area is the best continuing insurance against political and economic intrusions from the Communist bloc. Any major attempt by Washington to dictate anti-Communist foreign policies to the more powerful states of the region is liable to have reverse effects.

5. Brazil

Although we have been considering Latin America as primarily one stategic unit, it is actually an area composed of over thirty nation-states that have had very little in common except their historic association with American hegemonic power. Political and cultural diversity is far more characteristic, even within specific regions like the Caribbean and South America, than any shared or community feelings. Consequently, the United States must carefully manage its bilateral dealings, mindful of the fact that in terms of overall military power it will remain the area's superpower.

In South America the most important state of the future will be Brazil. It is the only country that has the potential to achieve great power status by the year 2000. The present military government has not disguised its intentions to make Brazil a modern, wealthy, powerful, and respected country. Brazil's land mass, population, natural resources, endowment, and economic growth rate should combine to make it the new South American great power, outstripping all rivals including Argentina.

Historically, Brazil has an almost unbroken record of friendship with the United States. In the special relationship with Latin America, the United States has always assigned Brazil a unique role, viewing it as the necessary pillar of stability on the southern continent. This traditional importance will be enhanced markedly as Brazil acquires greater power and international status. The United States has already acknowledged Brazil's growing role in the hemisphere of the 1980s. In 1975, the United States and Brazil signed a bilateral agreement establishing procedures for special consultation. In reporting on the negotiations to Congress, Secretary of State Kissinger noted that the agreement, unique in Latin America, elevated Brazil's status in the United States hierarchy of interests to the same level as that of the nations of Western Europe, Canada, and Japan.[18]

In its bilateral relations with Brazil, however, the United States must not create a Washington-Rio axis to the detriment of the other countries of South America. While Brazilian-American cooperation is a *sine qua non* for stability in Latin America, it cannot be a cover for an undue expansion of Brazilian power and influence. Several of Brazil's neighbors genuinely fear her ambitions. In its relations both with them and with Brazil, the United States must act as a stabilizing factor. United States diplomacy must find constructive and imaginative ways to oversee the pattern of emerging bilateral relationships in Latin America in 1980 and beyond. It remains to be seen whether the strong reaction in Brazil against President Carter's unsuccessful efforts to block Brazil's purchase of advanced nuclear technology from West Germany will inhibit the development of the Rio-Washington relationship in the long term. For the short term, the Carter administration is off on a bad footing with this potential giant of the Southern hemisphere.

CONCLUSION

The United States has reached a crossroads in its policies with the other states of Latin America. The hegemony that held true throughout most of this century is currently in a period of transition. What it will become will depend largely upon the nature of Washington's responses to the new political and economic trends in the region. The United States could attempt to maintain its traditional domination, but such an effort would certainly antagonize the majority of the more important states and, in the long run, would succeed only in isolating America from hemispheric politics. At the other extreme, the United States could disassociate itself from the area, refuse to become involved with "reactionary" governments, denounce anti-American nationalism, and withdraw into a continental shell. In effect, this would leave the rest of Latin America on its own, subject to the political or military domination of the most important states and, in the process, subject also to possible interventions from the Communist bloc. The course outlined in the preceding pages offers a broad program of continuing American strategic involvement in the region without the presumptuous political and economic hegemony of the past. In any event, it is impossible for the United States to treat the area as it always has. Nor can Washington realistically expect cooperation from the states of the region if the United States ignores their desire to be respected as equals, or preaches to them as though they were children.

The United States has a national interest in Latin America, and that interest, fundamentally, is to regulate the transition of the regional system from one dominated by Washington to one in which the

United States acts as *primus inter pares* in a multipolar system. Related to this fundamental interest are others supportive of it: a hemisphere free from outside military intervention, a system in which the Communist states can make no further political or economic inroads, an area that promotes peaceful change among the leading states, a region in which nations can move toward economic modernization without internal strife and violent revolution. In short, the United States must support a peaceful regional political system in which Washington exercises leadership but eschews a hegemonic role.

It should be remembered that the American experience with Latin America goes back much further than Washington's strategic involvement with either Europe or Asia, which only began on a sustained basis after World War II. Throughout this century there have been periods of intelligent and farsighted diplomacy by the United States in its dealings with the other states of Latin America. In the early 1920s, for example, the United States began to reevaluate its military interventions in Central America and the Caribbean. This was a direct result of the new power realities of the post–World War I era and led indirectly to the Good Neighbor Policy of the 1930s. That policy, as another example, constituted an important transition in Latin American relations. By offering the hand of friendship instead of the bayonet, the administration of Franklin D. Roosevelt secured the goodwill of Latin America, not only throughout the 1930s but also through the trials of World War II and well into the Cold War with the Soviet Union.

In the political atmosphere of the late 1970s there is a further need for the United States to secure the goodwill of its partners in Latin America. Not only has the United States lost political ground in the Caribbean and South America, but both Canada and Mexico on the North American continent are restless under the American shadow. Both of these countries are also facing crises of an economic and social nature that will take years of patience and American cooperation to overcome. Canada faces rebellion in Quebec and economic nationalism throughout the country. Mexico has severe economic problems plus a growing possibility of peasant revolt in the northern provinces. The flood of Mexican immigrants into the United States may soon make this country the fourth largest Spanish-speaking nation in the world.

The stability of Mexico and Canada is crucial for the United States, and during the next few years, each will need careful attention from Washington. United States diplomacy with Canada and Mexico must be active and constructive. The United States is deeply involved in the fate of both, but at the same time, Washington must be especially sensitive to the economic and cultural autonomy which each country has manifested.

The same holds true, in general, for United States policy in the Caribbean and in South America. Overall, United States policymakers face a challenge similar to that which their predecessors between the two World Wars faced: how to translate a historic frustration against United States power into positive and constructive channels of mutual self-help. The United States can take the lead in this endeavor by providing a strategic shield behind which the nations of the hemisphere can, either separately or individually, discover their own paths to political and economic modernization.

NOTES

1. For a history of United States strategic policies in the Western Hemisphere during this century, see the author's article, "The State System of the Western Hemisphere: A Strategic Analysis," *Lugano Review*, no. 4 (1975).

2. Recent books that demonstrate such changes are: Harold E. Davis, Larman C. Wilson, et al., *Latin American Foreign Policies* (Baltimore: The Johns Hopkins University Press, 1975); and Ronald G. Hellman and H. Jon Rosenbaum eds., *Latin America: The Search for a New International Role* (New York: John Wiley & Sons, 1975).

3. Abraham F. Lowenthal, "The United States and Latin America: Ending the Hegemonic Presumption," *Foreign Affairs*, October 1976.

4. For a series of expert statements on this, see: Committee on Foreign Relations, U.S. Senate, 94th Congress, 1st session, *U.S. Relations with Latin America, Hearings Before the Subcommittee on Western Hemisphere Affairs*, February, 1975 (Washington, D.C.: Government Printing Office, 1975).

5. Donald F. Ronfeldt, *Future U.S. Security Relations in the Latin American Context* (Santa Monica, Calif.: The Rand Corp., 1975).

6. Roger W. Fontaine, *Brazil and the United States* (Washington, D.C.: AEI-Hoover Policy Studies, 1974), and Norman Gall, "The Rise of Brazil," *Commentary*, January 1977.

7. Ironically (or deliberately), the best-selling history of the construction of the Panama Canal appeared just three months before the new treaty was signed. See David McCullough, *The Path Between the Seas, The Creation of the Panama Canal, 1907-1914* (New York: Simon & Schuster, 1977).

8. The domestic debate on the canal issue transcends both party and ideological boundaries. Many prominent Democrats, especially in the House of Representatives, oppose the treaty, while several prominent Republicans of both houses are in favor. At the same time, influential conservatives who would normally see eye-to-eye on foreign policy, such as Ronald Reagan and William F. Buckley, are on opposite ends of the issue regarding Panama.

9. It is strongest in Venezuela, Colombia and Mexico and weakest in Brazil and southern South America.

10. The only South American wars in this century occurred between the two World Wars: Bolivia versus Paraguay from 1932 to 1935, Colombia versus Peru in 1932, and Ecuador versus Peru in 1941.

11. Indeed, the idea that the United States *ever* had more than marginal influence on the internal policies of South American regimes is probably an American myth, born out of utopian desires to expand the American ideology and to exaggerate United States political and social influence. See Mark Falcoff, "Our Latin American Hairshirt," *Commentary,* October 1976.

12. Three years after its inception, the Chilean military government is beginning a rehabilitation of civil liberties, but at its own pace according to its own needs. See a report by John Chamberlain, "Evolution Within the Form," *National Review,* 24 December 1976.

13. This agency can only operate with the permission of the government against which a complaint had been lodged.

14. See, for example, the testimony of Professor Martin C. Needler, *Hearings,* op. cit., p. 180.

15. James D. Theberge, *The Soviet Presence in Latin America* (New York: Crane, Russak, 1974), esp. chap. 1.

16. See, for example, the testimony of Hon. Sol M. Linowitz, *Hearings,* op. cit., pp. 4–13.

17. Leon Goure, Mose L. Harvey, and Morris Rothenberg, *Soviet Penetration of Latin America* (Washington, D.C.: Center for Advanced International Studies, University of Miami, 1975).

18. U.S. House of Representatives, 94th Congress, 2nd Session, "Report of Secretary of State Kissinger on his trip to Latin America, *Hearing Before the Committee on International Relations,* March 4, 1976, p. 3.

Chapter Twelve

Africa and United States Foreign Policy: A Realist's View

Anthony Harrigan

Africa poses special problems for United States foreign policy. It is a continent where this nation has limited experience, as compared, e.g., to Latin America and even to Asia, where the United States has been involved in varying ways since the nineteenth century. This situation is in marked contrast to that of several of our NATO allies, who administered vast African territories until recent years and who, as colonial powers, were responsible for bringing contemporary civilization to Africa. In the post–World War II period the United States pressured these NATO allies to speed up the decolonization process, which, in many cases, became an unfortunate, precipitate retreat of the West that created both a power vacuum and a civilizational vacuum in large portions of the underdeveloped world. America exerted such pressure against its allies in part because it believed that the new states of Africa would develop into nations in the democratic mold. This assumption, it is now clear, was based on a fundamental lack of understanding of African realities and on a misperception of the possibilities for the creation of political and civilizational order in sub-Saharan Africa in the foreseeable future. Americans failed to understand, as Irving Kristol has recently observed, "that there are many nations where the American ideal of self-government in liberty is simply irrelevant."

In my view, the national interest of the United States, the interests of our NATO allies—France, Britain, Belgium, and Portugal—and, very definitely, the interests of the indigenous peoples of Africa themselves would have been much better served had the process of decolonization been stretched out over a lengthly period and had significant links been maintained between the emerging nations and the metropolitan governments in Europe. Indeed, this might have happened but for pressure from the United States that helped force instant independence on poorly prepared African territories.

In a sense, this is ancient history—an historical might-have-been. And it thus might be argued that it is futile to ponder the spilt milk of history—even that of recent history. I do not believe this to be a correct view, however. We learn from history, as Santayana observed, or we are condemned to repeat it. The root error of the fifties and sixties, as I see it, was unthinking American pressure for change in Africa that the circumstances did not warrant.

Unfortunately, the United States has made many mistakes in interfering with and intervening in various regions of the world. Our attitudes, our habits of mind, our institutional approaches, our moral idealism simply do not "take" in many situations and many countries. Our national conditions are unique. We frequently get into vast trouble by assuming that what works in the United States is applicable to far-away lands with very different traditions.

I fear that we will intervene more deeply in Africa in the next few years and compound our mistakes, damaging our national interests without truly helping the peoples of Africa. I fear the United States will intervene because the African nations south of the Sahara have moved to center stage in international affairs. The United States will be tempted to apply economic and political pressure in various ways, if not actually to commit troops, in support of the "one person, one vote" principle. Africa, after all, is a politically sensitive area for the United States. It is the ancestral home of 25 million Americans. The Carter administration will thus be under heavy pressure to develop foreign policy positions on Africa that are responsive to "racial" politics. Under the circumstances, it will be very difficult for the United States to maintain a foreign policy with respect to Africa that is balanced and in accord with the overall national interest, which involves a variety of complex considerations.

Obviously, individual groups of Americans cannot—and do not— ignore considerations of race, religion, and national origin in proposing policies toward a particular country or region. Americans who have family roots in the Baltic states, for example, have their views toward United States–Soviet relations colored by their special background— and understandably so. It is dangerous, however, for the United States government to allow ethnic or racial politics to influence decisively American foreign policy, for the safety and prosperity of the entire American people—not one section—may thereby be adversely affected.

In addition, there is the ideology factor. In the United States, as in other Western nations, there are numerous observers who believe that the West owes a moral debt to the Third World and that, more-over, the economic and political system of the West is unjust. Such persons believe that United States policy towards Africa should include at least preliminary steps—involving large transfers of funds through various types of aid programs and the like—toward the establishment of a new economic order worldwide. This is the position of prominent African leaders as well. President Nyerere of Tanzania, for example, in an address to the Royal Commonwealth Society in London in 1975, stated:

> In one world, as in one state, when I am rich because you are poor, and I am poor because you are rich, the transfer of wealth from the rich to the poor is a matter of right. It is not an appropriate matter for charity.

Not a few Americans share President Nyerere's view. Franklin H. Williams, president of the Phelps-Stokes Fund and a former United States ambassador to Ghana, writing in *Africa Report*[1] referred to "a twenty year period of American neglect" of Africa. He criticized what he described as the lack of American economic assistance to African nations, adding that he hoped Congress would loosen the purse strings "for more adequate aid allocations."

There is, in effect, a sizable Africa lobby in the United States that wants to make assistance to—indeed, the transformation of—Africa a major foreign policy goal of the United States. The journal *Africa Report* provides a forum for those Americans who share this outlook. Anyone pondering future United States foreign policy with respect to Africa should understand the extent of the ideological and emotional commitment of advocates of a deep American involvement in African affairs.

Indeed, as suggested above, Africa plays a symbolic role in the minds of many people who are ideologically committed to a radical restructuring of power and wealth on this planet. Richard Harris writes from this standpoint and asserts the following: "Our common humanity with the African people requires that we be intellectually and morally concerned with their interests and welfare."[2] Dr. Harris's viewpoint is highlighted by his attribution of "the underdevelopment of the Third World countries to their incorporation as dependent satellites within the international system." His remedy—one in which he would have the United States play a major role—is a "united and socialist Africa" established by means of "socialist revolution," including "armed struggle for liberation."[3]

This point of view is by no means an isolated example. Numerous American writers of a liberal-left persuasion advocate United States support for revolutionary movements in Africa. For example, Stephen S. Rosenfeld, editorial staff member and columnist for the *Washington Post*, recently wrote that "it makes a lot of sense to me ... for the United States to steal some of the Russians' advantage by coming more openly to the side of the black majority liberation movements in Rhodesia and Namibia. . . . In the same spirit, the United States ought to be more supportive of the black nations just north of South Africa— Zambia, Mozambique, Tanzania."[4]

This argument raises the basic question of United States objectives in Africa. What, for example, has the United States to gain from being "supportive" of a one-party, Marxist state such as Mozambique, which styles itself a "people's republic"? Surely, the American people do not approve of Soviet or Chinese-style people's republics, or of regimes that are collectivist in character and which consistently vote against the United States in the United Nations.

C.L. Sulzberger of *The New York Times* has written that the State Department is "now engaged in a long-overdue restructuring of United States African policy." But to what end? Is the toppling of the governments of Rhodesia and South Africa to constitute the end purpose of United States foreign policy? If that is the case, what is the rationale? It hardly seems appropriate for the United States to fashion a foreign policy toward an entire continent that is based on the sole object of ending white rule in two countries. How this would promote the national interest of the United States is not self-evident.

Those charged with the formulation and management of American foreign policy have the responsibility for determining how relations with the countries on the African continent affect the safety and prosperity of the American people and how relations with African nations should be conducted so as to assure the safeguarding of United States national interests. Ill-defined policy objectives in Southeast Asia in the 1960s involved the United States in an immensely costly and futile war. The Carter administration has an obligation to prevent a repetition of similar errors in Africa. Moreover, it seems abundantly clear that the United States public is in no mood to support interventionist activities in Africa—either military blocking actions against Soviet involvement, or economic and political actions that amount to interference in the internal affairs of countries in South Africa.

George Kennan, the author of America's postwar containment policy, recently stated flatly: "We should come out firmly and frankly in the United Nations and say: 'We are prepared to have nothing to do with this area.' "[5]

I suspect that Mr. Kennan's position is a bit too isolationist for the public mood today, but I am confident that it is closer to the mark than Mr. Rosenfeld's call for support for revolutionary "liberation" groups.

In general, I believe that the American people are tired of foreign adventures and grandiose gestures aimed at various regions of the world. On the whole, they display no eagerness to make Africa a centerpiece of United States foreign policy. They will be concerned, however, if they find that a changed orientation in foreign policy results in American industry being deprived of strategic materials vital to employment and the maintenance of prosperity.

Prof. W.A.E. Skurnik of the University of Colorado asserts that "the American public seeks retrenchment from international affairs. . . ."[6] I believe this is the central truth that must be borne in mind in considering future United States policy toward Africa. In this connection, I am convinced that the vast majority of Americans were pleased that the United States Senate barred the use of funds for support of one of Angola's warring factions. There was no public desire for direct or indirect American involvement in that African territory.

Following Senate rejection of administration efforts to affect the situation in Angola, the then-secretary of state produced a new African policy that was enunciated at Lusaka, Zambia, on 27 April 1976. He pledged United States financial support for nations where guerrillas are being trained for the struggle in southern Africa. This position, also, did not appear to arouse widespread public support in the United States. The *Wall Street Journal* termed Dr. Kissinger's sudden shift, in an apparent attempt to be on the winning side, "cold-blooded *realpolitik*."[7] It pointed out that "inalienable rights are not guaranteed for blacks in Rhodesia or South Africa, but neither are they guaranteed for blacks in most of black Africa," adding that "all but about five of the 49 members of the Organization of African Unity are either military or civilian dictatorships." Indeed, the *Journal* noted that "some black African states 'solve' their racial problems by exterminating or expelling religious, tribal or racial minorities."[8]

The conditions in many African countries underline the absurdity of any new American policy toward Africa that is based on a crusade for racial justice in southern Africa while ignoring injustices to racial, religious, and tribal groups elsewhere on the continent. It is hard to believe that the American people would support a policy that was based on such a narrow view.

Now the objection may be raised that if the United States follows a policy of noninterference in Africa, it will lose its influence, and that passivity on the part of America will enable the Soviet Union to become the dominant force in African affairs.

It is of course possible that noninterference on the part of the United States *will* make it possible for the Soviets to repeat the Angola military operation in other African countries. But the fact remains that Americans do not want to fight for Africa, and they do not appear anxious to support, financially or militarily, the efforts of others who do.

It is nonetheless true that the United States has a considerable economic stake in Africa and a demonstrated need for many of the raw materials produced in African countries. It is this need that prompted Vice Adm. John M. Lee, USN (Ret.) to cite, in a 1974 address at the Naval War College, the importance of a "resource control strategy." He pointed out that "as the resource problem develops in industrialized nations, the primary military task after physical defense of the homeland will be support of access to needed resources against constraints, interruptions or denials. . . ." The United States, it should be noted, imports some one hundred minerals, at least half of which are imported in large quantities, many of these from African countries. As Sanford Rose pointed out in the November 1976 issue of *Fortune,* "African countries have huge deposits of chromium, bauxite, copper, manganese, and cobalt."[9] For example, Zaire accounts for more than half the world cobalt output, with Zambia and Morocco accounting for much of the rest. Africa also is an important producer of oil. Nigeria, for example, derives 85 percent of its revenues from oil exports. Any serious consideration of America's foreign policy objectives in Africa must thus focus on the special role that the Republic of South Africa plays in meeting the raw materials needs of the United States, its NATO allies, and Japan.

South Africa has been called the Saudi Arabia of the 1980s, due to the extent of its mineral reserves and their importance for the industrialized nations of the world. South Africa ranks with the United States, Canada, and the Soviet Union as one of the four major suppliers of minerals to the entire world. One statistic suggests the country's importance: South Africa is the major supplier of seven out of the twenty minerals of which the United States imports more than 50 percent of its requirements. Therefore, it would be a severe setback for the United States if an anti-American regime were to seize power in South Africa. A pro-Soviet regime in Pretoria would give the Soviet Union control of 90 percent of the platinum, 75 percent of the manganese, 80 percent of the gold, 60 to 80 percent of the diamonds, 50 percent of the chrome, and 50 percent of the copper production of the world.[10] Dr. Peter Janke of the Institute of the Study of Conflict has pointed out that by the mid-1980s South Africa will replace Canada as the non-Communist world's second largest producer of uranium.

It is true that the United States could make adjustments if denied access to African metals. In addition, it is possible for the United States to substitute metals from non-African sources. For instances, nickel and tungsten, which are available outside Africa, will serve as well as cobalt for alloying purposes. The United States also can turn to Brazil and Mexico for manganese, and United States reserves of bauxite can be developed. The search for alternative sources would be costly, however. Therefore, it would be imprudent in the extreme to adopt foreign policy positions on Africa that could result in the loss of

American access to strategic raw materials required by our industrialized society. That the adoption of such positions is even a possibility is indicative of the largely emotional climate in which United States policy towards Africa is debated.

Part of the problem lies in thinking of Africa as a consistent whole—as an economic, political, and spiritual entity. It is no such thing. The beginning of wisdom about Africa is recognition of its vastness and diversity. A few African nations are very rich; most, however, are among the poorest nations in the world. The nations of Africa are extraordinarily dissimilar. They are separated by language, tribal character, and history. It really makes very little sense to talk about "African" problems, though it is now an ingrained habit. There are approximately thirty countries in sub-Saharan Africa alone. Many of these countries are insignificant—Gambia, Sierra Leone, Equatorial Guinea, Upper Volta, and Malawi. On the other hand, there are a handful of truly important states—important because of their size, natural wealth, and strategic location. One of these is South Africa, which covers just 4 percent of the area of Africa and has only 6 percent of its people, but which accounts for more than a quarter of the Gross National Product of the African continent. Another key African country is Nigeria, an important supplier of crude oil to the West. With a population of 82 million, Nigeria is Africa's most populous country. It also is one of Africa's wealthiest nations, with a GNP of $25 billion. United States business has at least $1 billion invested in Nigeria, as compared to $1.5 billion in South Africa.

If South Africa's social and political system is offensive to many Americans, it should be recognized that that of Nigeria—the premier black African state—has profound flaws as well. Levi Nwachuku asserts that there is "deep-seated and widespread corruption" throughout the nation's bureaucratic apparatus. Gen. Yakubu Gowan, the former head of state, Professor Nwachuku asserts, had between $122 and $320 million in foreign bank accounts.[11]

The new leader of Nigeria, Lt. Gen. Olusegun Obasanjo, in May of 1967, ordered the execution of seven people accused of taking part in an abortive coup d'etat. Two months earlier, the regime had executed twenty others for their alleged roles in the coup attempt. Clearly, Nigeria is a long way from anything resembling a democratic government with full civil rights.

Military rule, arbitrary arrests, reprisals, and executions are the order of the day in numerous African countries. In Ethiopia, the recent events have been noteworthy by any standards. According to one report, "reprisals have included public hangings, bombing of villages, mass arrests, and the shooting of villagers herded into mosques."[12] The same journal told of nine persons sentenced to death in Niger following an attempted coup.[13] Such is the political pattern in much of black Africa.

Nevertheless, whether one is considering the Republic of South Africa or Nigeria, or any other African country, something more than moral indignation is required if one is concerned with the shaping of American foreign policy. Moral perfection will not be found in the political systems on the African continent, whatever their racial composition. Indeed, where in the world will one find states that are models of moral behavior? It is well to bear in mind the statement of Hugh Seton-Watson, the distinguished British historian, that "states do not exist for bringing about moral perfection on earth." The United States, therefore, cannot base its foreign relations on the position of nations on the scale of virtue. If this were the case, Switzerland would be America's Number 1 ally, and the United States would not have diplomatic relations with numerous countries around the globe. As Prof. Seton-Watson has observed:

> Now take a look at the South Atlantic. There are two potentially important powers there: Brazil and South Africa. Brazil is an unpleasant, oppressive dictatorship, though economically rather successful. South Africa, though not perhaps strictly speaking a dictatorship, is a regime based on a loathsome doctrine of racial superiority. Should we proclaim that these countries can never be our allies because we disapprove of the way in which they run their domestic affairs? Should we allow Soviet influence to intrude into the South Atlantic because we find the Brazilian and South African regimes to be lacking in virtue? Or should we think in terms of which power is going to do more, or less, damage to our interests?[14]

These comments should help Americans understand the proper basis of a foreign policy for the African continent. That basis is the national interest of the United States. The United States purposely aligns itself with countries whose interests coincide with those of the United States, and rejects or works against those countries whose interests are contrary and harmful to our own.

It might be argued that these comments do not provide much in the way of concrete guidelines for United States policy toward Africa, or for preventing Soviet gains on the continent. It is true that the Soviets now have two treaties with Angola—a friendship and cooperation agreement, as it is called, and a party-to-party pact linking the Soviet Communist party and Agostinho Neto's Popular Movement for the Liberation of Angola. This is the first time such agreements have been signed with a sub-Saharan African government. More recently the Soviets signed a similar agreement with Mozambique.

In 1975, the United States provided limited military grant assistance to Ethiopia, Zaire, Liberia, Ghana, Senegal, and Kenya. In addition, there were commercial sales of United States military equipment to Africa (totaling $5.4 million), with 40 percent going to Nigeria, 35 percent to Kenya, and smaller amounts to Gambia, the Ivory Coast, Tanzania, and Zaire. It is scarcely possible to object to commercial sales of arms to those African countries that are not planning military operations against their neighbors—Kenya, for example. A massive expansion of military grant assistance to African countries, however, is not a wise course for the United States. In the first place, serious questions can be raised concerning the ability of the African countries to make effective use of sophisticated weapons. Bear in mind that the decisive factor in Angola was not the MPLA and its forces, but the 14,000-man Cuban expeditionary force dispatched to Africa. Beyond that, there is a real question whether United States military grant assistance is an effective barrier to Communist expansion anywhere in the Third World where insurgent forces are directed by Communist military cadres. And no one is suggesting that the United States revive the Vietnam-era military-adviser system in such countries as Kenya or Zaire, or that America urge NATO countries to provide such advisers.

It can be said that by failing to provide arms to countries such as Zaire and Kenya, and by refusing to furnish advisers, the United States will be unable to block the further expansion of Soviet influence to Africa. In other words, it can be argued that a policy of nonintervention in Africa is a no-win policy.

That may be, and America may have to pay a penalty for refusing to deploy military power overtly or covertly on the African continent. But I return to my fundamental point, namely that such involvement appears, at the moment at least, to be held in disfavor by the American people. It is very clear that Americans, while strongly supporting continental and oceanic defense measures, are firmly opposed to new involvements in remote regions, except in very special circumstances where national pride and interest are concerned. The *Mayaguez* incident met that test. If the oil-producing nations were to deny vital oil to the United States, moreover, the American populace would support the strongest possible action to start the oil flowing again. Short of such a crisis situation, the United States public opposes military intervention, large-scale CIA-type paramilitary operations, or assistance to revolutionary movements proclaiming national "liberation" as their goal. This attitude cuts both ways, affecting the favored objectives of both American conservatives and American liberals. Only such bold actions as are designed to protect America's vital economic interests are likely to receive public approval. This means that America must leave the Africans alone to settle their own affairs.

As noted above, of course, it can be argued that such a noninterventionist posture is a poor one for a nation that is dependent on resources from the African continent. Nevertheless, the United States public has indicated what it will and will not do, and what policies it will and will not support. And United States foreign policy has to be built on the bedrock of the people's will. If the American people are shortsighted and unwilling to make the commitments necessary for their well-being or security, they will ultimately have to pay for it.

It may be, however, that a nonintervention policy toward Africa will not prove so costly after all. The security of every state on the African continent is clearly an American concern. For much of the continent is of little strategic value. That is to say, events in Chad or Upper Volta are unlikely in the extreme to have any serious impact on United States international interests. Moreover, many African countries are considered nations only out of international courtesy, for they are nonviable, lacking adequate resources for self-supporting nationhood. The United States can legitimately narrow its concern for sub-Saharan Africa—at least its economic and strategic concern—to a handful of countries, chiefly Nigeria, Zaire, and South Africa. These are the key African countries because of their natural wealth.

Incidentally, both Nigeria and South Africa are fully capable of defending themselves against, e.g., Cuban-type expeditionary forces. Nigeria can call on Britain for military assistance if necessary. South Africa builds the most modern armaments, including missiles and jet aircraft. Israel is building fast missile ships for the South African Navy. Moreover, the South Africans have the capability to construct nuclear weapons within a relatively short time if they decide to do so.

The difficulties that confront the United States in developing a cogent policy for sub-Saharan Africa are clear. Policymaking for the region is complicated by domestic politics, by differing views as to the place of moral judgments on social systems in the making of foreign policy, by concern over Soviet policy in Africa, by varying concepts of the proper world role for America, by United States economic dependence on many African resources, and, finally, by ignorance of the conditions of African life and the history of the African continent.

I am not optimistic about our ability to resolve these various difficulties and controversies. It is only in connection with Western Europe that the United States has a relatively easy time in fashioning its foreign policy. This is because of the close, historic ties between Europe and European culture and America and American culture. The United States confronts difficulties even in dealing with the countries of Latin America, a continent with which the United States has been involved for a long time, because of cultural and economic differences. And the history of the domestic political struggle over United States involvement in Vietnam testifies to the unsettled nature of American foreign policy with respect to Asia. Africa looms as the least known, the most remote continent in cultural and political terms, and the most profoundly alien to the American experience.

Africa, as I noted at the beginning of this essay, historically has been within the sphere of influence of Europe and the Muslim world. The United States is not prepared to fill the role in connection with Africa played by other great nations that, in the past, were deeply involved on that continent. On the one hand, the American people appear to have little sympathy for the so-called African liberation movements, many of whose leaders espouse Marxist philosophies and articulate economic objectives perceived as antagonistic to the interests of the industrialized Western world. At the same time, many Americans are made uncomfortable by proposals that the United States cooperate more closely with South Africa, despite its economic and strategic importance for the West. Under the circumstances, a hands-off, nonintervention policy on the part of America seems the only policy acceptable to the United States public.

It is a policy that would be in accord with the general wish for a moderate retrenchment in foreign affairs, which appears to represent the popular consensus at this point in our nation's history.

NOTES

1. Franklin H. Williams, "Towards an African Policy," *Africa Report* 21, no. 4 (July-August, 1975).
2. Richard Harris, ed., *The Political Economy of Africa* (Cambridge, Mass.: Schenkman Pub. Co., 1975).
3. Ibid.
4. *Washington Post,* 20 February 1977.
5. "From Containment to . . . Self-Containment: A Conversation with George F. Kennan," *Encounter* 47 (September 1976).
6. W.A.E. Skurnik, "Africa and the Superpowers," *Current History* 71 (November 1976).
7. *Wall Street Journal,* 3 May 1976.
8. Ibid.
9. Sanford Rose, "Third World 'Commodity Power' Is a Costly Illusion," *Fortune,* November 1976, p. 148.
10. See P.C. Roberts, "The Economic Importance of South Africa," in *South Africa: The Vital Link,* ed. Robert L. Schuettinger (Washington, D.C.: Council on American Affairs, 1976), pp. 37–39.
11. Levi A. Nwachuku, "Nigeria's Uncertain Future," *Current History* 71 (November 1976).
12. "African Update," *African Report* 21, no. 4 (July-August, 1976): 23.
13. Ibid., p. 24.
14. Hugh Seton-Watson, "George Kennan's Illusions: A Reply," *Encounter* 47 (November 1976).

Chapter Thirteen

United States National Security Policy: Retrospect and Prospect

James E. Dornan, Jr.

I

To a greater extent than most Americans care to acknowledge, the past of every nation is prologue. At one level, this assertion merely restates the obvious. Quite clearly the manner in which a nation over time defines its objectives, deals with its adversaries, capitalizes on opportunities, and in general conducts itself in international relations will in considerable measure determine its present course and future possibilities in world affairs. More fundamentally, a nation's history reveals much about what it is—its values and outlooks, its temperament and character, its characteristic manner of conceptualizing political reality—and therefore reveals something of the inherent factors that shape and constrain its international behavior and that significantly affect its prospects for successfully achieving its objectives under the variegated circumstances of world politics.

It is in this connection that the distinctive character of the American tradition in foreign policy becomes a factor to reckon with. Since very early in American history our statesmen—and, to the extent that it is possible to generalize on the matter without the benefit of extensive survey research, the American public as well—have conceptualized America's world role in a special way. The nation's characteristic way of thinking about its role in world politics, in turn, has had enormous impact upon United States foreign policy.

From the Republic's earliest days American political and social thought was characterized by an intense belief in the distinctive quality of the social order that had been established in the New World, and by a conviction that America had been selected by Providence to make a profound contribution to the amelioration of the human condition.[1] A free society had been established here, the Founding Fathers believed, which afforded to the average citizen unparalleled opportunities to develop his or her talents and pursue personal goals to the maximum extent possible. At the very foundation of the *weltanschauung* of the early Americans thus rested a self-conscious, often highly articulated image of two different worlds. One was dominated by monarchs and the nobility, and was characterized by the subordination of freedom and the rights of the person to the interests of the few, and by the conduct of foreign policy according to the base dictates of expediency; the other was inspired by the principles of republican virtue and was dedicated to individual self-fulfillment and the protection of personal liberty, and to the strict observance of settled moral principles in the conduct of its international relations. The United States is not as other nations are: both our goals and our practices serve to distinguish us sharply from other nations, for we had created on these shores a new kind of political community, essentially moral in character and untainted by the imperfections and deficiencies of the Old World. "In this legend," Cushing Strout has written, "America is the land of the Future, where innocent men belong to a society of virtuous simplicity, enjoying liberty, equality and happiness; Europe is the bankrupt Past, where fallen men wander without hope in a dark labyrinth, degraded by tyranny, injustice and vice."[2]

Such convictions, of course, reveal much about the general political outlook of early America and deserve further analysis from that perspective alone. But what is important for our present purposes is that the early Americans were also persuaded that there was a significance attached to the founding of the American Republic that far transcended this nation's borders. Precisely because America was a new kind of political society, they believed, she was to become the model society for the universe and ultimately was to make a profound contribution to mankind's political redemption: the United States was to become the vehicle for the realization throughout the world of the natural rights of man.

This vision of America's future in world politics, it should be noted, cut across the partisan and ideological divisions of the period. Few of the prominent Framers dissented from it, at least in its general formulation. Thus we find Benjamin Franklin observing that the cause of America is "the cause of all mankind . . . assigned us by Providence."[3] Thomas Paine perceived the American Revolution as "the most virtuous and illustrious revolution that ever graced the history of mankind" and a harbinger of a new world order, in which the "spirit of jealousy and ferocity" that had in the past been characteristic of world politics would give way to the "dictates of reason, interest and humanity," so that force would no longer be the prime arbiter of international quarrels.[4] Even those of the Founding Fathers with a reputation for realism and toughmindedness in political matters articulated their vision of America's future in such terms. Alexander Hamilton, for example, whose thought, of all the Framers, is closest to the European tradition of realpolitik, often expressed his conviction that America's cause was also "the cause of virtue and mankind." "The world has its eye upon America," he wrote in an essay published in 1784. "The noble struggle we have made in the cause of liberty has occasioned a kind of revolution in human sentiment. The influence of our example has penetrated the gloomy regions of despotism, and has pointed the way to enquiries which may shake its deepest foundations."[5] Quotations could be mustered at length, but enough has been said to show that a very expansive view of the nature and destiny of the American Republic pervades the thought of the Founding Fathers.

To be sure, no consensus developed among the early Americans concerning either the manner in which the political redemption of mankind would occur, or the precise nature of the role that the United States was to play in the process. Paine, one of the few authentic revolutionaries of prominence in the American political tradition, seems to have preferred the direct approach. Only republican governments, he believed, had a moral right to exist, and he frequently expressed his belief in the need for "a general revolution in the principle and construction of governments."[6] True to his principles, he left the United States after independence was assured and went to Europe, where he both participated directly in the French Revolution and offered verbal encouragement to Irish rebels and others seeking to free themselves from the yoke of oppressive regimes. Thomas Jefferson's approach was similar, if less consistent. Jefferson believed that liberty was indivisible. Not only would the success of the American experiment with free government have a profound impact upon events elsewhere, but the defeat of the cause of freedom abroad, he believed, would result ultimately in the collapse of the American Republic as well. Jefferson, however, as had Paine, believed that the United States of the late eighteenth century was in no position to participate actively in the overthrow of authoritarian regimes in Europe, although, in a statement seldom quoted by his admirers, he held out a different possibility for the future. "Not in our day," he wrote to a political associate, "but at no distant one, we may shake a rod over the heads of all, which may make the stoutest of them tremble."[7] At that point, he apparently believed, America could begin to make an active contribution to the political reformation of mankind. Consistent with the Jeffersonian view was the outlook of Woodrow Wilson, America's leading proponent of political reform abroad during the first part of the century, who proved himself quite willing to use America's military power to provide oppressed peoples with the opportunity to choose freely their own forms of government.

Even in the nation's early period, however, there were active and vocal proponents of a quite different approach. Charles Pinckney of South Carolina, in an extended debate with Alexander Hamilton at the convention of 1788, took direct issue with the latter's approach to foreign policy. He argued that an activist foreign policy—and the development of the national power requisite to such a policy—would involve this nation continually in foreign quarrels and ultimately threaten the survival of free and democratic institutions at home.[8] John Quincy Adams, perhaps the greatest of the early American statesmen, also doubted the desirability of a foreign policy that deliberately set out to reform the political world. Although throughout his life he conceived of the United States as the leader in a general struggle to establish a new and liberal international order, his most cherished belief was that the United States could best help change the world by the power of example. The American political order, he asserted, is a "beacon on the summit of the mountain, to which all the inhabitants of the earth may turn their eyes for a genial and saving light. . . . It stands for ever, a

light of admonition to the rulers of men, a light of salvation and redemption to the oppressed." Sooner or later all people will follow the
light, he believed, and "the American will triumph over the European
system."[9]

To be sure, in common with the views of Paine, Jefferson, and indeed with virtually all of the early American statesmen, Adams's
dictum that the United States should "not go abroad seeking dragons
to destroy"[10] was in part motivated by prudence. The isolationist impulse of early American statecraft was in considerable measure motivated by an awareness of the new nation's relative military and economic weakness, especially in comparison with the great powers of
Europe. The Framers were clearly aware that the ultimate destiny of
the United States could not be realized if the nation were destroyed
in the course of involvement in the conflicts of Europe, and they thus
chose to concentrate in their statecraft upon the problems involved in
forging political independence, guaranteeing the new nation's boundaries, stimulating national growth, and exploiting our fortuitous global
position for economic and political advantage.

From the beginning of American history, therefore, there developed
a gap between dream and design in United States foreign policy. From
the nation's earliest days American diplomacy was inspired by a noble
vision: a world of free and independent states, dedicated to maximiz-
ing the opportunities afforded their citizens for self-development and
cooperating with one another in their international relations. The objectives of United States foreign policy, insofar as they were inspired by
that vision, tended to be articulated in far-reaching terms. There was
thus an interventionist spirit implied in the American foreign policy
tradition from the outset. At the same time, the Framers paid little
attention to analyzing the means by which their noble vision was to be
realized. Not only was there no need to think about such issues; to do
so would in fact have been dangerous given the precarious position in
which the new republic found itself.

II

This gap between dream and design became a characteristic feature
of the American tradition in foreign policy. After the promulgation of

the Monroe Doctrine in 1823, the United States was spared both by its geostrategic situation and by the exhaustion of its potential enemies after the Napoleonic Wars any need to concern itself with international problems, and was thus able to devote its attention almost exclusively to domestic affairs. During the following three-quarters of a century, the course of both international and domestic events seemed to confirm the thesis that the United States was destined to achieve great things in the world. Such foreign policy concerns as developed in the nineteenth century were handled with relative ease; even the Civil War excited only fleeting interest in Europe, whatever the fears in Washington, and corresponding hopes in Richmond, at the time. Domestically, the United States achieved phenomenal rates of economic growth, particularly after the Civil War. Hundreds of thousands of immigrants left Europe to help swell our population, and were readily absorbed into the nation's social and economic fabric. By the close of the nineteenth century the United States had become a power capable of influencing developments outside its own boundaries in fact as well as in pretension; it began to do so with vigor and, as far as can be determined, with the full support of the bulk of the American population. Few Americans, in fact, appeared ready to quarrel with Herman Melville's mid-nineteenth-century assertion that "God has predestined, mankind expects, great things from our race; and great things we feel in our souls."[11]

It is worth remembering, however, that the United States came to global power without having learned, in Walt Whitman's phrase, "to chance the cold dirges of the baffled and sullen hymns of defeat."[12] Neither the American ideology nor the American political experience, foreign or domestic, had prepared the United States to exercise effective leadership in world affairs. Having had little experience with conflict or defeat, and having forgotten what little it had experienced, America was unprepared to deal with the reality of permanent and persistent conflict that is the essence of world politics. Progress, to the United States, seemed built into the natural order of things; peace was perceived to be the normal state of international affairs, expressing the harmony of nature, while war was perceived to be an abnormality, an aberration caused by evil men pursuing evil designs. These perceptions, as Correlli Barnett has pointed out, were reinforced by the ethical ideals and moral values derived from classical philosophy and from Christianity, which the United States had derived from its European heritage, and were relaunched by Victorian liberalism-cum-evangelicalism.[13] Peace and war, thus, came to be viewed as totally dichotomous states, to be dealt with by entirely different means. Peace is the realm of diplomacy, while war is the realm of violence. Totally alien to the American experience was the truth, understood instinctively by Europeans, which has been given its most forceful expression by Clausewitz: war and politics are a seamless web. It is therefore not merely because, as one commentator has recently argued, "strategy, like invention, is mothered by necessity,"[14] that there has been a paucity of relevant strategic thinking in the United States in the twentieth century. The United States, due to its characteristic way of thinking about world politics, lacks the intellectual framework necessary to think relevantly about grand strategy, here defined as the integrated utilization of political, economic, and military assets in the pursuit of national objectives.

It is for these reasons as well, although there is not space here to trace their origins in detail, that American thinking about foreign policy problems is characterized by what Stanley Hoffman has called "skill thinking," or the "engineering approach," in acordance with which our statesmen tend to ignore ends while fragmenting problems in such a way as to make them susceptible to the application of expert technique.[15]

The history of United States foreign policy in the twentieth century can be viewed fundamentally as a record of attempts by the United States to "unlearn" many of its most cherished assumptions about the nature of world politics. That America has in the process experienced as many defeats as victories, the former of late clearly outnumbering the latter, is a tribute both to the persistence of those assumptions and to the intractability of international problems. During the Spanish-American War the United States learned that in the course of bringing democracy and prosperity to the presumably benighted peoples of what is now called the Third World, it might be necessary to assume what elsewhere might be called imperial responsibilities—and to fight nasty "low-intensity wars" against those who would have preferred that the United States exercise its responsibilities elsewhere. During

World War I we should have learned—but apparently did not—that the replacement of authoritarian governments with regimes selected according to the principle of national self-determination guarantees neither democracy nor prosperity in the target countries. We should have learned as well that the policies of democratic as well as of authoritarian states can lead to international conflict, and that continuing participation by the United States in world politics on an extensive scale was essential to achieving whatever world order was possible in the twentieth century. We did learn that the American people become rather quickly disillusioned when their nation's foreign policy objectives are not easily achieved: the 1920s and 1930s represented the first of several attempts in the twentieth century by the United States to withdraw from a world that proved resistant to American attempts to reform it.

American policy during World War II exhibited a somewhat greater degree of realism. There can be no doubt, as FDR clearly realized, that Hitler's Germany represented a far greater threat to American ideals and American security than had the policies of the Central Powers two decades before. By the end of the war, however, FDR too had fallen victim to the American illusion that wise American policies could create a stable and peaceful international order. In order to make such a posibility seem real in the world of 1945, it was necessary for Roosevelt to ignore or define away the incipient challenge to world security represented by the rising power of the USSR. This he did, in the process contributing substantially to the world's predominant security problem of the present.

The challenge posed by the USSR to the security of the non-Communist world, in any case, ensured that the post–World War II United States withdrawal from the world would be brief indeed. By 1947, the United States had embarked upon a grand strategy for dealing with its Marxist-Leninist adversary, known as the containment policy. As is well known, the intellectual father of containment was George Kennan; less well known are the intellectual assumptions that lay behind Kennan's formulation of the strategy. Fundamentally a philosophical skeptic and ethical relativist, Kennan has made a career of opposing the formulation of foreign policy objectives in moral terms (although, to be sure, he has occasionally succumbed to the old

American illusion that, insofar as the world can be reformed, reform can best be accomplished by the power of American example.)[16] Concern for national interests governs the foreign policy calculations of states, in Kennan's view, and it was his assumption that if the United States succeeded, by vigilantly opposing all attempts by the Communist bloc to expand its sphere of territorial control, in containing the USSR, Soviet policies would eventually moderate and the Marxist states would learn to live peacefully with the West in a harmonious international order. The containment strategy, thus, was characteristically American in its essential features. Its core assumption was that relatively little effort by the United States over a relatively short period of time would bring about a fundamental transformation in the nature of international politics. Although Kennan never assumed that the Soviet Union would transform itself into a free-enterprise-oriented, Anglo-Saxon parliamentary democracy, he did expect the USSR of the future to turn its attention to improving the living standards of its people and to developing peaceful relations with its erstwhile adversaries.

The containment policy therefore did not fill the need for an American grand strategy appropriate to the challenges of the post–World War II world. Essentially defensive in nature, it left the strategic initiative and even the choice of battlegrounds and tactics largely to the adversaries of the United States. As James Burnham long ago pointed out, its expected outcome—the transformation of Soviet foreign policy objectives—depended on constant success, an impossibility given the strategy's defensive character.[17] In its expectation that, with relatively little effort, the United States could both protect its essential interests against the Soviet challenge and ultimately usher in a new world order, the containment policy was fundamentally utopian.

In practice, however, it is possible to judge containment somewhat more kindly. Under the rubric of containment the North Atlantic Treaty Organization and the other components of the Western alliance system were created as counterweights to Soviet power, and a series of strong points was developed around the Communist periphery in an effort to block the further expansion of the Soviet Union. Japan and West Germany were drawn firmly into the Western camp, and the economic recovery of Europe from the ravages of World War II was completed. While the Soviet Union can point to significant victories in its quest for expanded global political influence during the era of containment, it must acknowledge significant defeats as well. Communist-led guerrillas in Greece, Malaysia, the Philippines, and Thailand were turned back, at least temporarily. Indonesia, a state once strongly susceptible to Soviet influence, radically revamped its foreign policy after the death of Sukarno in 1965. With the exception of Egypt and to a lesser extent Syria, even Soviet policy in the Middle East achieved few successes during the containment period; such successes as it achieved were in any case due primarily to the dynamics of the Arab-Israeli conflict and not to the appeal either of Soviet power or of the Marxist-Leninist ideology.[18]

These Western successes, however, which in retrospect must be attributed as much to internal problems confronting the Communist bloc during the 1950s and 1960s and to the inherent caution of the Soviet leadership in the face of United States strategic superiority as to the effectiveness of Western strategy, were deceptive. They concealed the failure of the West to come to terms with the underlying realities of contemporary politics and obscured for a time the fact that the United States was only marginally more prepared for a sustained global struggle with determined adversaries than had been the case earlier. Throughout the containment period, if fact, there were episodes—responses to assorted Soviet "peace initiatives," and the like—that revealed the extent to which the United States continued to believe that peace is the normal, and war the abnormal, condition of international politics.

III

By the late 1960s, a combination of factors coalesced to destroy the intellectual and political consensus that had undergirded the containment strategy. The impact of the protracted war in Vietnam, which the United States military for a variety of reasons was singularly ill-suited to wage, was of course decisive; even before, however, the dominant wing of the United States foreign policy community had become persuaded that both the impact of nuclear weapons on world politics and changes said to be occuring within the Soviet political system made posible—indeed, made necessary—the abandonment of the containment strategy. Containment, in this view, had succeeded; the time had come for a new American strategy appropriate to changing international circumstances.

Initially, that new strategy took the form of the so-called Nixon Doctrine, articulated during the early days of that ill-fated administration.[19] The Nixon Doctrine was basically a rationale for American retrenchment. The world had changed radically since the early days of containment, it asserted, and the principal changes—the economic recovery of Europe, the breakup of the Communist bloc, and the emergence of stable regimes in the Third World—made possible a reduced American global role. While maintaining our military strength and our alliance commitments, the United States would turn toward negotiations with the USSR in an effort to stabilize definitively the world political system. Within a surprisingly short time, the Nixon Doctrine dropped from sight as the centerpiece of the Nixon administration's foreign policy, to be replaced by the detente strategy of the increasingly dominant Henry Kissinger. Considerations of space prevent a full treatment here of the intellectual assumptions underlying Kissinger's diplomacy; that task has in any case been accomplished elsewhere.[20] Fundamentally, Kissinger's diplomatic strategy brought to full flower the new intellectual consensus concerning world politics and America's role in it that had been emerging within the dominant wing of the American national security community since the mid-1960s or earlier. Like his peers, Kissinger (abandoning earlier views) had come to believe that internal changes in the Soviet political system, principally pressures generated by the desire of the Soviet population for higher living standards, had produced fundamental changes in the Soviet world outlook. Also in common with his peers, Kissinger was persuaded that nuclear weapons had revolutionized world politics. There had been at least since the 1960s, he argued, a nuclear stalemate between the superpowers (he in fact had been predicting the onset of that stalemate for more than a decade). The nuclear stalemate rested on the invulnerable second-strike forces in the arsenals of both powers and on their mutual awareness that neither side could win a nuclear war. In his phrase, the superpowers are thus "forced to coexist."

Considered as a grand strategy, detente was thus a program for capitalizing on changes believed to have occurred in the Soviet world outlook and on the revolutionary impact of nuclear weapons on world politics in order to bring into existence—or create, as Mr. Kissinger would prefer to put it—a stable world order. Negotiations with the Soviet Union were to be undertaken on a broad front, from strategic arms to specific problem areas such as the Middle East. The strategic arms talks were regarded as particularly important; their purpose was to stabilize the arms competition between the superpowers, thus improving the general environment of Soviet-American relations and facilitating progress in other problem areas. The details of the arms accords did not matter, nor did Soviet numerical preeminence in various areas of strategic weaponry, since the United States, in Kissinger's view, retained its invulnerable second-strike capability and since nuclear weapons had no political utility. Especially important, in Kissinger's view, were the economic agreements to be negotiated with the USSR. Their purpose was the creation of a network of interlocking agreements that would bind the two economies together and provide a continuing incentive to both to engage in cooperative behavior. Depending on the exigencies of the moment, of course, Kissinger employed a variety of formulations explaining both the nature of detente itself and the relationship between detente and arms control; his critics have enjoyed pointing out the often contradictory and self-serving nature of most of these arguments. From Kissinger's perspective, however, neither the arguments nor the fulminations of his critics were of any great consequence. What mattered was the opportunity he saw to at least begin a new era in Soviet-American relations and thus in world politics itself.

As other chapters in the present volume make obvious, Mr. Kissinger failed in his central objectives. To be sure, he achieved certain short-run tactical successes, primarily in the Middle East, but in the end, as George Will has suggested, he will most likely be remembered principally for having contrived to make America's retreat from world power appear glamorous.[21] There is no evidence whatsoever that there exists a true detente between the United States and the USSR, even if we define detente, in a minimum way, to mean acceptance by the Soviets of the pre-SALT military balance as a permanent condition of international life. Much less is there a true detente if that word is defined more broadly as a situation in which both superpowers agree to pursue foreign policies that are essentially status quo in nature. Kissinger failed because he was incorrect in his central assumptions concerning the nature of Soviet foreign policy, and was thus incapable of fashioning a strategy that could effectively counter the steady growth of Soviet strategic, conventional, and political power. In practice, therefore, Kissinger became the great accommodationist. During his tenure as secretary of state, America's position in the strategic and conventional military balances steadily worsened. He presided over the collapse of the American defeat in Vietnam, the most ignominious chapter in American foreign policy since the war of 1812. He began the process of United States withdrawal from South Korea, Formosa, and Panama. He saw United States influence in the United Nations and in the Third World generally decline to an all-time low. When, toward the end, he became alarmed over the Soviet adventure in Angola and the rise of Eurocommunism in Western Europe, and attempted to rally support for effective American responses, no one listened; Kissinger's credibility as an architect of anti-Communist policies had been largely destroyed by his eight-year fixation on detente.

The long-term trends for United States foreign policy as the new administration concludes its first year in office are therefore not encouraging. Initially, of course, the Carter administration, as had the Kennedy administration a generation ago, appeared to promise the nation something better. Indeed, in its opening moments, with the president's reaffirmation of the moral principles so long associated with the American political tradition and in its relatively well-designed proposals on limiting strategic arms presented to the Soviet Union in March of 1977, the administration gave indications that it sought to have the United States take the offensive on a broad front in international politics. Mr. Carter spoke out with a vigor that the world has not recently heard from an American president on the continued violations of the Helsinki Agreement, the United Nations Charter and the elemental laws of human decency generally by the USSR. Whatever the nobility of his pronouncements on human rights, however, moral rhetoric is no substitute for policy, and soon it became clear that the Carter administration, like its predecessor, intended to pursue an accommodationist policy in world politics. During the first year of the new administration the American retreat from world power has in fact accelerated in the Far East, Africa, Latin America, and elsewhere. The March SALT proposals have steadily been diluted, and it is now obvious that the SALT II agreement, when it is finally concluded, will be at best no worse from the American point of view than Kissinger's disastrous 1974 Vladivostok Accords.

IV

The record of post–World War II American foreign policy can in the main be looked upon as a record of missed opportunities. Until the middle to late 1960s the United States possessed absolute strategic preeminence over its principal adversary, yet was unable to capitalize on the advantages which that preeminence afforded it. The reason for this is not, as some have alleged, that it was impossible to do so. It is rather the case that, led astray by its characteristic assumptions about international politics and thus incapable of developing an appropriate grand strategy for dealing with the contemporary world, the United States failed to do so.

What then of the future? Can the United States discover in time the wisdom that is necessary both to be true to the best of its principles and traditions and to deal realistically with the world of the 1980s and beyond? Can we reverse extant trends in world politics, which, if long continued, will see us reduced, in the words of Henry Kissinger, "to a fortress America, in a world in which we had become largely irrelevant"?[22] On what basis should the United States attempt to conduct relations with the world's other superpower? Should the purpose of this nation's foreign policy in the late 1970s and in the 1980s be "victory over communism," as the then-leading and still prominent spokesman for American conservatism advocated more than a decade ago?[23] Or is the "containment" of the Soviet Union a sufficient task for United States foreign policy? Alternatively, should we drastically reduce involvement with the outside world, as the so-called limitationists of the Left and the Right advise, or should we perhaps even attempt a withdrawal to the Western Hemisphere, relying on our strategic nuclear forces to ensure our survival?[24] To raise these questions is ultimately to ask again: what are the national interests of the United States, and how can they best be protected under contemporary international conditions?

It is first of all clear that an effective American foreign policy capable of being sustained over the long haul requires a moral foundation. As the Kissinger era clearly demonstrated, it is not possible to develop the requisite political consensus behind a foreign policy that is unabashedly realpolitik in inspiration. Not only the American intellectual community but the American people as well think more of themselves than that; indeed, a policy of pure realpolitik would constitute a repudiation of the best aspects of the American political tradition. To set forth such assertions as these, however, is to provide little in the way of concrete guidance for the policymaker. Indeed it is inevitable that this be the case, as Irving Kristol has recently reminded us.[25] The unhappy truth—still unaccepted by most American intellectuals and by many Americans generally—is that there is no unequivocal "moral" answer to most social, economic, and political problems. So far as these problems are complex, the relationship between morality and reality is also inevitably complex. Doing the right thing cannot be easily divorced from doing the effective thing; and, to complicate matters even further, doing the right thing in one respect almost always means doing the wrong thing in other respects. To illustrate this central theme, Kristol analyzes the principle of the "self-determination of peoples," still a favorite of most Americans when they think about the outside world. What happens, he asks, when the principle of self-determination, if applied in a particular case, leads inevitably to majoritarian tyranny and massive infringements on personal rights and liberties? More concretely, it might be asked, should the United States back "freedom" for Rhodesia from the regime of Ian Smith if the result would be the accession to power of a totalitarian Marxist regime under Joshua Nkoma? The United States, Kristol concludes, whatever the "truth" of its original insights into the nature of man and politics, badly needs to think about the relationship between morality and reality more clearly than it has in the past.

Doing so, however, will constitute only a beginning. As John J. Tierney has pointed out in his essay on United States–Latin American policy in the present volume, many areas of the world at present do not constitute fertile ground for the introduction of American political principles. Some, indeed, may never be, which is why it may be a mistake to define away the problem by asserting, in patronizing terms, that such-and-such a country or continent is not "ready" for American-style democracy. The question is not one of readiness or goodwill, but rather the determining influence of history, culture, stage of economic and social development, and perhaps even climate on the development of political institutions. To make Anglo-Saxon parliamentary democracy the sole standard for evaluating political systems abroad is not morality; it is chauvinism.

Secondly, there is a vital need for the United States to remain actively involved in international politics on the widest possible scale, for reasons both of morality and of self-interest.

As the French scholar Raymond Aron has reminded us, only "a small power restricts its ambitions to physical survival and the preservation of its legal independence and its institutions."[26] A great power, on the other hand, "over and above physical security, moral survival, and the well-being of its inhabitants, acts to achieve an (often) ill-defined purpose, which I should call the maintenance or creation of a favorable international environment." Isolationism in the United States, he adds, has been largely discredited because five times in the twentieth century, in moments of profound crisis, the United States has found it necessary to undertake a major military intervention in Europe or Asia. The issue, he suggests, is not what the United States might prefer to do, but what it has done and will continue to do: "The real question is whether nonalignment and the refusal of 'entangling alliances' would not give rise some day to cries from which once again, however much it wished to abstain, the American Republic would be incapable of standing aside."[27]

In arguing that, whatever its formal doctrine, the United States would find a policy of isolationism impossible to maintain in practice, Aron is not succumbing to the determinism of the power realists or the neo-Marxists, who also assert—albeit for quite different reasons—that the United States is compelled to play a substantial role in world politics. Neither is he merely arguing, with Thucydides, that the interests of states tend to expand with their power. On the contrary, he is asserting that power is not the sole, and often not even the primary, determinant of human action, and therefore that the behavior of people and nations cannot be explained in terms of power alone:

> Drawing a distinction between physical security and the creation of an environment favorable to the expansion of the national values, though

valid analytically, is rather hazardous. No great power defines its national interest simply as its physical security. Diplomats think and act within a world already structured by animosities, principles, or sympathies which cannot be reduced to calculations of strength or considerations of balance.[28]

If this argument is correct—and the historical experience of all great nations goes far toward confirming it—it suggests at least the beginnings of an answer to the questions raised earlier concerning the purpose of American policy. Self-interest and principle are inextricably intertwined as motives for the foreign policies of all nations, although of course the mix will differ in each individual case; moreover, it is when the demands of self-interest and the demands of principle reinforce one another that policy tends to be most consistent and effective.

Third, there is a vital need for active leadership, in both the executive and legislative branches, in shaping American national security policy, and perhaps, as the chapters by John F. Lehman and Robert L. Schuettinger suggest, a need for rethinking organizational structures as well. Past experience suggests, however, that such changes will be a long time in coming; nevertheless, still another lesson of the Kissinger era in American foreign policy is that one person won't do. Perhaps some aspiring government reorganizer in the Carter administration may decide to examine seriously some of the highly valuable suggestions presently buried in the reports of the Murphy Commission on the reorganization of the government's foreign policy machinery.

In the process of rethinking America's global role it will also be necessary to reflect carefully on the role of public opinion in the policy formation process and the limits that public opinion places on the development of relevant international policies, in both the short and the long term. As has been suggested at length above, the American people are accustomed to thinking relevantly neither about values nor about strategic realities, let alone serious threats to this nation's survival. Although recent polls indicate that the public is now concerned about the rise of Soviet power and the concomitant decline in American influence in the world, the same polls suggest that the United States populace remains hopeful that what they have been often told in the past about the imminent onset of a new and more harmonious international order is true. There is certainly no consensus at present among the American people concerning either the threats which the United

States confronts in the contemporary world or the steps that ought to be taken to deal with those threats.[29] While public attitudes on such matters are surely susceptible to effective executive and congressional leadership, American history suggests that the capacity of the United States populace for sustained interest in foreign policy is limited. This truth clearly has implications for the development of a new grand strategy for the United States relevant to the realities of the late 1970s and early 1980s.

Unfortunately, there are external limits that constrain the options available to the United States in the international arena as well, at least for the short term. All of the authors who have contributed to the present volume are agreed that the Cold War is not over. Indeed, the problem precisely is that while the United States has been pursuing detente, Soviet miltary power and political influence have increased drastically in comparison with that of the United States. An immediate reversal of long-extant trends is not possible. Moreover, an overly sudden attempt to reverse these trends might well be destabilizing both at home and abroad. At home, while the American public might—indeed, certainly would—respond favorably to a presidential appeal for, e.g., higher taxes to sustain a 10 percent increase in the defense budget if over the short term a new defense posture appeared to lead to an improvement in America's global fortunes, the appeal of detente policies would soon become irresistable once again. What the United States needs above all is steadiness in international security policies, not constant swings of the pendulum. In any case an overly sudden shift in America's foreign policy posture might stimulate an over-reaction on the part of the Soviet Union—that, given the current state of the military balance between the superpowers, could put the United States in a precarious position indeed.

What is required, then, is an agenda for United States national security policy that defines both the essential interests of the United States and the means, economic, political, and military, necessary to protect these interests against existing threats, and those likely to arise in the near term. If these near-term measures are undertaken, a base will have been created for a more active and offensive posture, as needed, over a longer period. The agenda set forth in the previous chapters constitutes such an approach, articulated with respect to a variety of geographical and functional areas of United States national security policy. As an overarching strategic framework integrating the various policy proposals in each area, a revived form of containment appears called for—a doctrine of strategic containment, if you will.

This revived form of containment would be strategic in two senses. First, it rests on the assumption that the first priority for American national security policy in the decade ahead must be to reverse existing trends in the strategic balance between the United States and the USSR. William Schneider has carefully described the dimensions of America's strategic problem in Chapter Five, and has set forth the minimum steps necessary to rectify that problem. Others of similar outlook have established somewhat different priorities, but the point is in any case clear.

Secondly, United States national security policy must focus on containing the growth of Soviet military and political influence and power in those areas where such growth affects vital United States interests and the interests of significant allies. Several means, in turn, appear appropriate to that end. First, a point often made but seldom acted upon, and therefore in need of repeating: the United States must pay attention where possible and necessary to revivifying its alliance system and making that system more relevant to the problems of the present and the future. Despite the problems that have developed in intra-NATO relations in recent years, NATO remains central to the effort to resist Soviet expansionism and therefore deserves priority American attention. Efforts must be made to persuade our NATO allies to extend NATO's strategic perimeter, and thus the scope of its responsibilities, beyond Europe. Since Europe has become heavily dependent upon Middle Eastern oil, for example, military cooperation between NATO on the one hand and Iran and Saudi Arabia on the other, when contingencies warrant it, seems justified. At the tactical level, this may involve the provision of air- and sea-lift services, the exchange of intelligence, and even joint military exercises. Although some progress has been made in recent years toward improving NATO's own military capabilities, much remains to be done, as Colin Gray's chapter suggests, particularly in the area of weapons standardization and modernization and doctrinal innovation. New urgency should be imparted to such efforts at the highest levels of the United States government. NATO's theater nuclear arsenal and the doctrine governing its usage in the event of war, in particular, badly needs modernization; this too should be a matter of top priority in the alliance.

But the revivification of NATO alone will not be sufficient to deal with the growing Soviet challenge, which has now assumed global scope. Other alliance relationships, of both the bilateral and the multilateral variety, must be attended to; those involving Japan, South Korea, and Brazil come immediately to mind. Indeed, in deciding which of America's existing treaty relationships should be assigned priority in the near term, and which emerging or new relationships should be solidified or created, the United States should keep its priorities clear. The principal objective should be to prevent Soviet domination of key geostrategic regions of the world and at the same time to preserve American access to essential resources, critical sea and air lines of communication, and bases and military facilities that would make possible the swift introduction of military equipment and/or military forces if required either to prevent drastic changes in the local balance of power or to protect an essential ally.

Whenever possible, however, the United States should rely on local powers as initial lines of defense, employing in the process the sort of "bastion state" strategy apparently envisioned in early versions of the Nixon Doctrine. Possible candidates for the role of bastion states are numerous. Iran is an obvious choice in the Persian Gulf region; and Stephen P. Gibert in Chapter Eight suggests that we pay greater attention to Saudi Arabia in the future. Israel, however, will remain the favorite of many American analysts despite the heavy price that the United States has paid, and will continue to pay, in terms of reduced influence in the Arab world for our continued identification with the Israeli cause. In Latin America, John J. Tierney in Chapter Eleven quite properly suggests that we give particular attention to Brazil; Mexico and Argentina are other possible candidates, depending on domestic political developments in those countries. In Southeast Asia, the United States has, as Alan Sobrosky points out in Chapter Ten, been driven in disgrace from most of the mainland; possibilities for the development of effective relationships continue to exist, however, with Indonesia, Malaysia, and perhaps Thailand, although continued domestic turmoil makes the political future of the latter nation uncertain. In northeast Asia, again as Professor Sabrosky points out, Japan is obviously crucial; beyond that South Korea and Formosa possess stable governments and rapidly developing economies and occupy as well key geostrategic positions. To abandon either would be an act of folly. Africa is more problematic, for reasons that Anthony Harrigan has detailed in Chapter Twelve. As Robert Conquest points out in his contribution, however, the Soviets have chosen to make Southern Africa a key battleground in the new cold war, in the process creating severe pressures on the United States and its allies to respond. While we should be wary of allowing the zero-sum game, mentally associated with the earlier cold war, to dominate our thinking in the decade ahead, the West will almost certainly be compelled to undertake at least minimal measures to prevent effective Soviet political domination in black Africa in the near term. This probably means support—some of it perhaps best channeled through NATO Europe—for such anti-Soviet African states as Zaire in black Africa, South Africa (particularly if that nation can be persuaded to modify some of the more objectionable features of its internal policies), and, further north, the Sudan.

Other candidates can be identified; it is only necessary that they meet several criteria. Broadly speaking, states suitable for inclusion in a revivified Western alliance system must be willing actively to oppose the expansion of Soviet power and influence in their particular geographic regions. They must be viable regimes, politically and economically, and thus be capable of mobilizing power in the region, to oppose, with American help where needed, actions by the Soviet Union or by Soviet proxies. If possible, their leadership role should be acceptable to lesser states in the region that are not already a part of the Soviet collective security system.

Over the longer term, it may become possible to integrate the series of bilateral and multilateral relationships discussed here into a more unified whole, as suggested by Frank Barnett in his APIODA concept. If this proves to be the case, the West may over the longer term assume a more forward posture, in which we would seek, for example, to disrupt the Soviet alliance system and exploit other evident vulnerabilities in the international posture of our principal adversary. The outlines of such a strategy for the period beyond 1985, however, will have to be dealt with elsewhere.

Above all, however, if the United States is to fashion a national security policy relevant to existing and anticipated challenges, American leaders and the American population must begin to think realistically about world politics and national strategy and thus begin to bridge the gap between dream and reality that has been part of the United States foreign policy tradition since the beginning of American history. Along the way, certain shibboleths will have to be abandoned as well. Peace will not be achieved in our time, nor will a new structure of peace be ushered into existence during the final third of the twentieth century. The USSR is not a status quo power, nor are Soviet leaders appreciably more concerned about the presumed desires of the Soviet people for higher living standards than they were twenty years ago. The state of domestic virtue in the United States will not insure our survival, nor will the United States change the world by power of example. Military power has not lost its utility, and American security is not a function of the amount of money we spend on pollution control. The North-South conflict is not more important than the East-West conflict, and growing global interdependence is not leading to a more peaceful world. "One man, one vote" will not become the governing political principle in Central Africa, no matter what happens to Ian Smith. And not only should the United States not jump when Brezhnev sneezes, but we should ignore the respiratory ailments of Hua Kuo-fung and Julius Nyerere as well. To do so would indeed be the beginning of wisdom in American foreign policy.

NOTES

1. For a more complete discussion of the self-image of early America and its significance for United States foreign policy, see the author's "The Founding Fathers, Conservatism, and American Foreign Policy," *The Intercollegiate Review* 7 (Fall, 1970): 31–43.

2. Cushing Strout, *The American Image of the Old World* (New York: Harper and Row, 1963), p. 19.

3. Benjamin Franklin to Samuel Cooper, 1 May 1777, in Francis P. Wharton, *The Revolutionary Diplomatic Correspondence of the United States,* 6 vols. (Washington, D.C.: Government Printing Office, 1889) 2:313.

4. Philip S. Foner, ed., *The Complete Writings of Thomas Paine,* 2 vols. (New York: The Citadel Press, 1945) 1:123, 397.

5. Henry Cabot Lodge, ed., *The Works of Alexander Hamilton,* 12 vols. (New York: G.P. Putnam's Sons, 1904) 1:52 and 4:289.

6. Foner, op. cit., p. 341.

7. Thomas Jefferson to Thomas Leiper, 12 June 1815, in *The Works of Thomas Jefferson,* 12 vols., ed. Paul L. Ford (New York: G.P. Putnam's Sons, 1904–1905) 11:477-78.

8. For an analysis of the Pinckney-Hamilton debate see James E. Dornan, Jr., "The Search for Purpose in American Foreign Policy," in *The Confused Eagle: Division and Dilemma in American Politics,* ed. Lewis Lipsitz (Boston: Allyn and Bacon, Inc., 1973), pp. 491-94.

9. John Quincy Adams, *An Address Delivered at the Request of a Committee of the Citizens of Washington; On the Occasion of Reading the Declaration of Independence on The Fourth of July, 1821* (Washington, D.C.: Davis and Force, 1821), p. 21.

10. Ibid., p. 22.

11. The quotation is from *White-Jacket: or the World in a Man-of-War* (New York: Harper and Brothers, 1855), p. 181.

12. Quoted in Charles Burton Marshall, *The Limits of Foreign Policy,* rev. ed. (Baltimore: The Johns Hopkins Press, 1936), p. 53.

13. Correlli Barnett, "Strategy and Society," *RUSI Journal* 121 (September 1976): 12. One of the most thoughtful discussions of the origins of American strategic thinking is to be found in Robert E. Osgood, *Limited War* (Chicago: University of Chicago Press, 1957), chap. 1.

14. Daniel O. Graham, *A New Strategy for the West* (Washington, D.C.: The Heritage Foundation, 1977), p. 17.

15. See the discussion in his *Gulliver's Troubles, or the Setting of American Foreign Policy* (New York: McGraw-Hill, 1968), pt. 1.

16. See Dornan, "The Search for Purpose," pp. 495-99.

17. James Burnham, *Containment or Liberation?* (New York: John Day, 1952).

18. For a recent assessment of containment in terms similar to these, see Graham, op. cit., pp. 20-22.

19. See James E. Dornan, Jr., "The Nixon Doctrine and the Primacy of Detente," *The Intercollegiate Review* 9 (Spring, 1974): 77-97, for an extended analysis.

20. See James E. Dornan, Jr., "Kissinger's Foreign Policy: Grand Design or Grand Delusion?" *Washington Report,* American Security Council, December 1975, and James E. and Diane S. Dornan, "The Works of Henry Kissinger," *The Political Science Reviewer* 5 (Fall 1975): 47-128.

21. "How Kissinger Failed," *Newsweek,* 12 December 1976, p. 120.

22. *The Necessity for Choice: Prospects of American Foreign Policy* (Garden City, N.Y.: Anchor Books, 1962), p. 1.

23. See Barry M. Goldwater, *Why Not Victory?* (New York: McGraw-Hill, 1961).

24. For a trenchant statement of the Fortress America argument, see Robert W. Tucker, *A New Isolationism: Threat or Promise?* (New York: Universe Books, 1972).

25. Irving Kristol, "Moralism and Foreign Policy," *Wall Street Journal,* 19 November 1976.

26. Raymond Aron, "Is Isolationism Possible?" *Commentary,* April 1974, p. 41.

27. Ibid., p. 43.

28. Ibid., p. 42.

29. For analysis of public attitudes on foreign policy revealed by polls, see F. Clifton Berry, Jr., "National Survey Disputes Adult American Attitudes on Key Defense Topics," *Armed Forces Journal,* September 1976, pp. 24–25, and Charles R. Foster, "American Elite and Mass Attitudes Towards Europe," *NATO Review* 23 (June 1976): 13–15.

About the Authors

FRANK R. BARNETT is President of the National Strategy Information Center, Inc. of New York City and Washington, D.C.—a non-profit corporation engaged in education in national defense, geopolitics and international security affairs. He received his M.A. degree from Oxford University, and was awarded an LL.D. from the University of South Carolina. A former Wabash College professor, Mr. Barnett helped to initiate the first Defense Strategy Seminar for reserve officers at The National War College (July 1959) in Washington, and was on the summer school faculty of the College from 1961 to 1967. He has also served as a consultant on educational projects within the Department of Defense. He is the co-editor of a Doubleday book on national strategy entitled *Peace and War in the Modern Age* (1965), and contributed its concluding chapter, "Strategy, Public Opinion and the Private Sector." He is also the author of chapters in *American Strategy for the Nuclear Age* (Doubleday 1960) and *National Strategy in an Age of Revolutions* (Praeger 1959).

ROBERT CONQUEST is one of the world's most distinguished analysts of Soviet affairs. He has written countless books, articles, and reviews, including the widely cited *The Great Terror,* the definitive study of Stalin's purges of the 1930s. He spent 1976 at the Woodrow Wilson Center at the Smithsonian Institution, and is presently at the Hoover Institution.

JAMES E. DORNAN, JR., is Associate Professor and Chairman of the Department of Politics at the Catholic University of America, where he has taught since 1967, and Senior Research Consultant at the Strategic Studies Center of SRI International. He received his Ph.D. from The Johns Hopkins University. He has contributed articles and reviews to many professional journals, including the *Armed Forces Journal,* the *Journal of Politics,* the *Political Science Reviewer,* the *Intercollegiate Review, Brassey's Annual, Sea Power,* and *Survival.* His monograph on

SAT I, *Detente and the Impending Strategic Crisis*, was published in 1975 by the ACU Education and Research Foundation, and he has contributed chapters to several other books and monographs, including *The Soviet War Machine*, *The Confused Eagle*, and *The American Military Machine*.

EDWIN J. FEULNER, JR., new President of the Heritage Foundation, received his master's degree from the Wharton School at the University of Pennsylvania, was then a Weaver Fellow at the London School of Economics, and pursued further graduate studies in economics at Georgetown University. He has written extensively on various aspects of economic warfare, including articles on Cuba and the trade embargo (1967), and on Vietnam and East-West trade (1969). He is a co-author of *Trading With the Communists* (Washington, 1968), a contributor to *America-East European Trade* (Washington, 1969), author of *Congress and the New International Economic Order* (1976), editor of *China—The Turning Point* (Washington, 1976) and author of numerous other articles and reviews. He was formerly Executive Director of the Republican Study Committee in the U.S. House of Representatives.

STEPHEN P. GIBERT is Professor of Government at Georgetown University and Senior Research Consultant at the Strategic Studies Center of the Stanford Research Institute. Professor Gibert received his B.A. degree at Wofford College (South Carolina), his M.A. at Harvard University, and his Ph.D. at Johns Hopkins University. He was for five years the Director of the Master of Science in Foreign Service Program at Georgetown. Professor Gibert has served as an advisor to the Asia Foundation and the Government of the Union of Burma and has been a Visiting Professor at the University of Rangoon and the U.S. Naval War College. He has published a number of articles on foreign policy and international security affairs and is the co-author of *Arms for the Third World: Soviet Military Aid Diplomacy*, and author of *Soviet Views of America*.

COLIN GRAY is a widely published defense analyst who is now on the staff of the Hudson Institute. He received a D.Phil. from Oxford University, and has previously served as Assistant Director of the International Institute for Strategic Studies. His articles have appeared in such publications as *World Politics, Foreign Policy,* the *British Journal of International Studies, RUSI Journal,* and the *Journal of Political and Military Sociology.* Among his recent books is *The Soviet-American Arms Race* (1976).

ANTHONY HARRIGAN writes a newspaper column published in more than 250 newspapers. He is the author of six books, including *The Editor and the Republic, Red Star Over Africa,* and *A Guide to the War in Vietnam.* He has lectured before the Executives Club of Chicago, the Institute of Politics at Harvard University, and the U.S. National War College. He has been a recipient of a Relm Foundation Travel Grant to study the Canadian Far North and has received numerous awards for his publications. He is an advisory editor of *Modern Age* and a member of the national advisory board of Young Americans for Freedom. Since 1970, he has been Executive Vice President of the Southern States Industrial Council.

JOHN LEHMAN received his Ph.D. from the University of Pennsylvania, where he worked at the Foreign Policy Research Institute. In 1969 he joined the staff of the National Security Council. He later moved to the Arms Control and Disarmament Agency, serving as its Associate Director in 1975–76. He is now with the Abingdon Corporation. He has authored numerous articles, and is the co-editor of *Arms Control in the Sixties.*

FRANZ MICHAEL is currently Professor Emeritus of Far Eastern History and International Affairs at the Sino-Soviet Institute at George Washington University. He was Director of the Institute from 1970 to 1972 and formerly taught at the University of Washington. He holds the Doctorate of Jurisprudence from the University of Freiburg. He has contributed to numerous periodicals and is the author of *The Far East in the Modern World, Asian Alliance, Japan and U.S. Policy* (with

Gaston Sigur), and the forthcoming *Mao and the Permanent Revolution.*

ALAN NED SABROSKY holds a Ph.D. from the University of Michigan. He is Assistant Professor of Politics at the Catholic University of America, and Research Associate at the Foreign Policy Research Institute, Philadelphia. A specialist in international security affairs and civil-military relations, he has published in numerous anthologies and professional journals, including *Asian Affairs, Orbis, South-East Asian SPECTRUM, Intercollegiate Review,* and *Journal of Conflict Resolution.* Dr. Sabrosky is editor of *Blue-Collar Soldiers? Unionization and the U.S. Military;* author of *Defense Manpower Policy: A Critical Reappraisal;* and co-author of *The Conventional-Revisionist Controversy and the U.S. Role in World Affairs.*

WILLIAM SCHNEIDER, JR., has a Ph.D. in economics from New York University. He is an aide to Rep. Jack Kemp (Rep., N.Y.), and is associated with the Hudson Institute, New York. He is co-author and co-editor (with J. J. Holst) of *Why ABM? Policy Issues in the Missile Defense Controversy,* co-author and co-editor (with Francis P. Hoeber) of *Arms, Men and Military Budgets,* and author of *Food, Foreign Policy and Raw Materials Cartels* and of numerous articles.

ROBERT L. SCHUETTINGER is currently Director of Studies for the Heritage Foundation in Washington, D.C. and Editor of *Policy Review.* He was formerly Senior Research Associate for National Security Affairs of the Republican Study Committee in the House of Representatives. He has been a Visiting Lecturer in Political Science at Yale University and formerly taught international relations at The Catholic University of America and St. Andrews University in Scotland. He studied at Columbia University and Exeter College of Oxford University and holds the M.A. from the University of Chicago and the advanced degree of B.Phil. from St. Andrews University. Schuettinger is the author of *Lord Acton: Historian of Liberty, A Brief Survey of Price and Wage*

About The Authors

Controls from 2800 B.C. to A.D. 1952 and *A Research Guide to Public Policy*, editor of *The Conservative Tradition in European Thought*, and coauthor of *Point-Counterpoint*. He has contributed to a number of scholarly publications.

JOHN J. TIERNEY, JR., is Executive Director of the bipartisan National Security Research Group in the U.S. House of Representatives. He is the former Chairman of the Department of Politics, and currently Adjunct Associate Professor at The Catholic University of America in Washington, D.C., and has also taught at The Johns Hopkins University. He has held a Public Affairs Fellowship from the Hoover Institution, and has written articles and reviews on international relations in *Orbis, World Affairs, Lugano Review, Modern Age, Intercollegiate Review* and other journals. He is co-author of *China—The Turning Point*. Dr. Tierney received his Ph.D. in international relations from the University of Pennsylvania.

Index

Index

human rights, 4-5, 13, 36, 105, 119, 235,
243-45, 279
Hungary, 132

Iceland, 4
India, 23, 112, 113, 153
Indian Ocean, 4, 8, 102, 163, 178, 179
Indochina War. *See* Vietnam War
Indonesia, 14, 174, 276, 286
Institute of the Study of Conflict, 259
Inter-American Commission on Human
Rights, 244
Inter-American Development Bank, 41
International Development Association, 43,
67
Iran, 14, 161, 162, 165, 167, 176, 177, 178,
285, 286
Iraq, 149, 162, 163, 166, 167
Ireland, 4
Israel, 33, 93, 108, 115, 143-52, 156, 157,
160, 161, 162, 163, 164, 165-66,
167, 168-73, 176, 177, 178, 179, 180,
227, 263-64, 265, 276, 286
Italy, 4, 103, 108, 111, 128, 129, 175
Ivory Coast, 262

Jackson-Vanik Amendment, 38
Jamaica, 232
Janke, Peter, 259
Japan, 4, 8, 10, 13, 14, 33, 37, 37, 39, 108,
150, 151, 153, 157, 160, 161, 163, 178,
197-98, 202, 203, 207-11, 227, 231,
238, 259, 275, 286, 287
Jefferson, Thomas, 270, 271
Jerusalem, 146, 149, 150, 170, 172
Johnson, Andrew, 59
Johnson, Harry, 114
Johnson, Lyndon B., 21, 36, 55, 59, 65,
229
Jordan, 147, 148

Kennan, George, 257, 274-75
Kennedy, John F., 1, 3, 37, 55, 279
Kenya, 102, 262
Kenyatta, Jomo, 102
Khrushchev, Nikita, 108, 190, 194
Kilpatrick, James, 55
Kipling, Rudyard, 112

Kissinger, Henry, 2, 20, 23, 25, 35, 40, 46,
69, 107, 108, 121, 124, 143, 152, 165,
170, 171, 172, 196, 200-01, 247, 258,
277-78, 279, 281, 283
Korea, *See* North Korea; Republic of Korea
Korean War, 54, 67, 199, 200, 215
Kristol, Irving, 253, 281

Laird, Melvin, 6
Laos, 3
Latin America, 8, 227-51, 264, 279, 286;
Brazil, 247-48; critical issues, 235-48;
Cuba and Soviet power, 245-46; decline
of hegemony, 228-35; human rights, 243-
45; Panama Canal, 235-41; security assis-
tance, 241-43
Latin American Free Trade Association
(LAFTA), 231
Law of the Seas Conference, 47
Lawrence, David, 55
League of Nations, 54-55
Lebanon, 147, 148-149, 151
Lee, John M., 258
Lenin, Vladimir I., 110, 113, 117, 211
Leninism, 6, 8, 110, 111, 113
less developed countries (LDCs), 3, 41,
44-45, 156
Liberia, 262
Liberty Lobby, 59
Libya, 149, 164
Lincoln, Abraham, 52, 59, 103
Lin Piao, 191
Lippmann, Walter, 27
Locke, John, 52
Lodge, Henry Cabot, 65
Lovett, Robert A., 22

McGovern, George, 128
Madison, James, 51, 64
Malawi, 260
Malaysia, 3, 276, 286
Mallet, Sir Charles, 23
Manila Declaration, 44
Manley, Michael, 232
Manning, Bayless, 26
Mao Tse-tung, 3, 6, 9, 15, 185, 186-88,
189, 190, 191, 192, 194, 205
Marshall, George, 55